T0305632

Leading and Transforming Organizations

Businesses must stay agile and be responsive to the complexities and disruptions brought about by digital transformation. The recent pandemic has also accelerated business digitization. Packed with insights and strategies, this book breaks down the roadmap to organizational success into core areas. It explains how companies can adapt, prepare, and optimize their business performance through strategic positioning, business sustainability, and crisis management.

Rajaram describes strategic positioning as a mix of strategies for organizations to gain competitive advantage and ensure long-term success. He also talks about business sustainability and explores how organizations need to re-innovate their approaches to tap into opportunities created by the rapid changing customer needs and evolving environmental interventions. The book also illustrates how companies can navigate out of a crisis successfully.

This book will be an excellent, essential guide for leaders, practitioners, and anyone who is formulating effective organizational strategies.

Kumaran Rajaram, PhD, is Senior Lecturer with the Leadership, Management, and Organization Division at Nanyang Business School, and Deputy Academic Director (Liaison) with Nanyang Technoprenuership Centre, Nanyang Technological University, Singapore.

"Dr. Kumaran Rajaram provides excellent insights on effective leadership from his experiences in large organizations, in academia, as an entrepreneur, and consultant. This book gives leaders tools and skillsets to resolve various dilemmas. The dilemma of dealing with current pressing needs and strategizing for the future; dilemma of being agile yet developing a strong culture; dilemma of being competitive/bottom-line driven yet managing with strong ethical foundations. While other management/leadership books exist, Dr. Rajaram's book astutely shows how his insights can be applied in the context of fast technological advancement, digitalization, and new work arrangements such as remote work."

FOO Maw-Der, PhD (MIT), *Professor, Nanyang Business School, Nanyang Technological University, Singapore; Director, Nanyang Technopreneurship Center; Director, Asian Business Case Center*

"This book astutely examines and discusses strategic issues concerning leaders in contemporary volatile times. The concepts and examples provided are relatable to both scholars and practitioners, thus offering both theoretical and practical insights. It is a highly recommended read for instructors and researchers who are keen to adopt sustainable and agile leadership strategies to navigate dynamic business environments!"

Chong SinHui, PhD, *Assistant Professor, Division of Leadership, Management and Organization, Nanyang Business School, Nanyang Technological University, Singapore*

"Current executives and business leaders are experiencing greater change, pressure, uncertainty, and complexity than ever before. And, it seems likely that the presence of these factors will only increase. This may be the biggest threat to organizations and the biggest challenge for organizational leaders. To prepare future leaders to navigate this environment successfully, different approaches to developing leaders and leading are necessary. *Leading and Transforming Organizations: Navigating the Future* is a unique scholarly/practice-oriented book that informs both current leaders and next-generation leaders on the cutting-edge ideas that are necessary for navigating the tumultuous now as well as the increasingly tumultuous future."

Ryan Gottfredson, PhD, *Associate Professor, College of Business and Economics, California State University, Fullerton, United States*

"Dr Rajaram's book discusses cutting-edge topics and latest skills with which leaders, strategists, and managers need to be well-versed and equipped to face twenty-first-century challenges, including developing transformative leadership skills in a remote VUCA work environment, meeting ethical and sustainable business standards, and adapting to and striving in digital ecosystems. I recommend Dr Rajaram's book to any leader, strategist, and manager involved in leading and transforming an organization for the twenty-first century."

Ludvig Levasseur, PhD, *Assistant Professor in Entrepreneurship, Indian Institute of Management Bangalore and Junior Research Fellow, Institute for Development Strategies, O'Neill School of Public and Environmental Affairs, Indiana University*

"This book is a timely reminder of the importance of leadership in the organizational context. The world is going through rapid changes due to nationalism, the pandemic, climate change, war, and economic upheaval. Organizations must adapt to such socio-political changes. This book raises important factors that can help organizations succeed in such changing circumstances. Leaders play a vital role in this process. The book provides novel leadership strategies in re-evaluating organizational strategies and commitments that can incorporate the changing nature of employees and work, management, and governance in the face of crises and change."

Sarbari Bordia, PhD, *Professor, Deputy Director Research, Research School of Management, Australian National University*

"Dr. Kumaran is spot on in identifying the three pillars for transformative change – leadership (self and team), innovative culture and dynamic strategizing for value proposition. The topics are timely for a post-pandemic era where the corporates are trying to find the fine balance between the internal challenges around the future of work and the external ones driven by disruption, high-competitive intensity, shorter life cycles, shifting customer preferences and macro-economic factors. Innovation is oxygen for companies – and Dr. Kumaran lays down both the big picture and a detailed playbook that make corporate transformation a reality."

Manish Sinha, PhD, CFA, *Director and Head of Venture Building, Nanyang Technological University – NTUitive Pte Ltd*

"Dr. Rajaram's book is a very resourceful one for professionals in any industry that try to cope with and navigate the turbulent and complex landscape in the digital era. It is also a perfect resource for researchers and teaching faculty to understand some of the key challenges and concepts that the business leaders deal with today. Delivering a mix of deep-dive theories and real-world applications, the book provides a set of evidence-based and practice-oriented frameworks as well as recommendations. I highly recommend this book to anyone trying to gather knowledge in this subject."

Mr. Paul Li, *Head, Strategic Partnerships, Nanyang Executive Education, Nanyang Business School, Nanyang Technological University*

"Dr. Kumaran's book on *Leading and Transforming Organizations: Navigating the Future* comes at the right time of unprecedented global change. As organizations scramble to adapt to the digital economy transformation, they must be agile. From a holistic perspective, strategic positioning is about how a company differentiates itself from its competitors and delivers value to its targeted markets. In my capacity as head of strategy at my organization, I recognize the significance of strategic positioning in advancing its development. While a strategic positioning approach enables an organization to devise the right mix of strategies that can help them gain an edge over their competition, the book's greatest value is that it teaches readers how to restrategize through re-value propositions, enabling organizations to be agile and responsive and promoting strategies that allow them to do so."

Dr. Samson Tan, *Head, Strategic Development, Libraries and Education, Civica Pte Ltd, Singapore*

"This nine-chapter book on Leadership and Transformation is an excellent book intended for researchers and practitioners, as well as teachers and students of Leadership and Strategy. It covers a wide gamut of topics and issues that are faced by business leaders: the future of work, innovation to address grand challenges, strategizing the value proposition, ethics and corporate governance, digitalization and technology management, change management, crisis management, sustainability and preparing for the future. The book can be used as a valuable reference by practitioners and researchers alike and as a reference resource at both undergraduate and graduate levels by students and instructors. The beauty of Dr. Rajaram's book is that it covers both long-term strategic issues such as leadership, innovation, change management and preparing for the future, as well as operational issues such as crisis management, sustainability and agility."

Professor S. Viswanathan, *Nanyang Business School,*
Nanyang Technological University, Singapore

"This book is a mind-opener for an audience that cares about the vital issues leaders and strategy-makers of organizations are facing today. In particular, it elaborates on the need for transformation and adaptation in a business environment that has never been more 'VUCA' (volatile, uncertain, complex, and ambiguous) before. It contextualizes crucial leadership responsibilities against the backdrop of the COVID-19 pandemic; the digital transformation bringing about various opportunities and threats; and the changing world of work. I highly appreciate the hands-on approach combining a rich theoretical underpinning with illustrative examples and outcome orientation. Leadership scholars will find plentiful inspiration for research strengthening their expertise in innovative value creation and strategy re-design, which will also enable them to support their business constituencies even better. Organizational leaders will find encouragement and practical guidance to design strategic transformation and to strengthen their crisis management capabilities."

Prof. Dr. Volker Rundshagen, *Management and Tourism Studies,*
University of Applied Sciences Stralsund, Germany

"A thoughtful book that niftily guides organizational leaders through complex transformation journeys. Readers involved in enormous transformation efforts will find this book indispensable. The book helps navigate the complexity of change by making sense of the situations, examining personal readiness, heightening awareness of people engagement, and charting multiple workstreams to drive implementation. Relevant theories and models are explained and linked closely to real-world examples. The book synthesizes the complex and competing ideas about leading and transforming organizations into a succinct yet complete framework that leaders can apply immediately. Rich in illustrations and broad in scope – this is a must-have resource for students and practitioners."

Phang Yew Keong, Nigel, Associate Professor (Practice)
and Associate Dean (Executive Education), *Nanyang Business School,*
Nanyang Technological University, Singapore

"This is a unique book. Most books on leadership focus only on organizational issues and/or traits of a good leader as though the firm strategy is a separate factor. And most books on strategy treat the firm itself as key actor and downplay the charisma, the style, and the behavior of individual leaders within the firm. In contrast, this book addresses the intersection between leadership, strategy, and management. The book provides insights into how it is the firm leader (or the leadership team) who shapes the culture of the firm, directs the transformation process, and guides the firm in re-strategizing and re-positioning itself to achieve a competitive advantage in its chosen market. The leader or the leadership team is also the one that keeps the firm agile, well-governed, and constantly prepared to deal with current and future disruptions. Each chapter is infused with deep discussions of contemporary issues that enable strategy and management scholars to rethink the validity of existing theories. Each chapter also offers practical frameworks and in-depth case studies that enable practitioners to derive useful prescriptions for their actual leadership work. The book serves as an excellent guide to practicing enlightened leadership in today's volatile business environment and within organizations that are populated by a new breed of workers that hold a whole new set of values."

Lewis Lim, PhD, *Associate Professor of Marketing (Practice),*
Academic Director, Nanyang Professional MBA Programme,
Nanyang Business School, Nanyang Technological University, Singapore

Leading and Transforming Organizations

Navigating the Future

Kumaran Rajaram

Routledge
Taylor & Francis Group

LONDON AND NEW YORK

First published 2023
by Routledge
4 Park Square, Milton Park, Abingdon, Oxon OX14 4RN

and by Routledge
605 Third Avenue, New York, NY 10158

Routledge is an imprint of the Taylor & Francis Group, an informa business

© 2023 Kumaran Rajaram

British Library Cataloguing-in-Publication Data
A catalogue record for this book is available from the British Library

Library of Congress Cataloging-in-Publication Data
Names: Rajaram, Kumaran, author.
Title: Leading and transforming organizations : navigating the future / Kumaran Rajaram.
Description: 1 Edition. | New York, NY : Routledge, 2023.
Identifiers: LCCN 2022038691 (print) | LCCN 2022038692 (ebook)
Subjects: LCSH: Organizational change. | Management—Technological innovations. | Strategic planning. | Organizational effectiveness.
Classification: LCC HD58.8 .R3435 2023 (print) | LCC HD58.8 (ebook) | DDC 658.4/06—dc23/eng/20221027
LC record available at https://lccn.loc.gov/2022038691
LC ebook record available at https://lccn.loc.gov/2022038692

ISBN: 9781032260501 (hbk)
ISBN: 9781032260488 (pbk)
ISBN: 9781003286288 (ebk)

DOI: 10.4324/9781003286288

Typeset in Adobe Garamond Pro
by codeMantra

Contents

NAVIGATING THROUGH SUCCESSFULLY IN CRISIS MANAGEMENT

Illustrations

Figures

Table

About the Author

 **Kumaran Rajaram** is a Senior Lecturer with the Leadership, Management and Organisation Division at Nanyang Business School and Deputy Academic Director (Liaison) at Nanyang Technopreneruship Centre, Nanyang Technological University, Singapore. He specializes in Global Leadership and International Management where he lectures, leads a team of senior instructors, and is responsible for the curriculum and learning design of management and leadership courses. He is a REP Fellow and teaches in the Renaissance Engineering Programme, which is one of the NTU's Premier Scholars Programmes (PSP). He is also a CRADLE Fellow with the Centre for Research and Development in Learning, where he performs cutting-edge research in Organizational Science & Management Science, People & Culture, Cultural Intelligence, Change Management, Learning Analytics, Culture of Learning & Learning Culture, Learning Intelligence and Internationalization of Business Higher Education. He is also the Founder and Executive Director of Research Lab for Learning Innovations, Learning Culture, and Culture of Learning – InnosolvLearn, Creative Solutions (www.innosolvlearn.com). He is currently a practicing C-Suite Executive Coach and Management Consultant, whose expert advice focuses on Leadership, People and Culture, and Change Management.

He has a PhD with Distinction in Business and Management (majoring in leadership, cultural intelligence, organizational and learning science). As an acknowledgement for his quality performance, he was nominated for the 2012, 2013, 2014 Emerald Outstanding Doctoral Research Awards. He has received multiple competitive school-, university-, and national-level research grants and awards on topics related to pedagogical innovation and leadership competencies. He has guest-edited papers in Academy of Management Conference (Tier 1), European Academy of Management, and journals including *Cross Cultural Management: An International Journal, Asian Case Research Journal* led by National University of Singapore, and *Higher Education Research and Development Society of Australasia*; the *Journal of International Education in Business* (Emerald); *Management Teaching Review* (SAGE); the *Journal of Education for Business* (Taylor & Francis). He had served as an Editor in *Singapore Management Journal*. He has published articles in leadership, management education, learning science, learning culture in multi-disciplinary context, learning analytics, and internationalization of business education. Dr. Rajaram has written four books and two book chapters with established publishers like Springer, McGraw Hill, and Routledge and co-authored a self-development book on time mastery. His current research focus is on leadership and change management for transforming future organizations. He was instrumental in transforming and implementing the flipped-classroom pedagogy, adopting problem-based and team-based learning in the course that he chairs. Dr Rajaram is also the inventor of many innovative learning interventions (http://blogs.ntu.edu.sg/learning-innovations). He was nominated for the Outstanding USQ Academic and Research Alumnus 2014, 2015, and 2016. He was awarded the John Cheung Social Media Award 2016, NTU EdeX Grants 2016 & 2017, and MOE TRF National Level Grant 2017.

Dr Rajaram has over 20 years of corporate leadership and senior management experience in organizational development, change and strategic management, and organizational learning and training development and management consulting. He is an expert in leadership and international management, change management, cultural intelligence (business culture + culture of business and learning culture + culture of learning), internationalization and business development, management consulting, organizational learning science, and management education. He started his career with Republic of Singapore Navy in Engineering with his last appointment as Section Head. Thereafter transited to the corporate world where during his last stints served as the Director of Academic Affairs and Head, Strategy and Business Development for Asia Pacific where he championed evolving issues of corporate governance, internationalization and had implemented change strategies. Then as the CEO and Executive Chairman of a global leadership and change management consulting firm where he has travelled widely to execute business consultations which has diversified his experiential horizons, especially in the cross-cultural context before he made a transition as researcher and educator. Organizations that he has offered his consulting services include Microsoft, General Electric, Energizer, Siemens, NCS, Sim Global Education, Ferrero Rocher, SINDA, and many more. During his entrepreneurial stint, he was interviewed and featured in *SPAN* magazine in 2008 for being an exemplary and outstanding young entrepreneur, USQ Alumni Newsletter in 2009 – "Alumnus achieves professional training success", and *Inspire* magazine in 2010 for being an exemplary role model as a business practitioner.

Despite his busy schedule and heavy commitments, he is a staunch believer of work–life balance where he disciplines himself to exercise regularly, spend quality time with his family, write and read widely. He is an active jogger, plays street soccer, swims regularly, and occasionally involves in adventure sports. He enjoys good music and plays the flute. He is passionate and has a keen interest in personal development, and is an advocator on the art of motivation and time mastery as he strongly believes that adopting a winning mindset with embedded motivational strategies and effective time management is a vital skill for anyone who aspires to achieve greater success and happiness in life. He believes that leadership is empowering and enabling others to be committed in achieving a vision embedded with the nuances of cultural intelligence.

Foreword

Leading and Transforming Organizations: Navigating the Future is a wonderfully incisive and relevant new book by Dr Kumaran Rajaram, a distinguished and accomplished scholar.

This book aims to guide readers through the perils and opportunities encountered by organizations in creating and managing change and skillfully navigates readers through specific topics and themes relating to the positioning and transformation of organizations, sustainability concerns, crisis management, and the changing market landscape.

Leveraging on his vast experience and background in the fields of leadership, management, and organizational behavior, and through the use of case studies to explain and illustrate important concepts, this book sits at the sweet spot of being an academically sound work of impeccable scholarship and an intimately practical guide at the same time.

Leading and Transforming Organizations: Navigating the Future is an important and timely book, particularly given the increasing challenges faced by organizations and its impact brought about by rapid technological advancements, geopolitical rivalries and tensions, and other onslaughts such as the COVID-19 pandemic. Readers will have much to learn from the book.

Associate Professor Samtani Anil
Head, Division of Business Law, Nanyang Business School,
Nanyang Technological University

Preface

Hard work, resilience, discipline, focused mindset, determination, and imperative consistency in upholding an ethos of excellence in quality will see a leader through breakthroughs despite the immense challenges that you have to navigate and overcome with patience, re-calibrating, adapting continuously, and with a clear actionable vision.

Kumaran Rajaram, PhD (Distinction), MBA; Former CEO, Global
Leadership and Cultural Intelligence Consulting Firm

Effective organizational leadership builds on trust. Trust is a word that has to be earned through sustainable actions, not merely words. A leader of an organization first needs to be exemplary in his actions, walking the talk. He shows that everyone at all levels including the senior leaders are vulnerable and subjected to the same treatment in terms of integrity and upholding ethos values, starting from top management to the employee on the ground. That creates a strong culture in the organization that focuses on building values that empower one rather than through mere rules that may not always resonate well across multifaceted complexities. The emphasis on transparency and accountability reiterates the values to be expected shaping one's behavioral and cognitive inclination. Management or managerial communication plays a vital role to enable managers to communicate efficiently and effectively with their teams, enhance employees' experience and psychological wellbeing, build stronger relationships, and continuously drive employees' success in the workplace.

Leaders must focus on the fundamentals to reflect and review on how to assist their employees to transit this challenging phase addressing two key aspects, namely the technical work-related aspects as well as social, emotional, and psychological elements embedded within the job responsibilities and role. Leaders must have a crystal-focused goal and purpose devised, find a creative way to advocate, and get the employees buy-in for their commitment. They must listen carefully and mindfully to their challenges and limitations and try how best you could assist them to work around them. Leaders' key role is to advocate, influence, and make others see the "light in the dark tunnel", engage them, and together come out with solutions that are feasible which may not necessarily have the best but workable ones, without putting people under too much of discomfort and stress. So, it is about getting the right balance by understanding the socio-cultural context between task and people's well-being and motivation. By prioritizing and placing the organization's mission and values at the core, leaders are able to provide clarity, communication, and decision-making that affect both themselves and their organization. Leaders are to take time to re-build credibility, trust, and loyalty with their stakeholders, i.e., employees, customers, distributors, suppliers, and others who are vital to an organization's growth and sustainability. A crisis like COVID-19 is where it reveals and puts organizational leadership under undue test of one's competence and values. An effective leader truly cares about his people and able to navigate, lead others not only through the tasks at hand but with compassion and empathy while addressing the evolving issues in the organization. In today's rapid evolving world, organizations have to be agile and creative to embrace changes with the moral courage, grit, and fortitude to continuously challenge the norms and innovate for the betterment that makes a positive impact on people, increases productivity, and enhances organizational effectiveness. This allows one to think, reflect, and strive toward the process of finding the answers to the queries and unanswered issues. The process of the effective, seamless, consistent, and continuous change management must be the emphasis if the organization is to stay highly relevant, productive, and performing to stakeholders' evolving needs.

It has been my motivation to put my years of practice work as a corporate senior leader, an entrepreneur, and a practicing management consultant, embedded with scholarship research insights and reflections together to benefit the larger academic community in a book titled *Leading and Transforming Organizations: Navigating the Future, Creating and Managing Change*. The insightful journey commenced back then in 2012 when I was invited to join as a faculty with Nanyang Business School, Nanyang Technological University, Singapore. Being appointed as the course chair, I am responsible to lead and oversee 8–10 senior instructors and over 450 students, including exchange students from various countries globally. I was intrigued by the rapid changes to explore and experiment ways to transform the learning culture and re-design the curriculum to enhance the competencies through addressing the complex learning challenges that emerge and were embedded in the pursuit of students' university studies, and more imperatively, to incorporate authentic learning design with a high emphasis of team-based and collaborative learning.

The primary goal is to train and nurture the students to be "job ready" equipped with the relevant "practical-oriented" skills and applied knowledge. The reflection on my values and beliefs on teaching and learning drives my mission that unfolds in three key dimensions: (a) inculcate positive and nurturing learning environment; (b) stimulate learner's interest for learning; and (c) ingrain a mindset of life-long learning; I constantly attempt to understand students' learning preferences as well as the course's key learning objectives. This allows me to customize the instructional techniques to meet students' expectations so that effective acquisition of knowledge will be achieved. I believe effective teaching happens when there is a good balance of interactivity, dialogue and exchange of perspectives between the teacher and students. Hence, by endeavoring to appreciate the varying students' aspirations, I am able to facilitate a conducive learning environment that inspires and encircles everyone's aspirations in the class. We should be creative to utilize varying instructional approaches, both via the traditional approaches and technological interventions that stimulate optimal learning in the students. I trust collaborative learning enables one to grow intellectually, develop internally, and enhance their individual personality. It is imperative for me to develop a culture of innovation and creativity, developing an entrepreneurial and problem-solving mindset. This encourages students to not only optimize their inner talent and potential but also nurture them to be enterprising, enabling them to be critical thinkers with diverse perspectives. I am also concurrently serving as a CRADLE Fellow with the Centre for Research and Development in Learning, where my research interests lie in the area of management, organizational learning science, culture, analytics, and internationalization of higher education. The inspiration to dive deeper on these management and organizational science areas was derived from the varying questions that emerge through the real-life challenges that I had to deal with and have experienced from both as the macro level (as a CEO, Director of Academic Affairs, Strategy and Business Development – Head) and micro level (as a professor who dealt directly with the students and a researcher to create new scholarly and applied knowledge). Back then, the immediate goal was to resolve the issues by addressing the contributing factors, but perhaps I did not have the bandwidth to dive deeper to explicitly address the root causes of the problem. However, now as an active researcher, I have since embarked tackling these vital and pressing research questions and having them put together in this book. In today's rapid changing environment with evolving expectations, educators in higher education need to carefully design its course curriculum to achieve quality, depth, and rigor of training in any context of specialization. Today's higher education at university requires to nurture students to become competent and globally employable business leaders and managers, having them realize and internalize their role as change catalysts in building a productive and sustainable world, where enterprises of all sorts can be leveraged on humanistic as well as economic conventions.

Organizations must be agile through their preparedness and readiness for the digital economy transformation. Strategic positioning is concerned with the way in which a business from a holistic perspective differentiates itself in a significant way from its competitors and delivers value to the targeted customer segment. Strategic positioning is a contributing factor that motivates the development and transformation of an enterprise. Transformation is seen as a sustainable process to ensure a company is positioning itself for long-term success. Strategic positioning allows the correct mix of strategies to be devised that enable organizations to get ahead of industry through its value-proposition and competitive advantage and environmental trends, adapt to evolving business models, exit businesses that no longer make sense, and enter new markets that they have the right to win. Three key pillars, namely "transformative leadership", "re-strategizing with re-value proposition", and "innovative culture and outcome-based approach", are core aspects that come under the purview of strategic positioning and transformation. The positive change in organization starts with self-leadership at all levels, i.e. strategic (chief executive officer, chief operating officer, chief financial officer and chief human resource officer), tactical (managers, supervisors), and operational (first line managers), where each of them is leaders in their own rights. Next, as changes rapidly intervene, organizations require to re-look and examine how to improvise their current strategies by re-evaluating their value proposition. For instance, re-strategizing with "re-value proposition" and "innovative culture and outcome-based approach" could be categorized under the purview of strategic positioning. This could serve as an opportunity in examining thoroughly on what needs to be done to respond to the digital economy. Next, organizations are to create an innovative culture filled with value systems that could potentially help to have employees buy-in in terms of their commitment to drive and attain the transformation.

Business sustainability and leading future markets entail three primary aspects, namely "re-assessing and re-innovating business strategy", "corporate governance and ethics", and "agile to digitalization and technological change". With rapid changing customer needs and evolving environmental interventions, new markets emerge enabling much more opportunities to tap on where companies need to re-innovate their approaches to be relevant and contemporary. Hence, this allows re-evaluating of a company's competitive advantage, its core capabilities, and customer value proposition and having it aligned to the target customer segments respectively. Organizations must realize, acknowledge, and be proactively mindful on the vitality, challenges, and complexities in maintaining good corporate governance, issues related to ethical dilemmas, and so on to effectively operate in the digital era.

Organizations' ability and agility to respond to rapidly evolving digitalization and technological change has now become a survivability need. Organizations need to tackle the ripple effects on businesses arising from external interventions, for example, new emerging markets and prospective market disruptions as well as industry changes. Companies have to navigate through successfully in a crisis management situation, where three core aspects should be taken into due consideration, namely "leadership competencies for crisis management", "sustainability and agility in navigating an unprecedented phase", and "re-strategizing and preparing for future businesses". The pressure on companies is to be able to deal with, navigate, and sustain through the unprecedented circumstances, for example, COVID-19 pandemic and more predictable future trends, say digital economy transformation. The leaders to be equipped with relevant and contemporary competencies play a crucial role to comprehend the rapid evolving and dynamic situational context more effectively. Imperatively, companies must adopt strategies by being agile to sustain against the challenges in an unprecedented phase. The mindset of leaders and the ability to create an ecosystem with the right operational processes to address the issues in an organized and scaffolded manner is vital to sustain the challenging circumstances and situational context. Organizations must continuously and consistently re-strategize and prepare for future business.

This book serves as an essential and timely intervention where the innovative, evidence-based, and contemporary strategies embedded with relevant insights and discussions on leading and transforming organizations are presented. These are validated strategies that have been executed successfully in various types of organizations in context aimed towards creating and leading change processes, explicitly in sustaining organization's growth and productivity. The book will address the complex challenges and limitations in practice supported with evidence, hence providing possible strategies and approaches to address them. The book addresses an interesting scope of topics that are both contemporary and essential to almost all academics who have a high responsibility to nurture, develop, train, and equip learners both at the undergraduate and post-graduate levels at the university with the relevant contents' knowledge, skills, and competencies.

There is combination of practice-oriented strategies with proposed holistic frameworks advocated to address varying challenges and issues in organizations. This will be of large interest for the academic community and practitioners to explore and examine how these organizational learning strategies, approaches, interventions, and innovations could be adopted. There is a high focus and inclination on outcome-based approach, focused on how to better perform the transformation in organizational context and setting that is able to sustain and deliver high-level impacts. I aim to value-add through the scholarly work in this book as an avenue of contribution to academics, practitioners, and other stakeholders in this field to help them attain their institutional, organizational, and individualized goals.

Kumaran Rajaram, PhD
Division of Leadership, Management and Organisation,
Nanyang Business School, Nanyang Technological University, Singapore

Acknowledgments

I sincerely express my heartfelt appreciation to the following people who have contributed to the successful publication of this book.

- My spouse and family for their unwavering support and encouragement
- All other people who have contributed to this book in one way or another

STRATEGIC POSITIONING AND TRANSFORMATION

I

Chapter 1

Leadership and the Future of Work

Lead with value-driven principles embedded with growth, open, promotion and outward mindset, nurturing others through vertical development. Attitude, character and excellence are primary core values that serves as the underpinning advocate and ethos to create the self-leadership framework that is adopted to nurture and shape future business leaders

Kumaran Rajaram, PhD

1.1 Introduction

The basic premise of transformative leadership is that everyone can lead (Montuori & Donnelly, 2017). Whether intentional or not, everybody contributes to and co-creates the world as we know it. Every action, discussion, and interaction can be perceived as leadership by others to the degree that it influences them both consciously and unconsciously. Transformative leadership is essentially a participatory process of creative collaboration and transformation which is beneficial to all parties involved. It emphasizes the significance of small actions and advocates that they can have a big and cumulative effect. Transformative leadership is increasingly relevant in today's more complex, rapidly evolving, challenging, and competitive work environment where leaders are struggling to maintain followers' trust (Caldwell et al., 2012). The sad truth that requires urgent attention is the adoption of outdated,

DOI: 10.4324/9781003286288-2

ineffective, and irrelevant leadership models in today's fast changing work climate. While leading others effectively is important for the success of an organization, one cannot lead others well without first being able to lead themselves. The concept of self-leadership poses that actions are ultimately controlled by internal rather than external forces (Stewart, Courtright, & Manz, 2011). A study by Marques-Quinteiro, Vargas, Eifler, and Curral (2019) found that self-leadership improves adaptive performance and job satisfaction. Self-leadership can be a valuable strategy especially when faced with organizational crises, which is highly relevant in today's volatile and increasingly complex business environment.

Merging the two concepts, namely self-leadership and transformative leadership, it enables an individual to effectively lead both others and his- or her-self in the future workforce. In fact, results from a study by Andressen, Konradt, and Neck (2011) found that self-leadership is a process element that mediates the relationship between transformational leadership and employee motivation. Self-leadership has a higher impact on motivation in virtual work structures compared to a shared work environment. This illustrates the importance of self-leadership in times like the COVID-19 pandemic where most people are required to work remotely. The future of work is likely to skew towards remote working, with companies like Twitter, Square, and Microsoft allowing majority of their employees to work from home. Leaders should prepare themselves for the future of work that will bring about further radical changes that present both instability and opportunities.

1.2 Self-leadership

Self-leadership is first introduced more than three decades ago in management literature as a type of leadership styles that focus on the self instead of the management of followers (Manz & Sims, 1980). Broadly, self-leadership is about "leading oneself toward performance of naturally motivating tasks as well as managing oneself to do work that must be done but is not naturally motivating" (Manz, 1986, p. 589). Self-leadership is however different from similar concepts like self-control and self-management, given its explicit emphasis on intrinsic motivation (Stewart et al., 2011). Extant research has pointed out a number of behavioral and cognitive implications of self-leadership in the context of work. Studies have shown that self-leadership is positively associated with job performance (regardless of being rated by self or others) by increasing one's self-efficacy, i.e., the extent to which one feels competent in performing work tasks (Prussia, Anderson, & Manz, 1998). Self-leadership is also positively associated with job attitudes like job satisfaction and organizational commitment (Harari, Williams, Castro, & Brant, 2021). Furthermore, self-leadership is not just the property of an individual but could also lie in a team. Team-level self-leadership enhances cohesion while promoting effective resolution of conflicts among team members (Stewart et al., 2011). Given the beneficial impacts of self-leadership at work, it is critical for organizations to recruit and cultivate individuals who engage in this leadership style. The earlier meta-analysis by Harari et al. identified several personality traits associated with self-leadership. Specifically, those with high conscientiousness, openness, and extraversion tend to be high on self-leadership. Also, self-leadership can be cultivated through management practice. One of the essential factors is transformational leadership (Harari et al., 2021) which focuses on leading subordinates with inspiration, idealized influence, intellectual stimulation, and individualized consideration (Avolio & Bass, 1995). There are also three types of strategies that employees can use to develop self-leadership – namely, behavior-focused (i.e., fostering positive behaviors while regulating negative ones through self-reflection and self-regulation), constructive thought pattern (i.e., creating a mindset that leads one to desirable behaviors), and natural reward self-leadership strategies (using forethought to identify naturally motivating elements about given tasks; Harari et al., 2021).

1.3 Transformative Leadership

One of the key notions of transformative leadership is that leaders need to inspire and encourage their employees to contribute to organizations, given the assumption that everyone can potentially act as a change agent or catalyst. Transformational leadership has four core components (Bass & Avolio, 1994), namely (a) intellectual stimulation (for example, encouraging followers to be creative and innovative); (b) individualized consideration (for example, caring and providing individual feedback to their followers); (c) inspirational motivation (for example, motivating their followers to commit to the organization); and (d) idealized influence (for example, being trusted and respected by their followers). This leadership style plays a critical role when organizations try to reinvent their businesses to be prepared for uncertainties, because each employee would play a key role in the process of organizational transformation. Transformational leaders are usually considered to be more effective and energetic and can help their followers to reach their optimal potential. As they can provide meaning and inspiration to their followers (University of Massachusetts Global, 2020), those led by transformational leaders should be more effective and adaptive during the time of organizational change. A recent meta-analysis indeed has shown such evidence. Specifically, transformational leadership is related to several types of reactions to organizational change including commitment to change, openness to change, readiness for change, and support for change (Peng, Li, Wang, & Lin, 2021). Further to that, the same meta-analysis has shown that transformational leadership is negatively associated with the negative reactions to organizational changes such as resistance to change and cynicism about change. Hence, this study reiterates that employees would become more motivated to engage in making changes in the organization, which could potentially have a positive ripple effect on self-leadership behaviors.

Though some might assume that certain people are naturally born to be a transformational leader who is charismatic and inspiring, research has shown that that is not necessary the case. For example, a review done by Sun, Chen, and Zhang (2017) has revealed a variety of predictors of transformational leadership. The first key antecedent is self-efficacy. When leaders have a strong conviction about themselves as a change agent in the organization, they should be more likely to initiate positive changes and/or encourage their followers to do the same to improve organizations. Another important predictor is emotional intelligence. It is important for leaders to understand how others feel that enables them to regulate their own negative emotions to inspire their followers. Kumar (2014) has also suggested the link between emotional intelligence and transformational leadership. Similarly, Lancefield and Rangen (2021) described that transformational leaders must be able to consider what others are thinking and going to do and to suppress their impulses. Furthermore, a recent empirical study provided evidence that behavioral cultural competence (CQ) has a positive impact on transformational leadership beyond personality traits (Crowne, 2019). Behavioral cultural competence concerns the extent to which individuals are able to exhibit culturally appropriate behaviors. Having high degree of behavioral cultural competence could potentially help leaders be trusted and respected by their followers. Given the potential positive impacts of these predictors on transformational leadership, organizations could consider providing training on building a sense of competence, emotional intelligence, as well as cultural competence for their leaders, so that they can act as an effective change agent to both the organizations and their followers.

1.4 Future of Work

We are now in the process of reinventing future of work every day (Gartner, n.d.) through technological advancement, the rise of artificial intelligence, as well as the implementation of automation in many spheres of business operations (Manyika et al., 2017; Deloitte, n.d.). Such rapid advancement of technology has certainly improved our lives, but also has been posing varying unique challenges. One of the most representative ones is the technologies that could potentially substitute employees, hence increasing unemployment rate. McKinsey (Manyika et al., 2017) reported that up to 50% of work that is currently done by human can be automated by utilizing technologies. Also, the COVID-19 pandemic has drastically shifted the way that businesses are conducted. For instance, the food industry is severely impacted by the pandemic, and the nature of work for food retailers and product suppliers has shifted to online shopping, e-commerce, and in-store pickups (Renner, Betts, & Cook, 2021). During such phases when we expect more changes to take place, employers are expected to take initiatives to lead the path to recreate the future workplace ecosystem. Specifically, employers can encourage their employees to engage in more upskilling opportunities so that they can keep pace with the technological changes that are rapidly evolving (Hancock, Lazaroff-Puck, & Rutherford, 2020). Continuous learning for employees is thus crucial to stay relevant and equipped with contemporary skills. It is not merely adequate and sufficient to enhance one's competence in technology, but employees should be equipped with essential abilities such as analytical and critical thinking, and interpersonal and leadership skills (Getsmarter, 2020; Brower, 2020).

1.5 Transformative Leaders: Case Studies

Steve Jobs, former CEO and co-founder of Apple, is often cited as a good example of a transformative leader with many describing him as a "visionary", "genius", and "iconic". This is due to his charismatic and inspirational qualities which allowed him to lead others in making the company successful. The New York Times reported that he had "led a cultural transformation in the way music, movies and mobile communications were experienced in the digital age" (Delaney & Spoelstra, 2015). He inspired and has been praised by many to an almost cult-like extent. The degree to which he influenced others was on a tremendous scale which had a ripple effect on people even outside of his organization. However, there was a dark side to Steve Jobs's leadership, where evidence shows that he may not necessarily be an inherently a full-fledged good-natured individual, as he was known to be manipulative, aggressive, and a bully to some of his employees. Another example of a transformational leader is Elon Musk who co-founded and leads various companies including Tesla, SpaceX, Neuralink, and The Boring Company. At Tesla, he takes lead in the areas of product design, engineering, and global manufacturing of the company's electric vehicles, battery products, and solar energy products. Elon Musk exemplifies all four facets of transformational leadership: idealized influence, inspirational motivation, intellectual stimulation, and individualized consideration (Asher, 2016). On the aspects of idealized influence or charisma, Elon Musk has well proven his confidence through his ideas by being a man of his word. Instead of convincing investors to fund his company like many other businessmen in Silicon Valley, he invests his own personal wealth into the varying company projects. This provides his followers with a model of the appropriate behavior he expects to see of them. Inspirational motivation refers to the degree to which a leader articulates a vision that is inspiring to followers. When SpaceX failed its third launch of its Falcon 1 rocket, an event that was extremely devastating to the company, Elon Musk directly addressed his employees and stakeholders of his organization instead of talking to the press. He went on to rally his team, encouraging them to push forward and said "for my part I will never give up, and I mean never". This motivated his team to work much harder and to be determined that enables them to immediately identify the causes of the accident, building a new rocket in six weeks and launching the world's first privately built rocket to achieve Earth orbit. The next facet, intellectual stimulation, is what many would say is his most obvious strength. It refers to how much a leader challenges assumptions, takes risks, and seeks followers' ideas. Not only did Elon Musk take a risk by investing a third of his wealth into one of his companies, but he did also so in an industry that was extremely and technically challenging and capital intensive. Further to that, his ability to question the status quo was noticed when he reduced the price to launch a rocket from $300 million to $60 million. Lastly, individualized consideration is the extent to which a leader deals with each follower's needs, acting as a mentor or coach. Elon Musk reportedly does this in a conventional manner pushing his employees to their breaking points. This is ingrained into the culture of SpaceX where people liken the company to the military or the "Special Forces". Elon Musk delivers both criticism and motivational talks strategically, though he never resorts to personal attacks and directs criticism to the matter at hand.

Masayoshi Son is another example who demonstrates the core qualities for transformational leadership – inspirational motivation and idealized influence. Masayoshi Son is the founder and CEO of SoftBank Group, which is a Japanese multinational conglomerate. Since he founded Softbank in 1981, he has had a strong vision of enabling a more connected world through investing in technologies (Pasztor & Martin, 2016). Son is committed to developing long-term visions. On the company website, Son introduces what he calls the next 30-year vision, but he actually regards his role as a leader to be designing "the DNA of the Softbank Group, which will last at least 300 years" (SoftBank Group, n.d.). To him, next 30 years are mere a stepping stone for their continued success that would last for next three centuries. Also, there is an employee testimonial that demonstrates his idealized influence. One former Softbank official had asked Son for a budget of 90 billion yen ($876 million) for the company's broadband business in the early 2000s. For that Son did not ask a single question but gave it immediately putting the trust and belief in his vision. The official later said, "He said, 'I trust you,' and all I could think was how I couldn't let him down" (Negishi, 2014). This episode illustrates how much strong influence and positive vibes Son gives to his employees through his actions and attitudes.

The value of transformational leadership has been increasingly recognized in not only developed countries but also in developing countries. For example, Al-Amri, Hassan, Isaac, and Masoud (2018) demonstrated that transformation leadership is positively associated with organizational innovation in higher education in Yemen. Especially, Africa presents a unique context for leadership research, given that the continent encompasses over 50 countries, territories, and states where people of greatly diverse backgrounds reside (Kets de Vries, Sexton, & Ellen, 2016). Sadly, Africa has seen some of destructive leaders in its history, such as Jean-Bedel Bokassa who declared himself as Emperor in the Central African Republic in 1966 and Idi Amin who was the third president of Uganda (Kets de Vries et al., 2016). However, there was indeed a transformational leader in Africa like Nelson Mandela. Such figure showcases that although there appears to be unique psychological and institutional factors that would induce leaders to act like dictators or despots in Africa (Kets de Vries, 2016), it is possible to foster more leaders like Mandela through the interventions at the levels of community, state and nations. The President of African Development Bank Group, Akinwumi A. Adesina, also expressed that it is necessary to ramp up the efforts of developing and growing the next generation of transformational leaders in Africa (allAfrica, 2021).

Recently, we have seen a good example of transformational leaders from developing countries. Ngozi Okonjo-Iweala, who is a former Nigeria's Minister of Finance, is another transformational leader. She was named one of the world's 50 greatest leaders by Fortune (Premium Times, 2015) for her contribution to the economy in Nigeria [i.e. for implementing a comprehensive economic reform and tripling its growth rate (Wilson, 2020)]. She graduated from Harvard University in 1976 and obtained a Ph.D. in Developmental Economics from Massachusetts Institute of Technology. She also served as a Managing Director of the World Bank Group from 2007 until 2011. During her term, she was responsible for the bank's operation in Africa, Europe, and Asia and did a pioneering work in assisting food and financial crises (Wilson, 2020). Currently, she is serving as the Director General (DG) of the World Trade Organization, as the first woman and African in the position (Business Daily, 2021). She is also active in fostering environments to promote future female leaders (Zhytkova, 2021).

Regarding her leadership competence, the Office of the US Trade Representative wrote, "She is widely respected for her effective leadership and has proven experience managing a large international organization with a diverse membership" (Office of the US Trade Representative, 2021). She possesses various qualities that make her a transformational leader, such as inspiring her followers with vivid visions and values (Lagosums, 2021). However, one of her most notable qualities as a leader lies in her spirit of empowering her followers to achieve the best outcomes possible. In her statement of being elected as the WTO General Director, she remarked, "At the WTO, the DG leads from behind working with the talented secretariat staff to help Members achieve results" (Okonjo-Iweala, 2021). This demonstrates that she sympathizes with a traditional leadership approach adopted by her predecessors at the WTO and that she would not force her followers to work in her own preferred ways but rather help them reach their own potential. Her statement seems to reflect the quality of individualized consideration of transformational leadership by serving as someone whom the followers can count on when the need arises.

An exemplary case of transformational leadership can be also identified in the context of Singapore. Mr. Lee Kuan Yew, Singapore's Founding Father, is said to possess various characteristics related to transformational leadership. Under his leadership, Singapore was transformed from a third-world country and became prosperous within three decades. There are several tips that can be learned from his leadership style (Business & Leadership, 2021). First and foremost, Lee Kuan Yew dedicated his life to a lofty vision of making Singapore great. One of the core characteristics of transformational leader is the ability to articulate a clear vision to their followers (Lancefield, 2020). Without being able to identify and promote the vision that can inspire and motivate followers, leaders cannot induce any changes from the followers and make any positive impacts on their organizations. Another key takeaway from Lee Yuan Yew as a transformational leader is his tenacious, consistent efforts in transforming Singapore. He is known for "his passion, his love of the Singapore people, his work ethic" (Business & Leadership, 2021). Such a quality as a leader should make followers trust and respect the leader. When leaders are able to successfully demonstrate their inspirational motivation in a relentless manner, they could better encourage and empower their followers to advance towards a common vision together. Overall, Lee Kuan Yew represents the two main aspects of transformational leadership, namely inspirational motivation and idealized influence.

As illustrated by the examples, transformational leadership can to a large extent drive a company to success. However, without self-leadership or an internal sense of awareness, a transformational leader may hurt others in the process of achieving greatness. Hence, a leader should engage in self-leadership as well to be a truly full-fledged transformational leader. Another primary concern would be the rapidly evolving business environment which influences the future of work.

The mission is to develop a multifaceted, holistic and validated framework that serves as a comprehensive guide for researchers and practitioners. Hence, the following multidimensional transformative strategies for the organization are recommended to meet the changing, complex and dynamic work landscape of the future. Figure 1.1 presents the Leadership and the Future Work Framework.

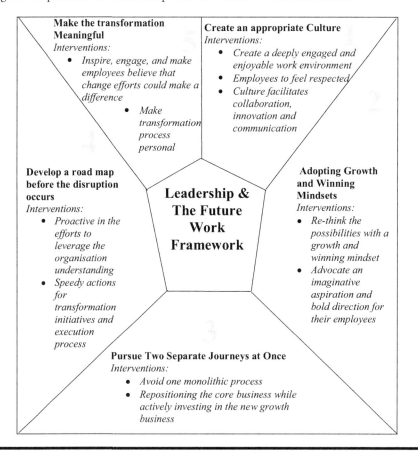

Figure 1.1 Leadership and the Future Work Framework

1.6 Strategy 1: Create an Appropriate Culture

The right company culture based on the business context and its dealings is imperative at the workplace as it has a large influencing effect on the overall work experience. This is primarily why many organizations put in a lot of effort in creating a work environment that employees could potentially be deeply engaged in and enjoy the work environment. As a result, employees feel appreciated and hence more motivated to work harder with increased level of commitment. Putting a high emphasis on the working culture from a transformational leadership perspective can be very beneficial in shaping the desired set of values and norms. Leaders who adopt transformational strategies must not only ensure that the company's culture allows employees to feel respected, but more explicitly reiterates that the culture facilitates collaboration, innovation, and communication. In the future, greater attention is required on the culture especially since the increase in virtual work environments may result in employees feeling less attached to the organization they are working for. In a nutshell, transformative aspects should be imbued into the company's culture to promote transformation. There are some empirical studies that indicate the importance for leaders to engage in some of the behaviors constituting transformational leadership to create an effective organizational culture and climate. For example, Sarros, Cooper, and Santora (2008) examined the six different types of transformational leadership behaviors, namely articulating vision; fostering acceptance of goals; intellectual stimulation; providing individual support; high-performance expectation, and providing appropriate role model and its implications in the organizational culture. Their findings indicated that among these eight behaviors, articulation of vision, individualized support, and high-performance expectation had significant positive relations with a competitive, performance-oriented organizational culture. They also found that such organizational culture is positively associated with climate for organizational innovation. The study thus demonstrates that adopting transformational leadership is critical in promoting a desirable organizational culture and climate that would contribute to employee creativity and firm innovation.

Similarly, Hartnell and Walumbwa (2011) emphasized the critical role played by CEO in influencing organizational culture. They argued that there are four specific ways that transformational leaders can affect organizational culture: (a) making broad strategic decisions to show the strategy and the landscape where the firm competes against others, (b) inspiring the followers with missions and values, (c) linking organizational success to the values and beliefs that the firm upholds, and (d) recognizing and rewarding the employees who exemplify the organizational values. Hartnell and Walumbwa (2011) argued that such transformational leadership adopted by the CEO would conduce to the development of certain organizational cultures (i.e., clan, adhocracy, and market cultures) which are related to firm effectiveness and innovation. To create a sustaining, long-lasting culture of transformation, there are a few strategies that McKinsey recommended (Cohen, Schrimper, & Taylor, 2019). First, organizations need to make expectations clear via role modeling. Cultural changes in organizations can be more effective when leaders demonstrate a set of expected attitudes and behaviors and convey them to their employees. McKinsey's research indeed showed that transformation is much more likely when employees could see the expected behavior being adopted by their leaders. Furthermore, CEO's active efforts in making transformation at the organization would enhance the effectiveness of organizational change. Put differently, *symbolic actions* of the company's executives would play a vital role in promoting a transformative culture within the organization. Unless employees have a clear understanding about what behavior is expected, building a sustained transformative culture would not be feasible. Towards this end, Cohen et al. (2019) suggested that organizations should develop a portfolio of symbolic action. More concretely, organizations can (a) define the purpose of and audience for potential symbolic actions, (b) brainstorm symbolic actions, and (c) review and prioritized ideas. Their symbolic actions should be consistent among organizational leaders and also should be in line with the culture that they want to promote. Equally critical is to share the vision for transformation with employees consistently (McKinsey & Company, 2020). In other words, transformative culture can be fostered when leaders repeatedly engage in desired behaviors and actions as well as constantly remind their employees of the type and form of organizational culture that they want to build within the organizations.

According to Liddle, there are five factors that are important for organizations to build transformational culture (Trapp, 2021). He claimed that organizations should be just, fair, inclusive, sustainable, and high performing to foster a positive culture. He also built the Transformational Culture Model that defines seven important characteristics that contribute to creating and fostering the culture. These seven characteristics are Collaboration, Courage, Common Purpose, Communication, Compassion, Curiosity, and Connection (7Cs). Most of these characteristics are in line with four key components of transformational leadership (idealized influence, inspirational motivation, intellectual stimulation, and individualized consideration). However, in order to sustain a transformational culture throughout the organization, all leaders in the organization need to base their attitudes and behaviors on these 7Cs. Also, adopting cultural changes in the organizations would require involvement from various stakeholders. Yohn (2021) argued that cultural changes can be made solely through the efforts of leaders such as CEO and senior management teams, but they can be achieved by involving board of directors, human resources department, compliance, risk, and ethics department, middle managers, and employees. When leaders aspire to adopt a new transformational culture, it is necessary to solicit endorsement from different parts of the organization. A positive culture is more effective when organizational members have consensus around a set of values and beliefs associated with the culture (Groysberg, Lee, Price, & Cheng, 2018). In spite of various potential benefits to which a transformational culture could give rise, when the values and beliefs relevant to the culture are not consistently practiced and shared across different levels and divisions of the organization, the new culture will not likely last or will not be sufficiently appreciated. It is thus critical for any cultural changes to be clearly communicated and shared within the organization across the board so that the culture will "stick" to the organization.

1.7 Strategy 2: Adopting Growth and Winning Mindsets

To re-shape an organization, you should adopt transformative leadership that requires you to rethink the possible and be inspired by adopting a growth and winning mindset. With the future bringing in new innovations and technology, it is crucial that organizations embrace changes and new possibilities. Leaders must re-iterate and direct their team to re-imagine the future (Dosik, Bhalla, &d Bailey, 2020). One way to do so is for leaders to set an imaginative aspiration and bold direction for their employees. This means reimagining how work gets done and what gets delivered. A good example to exemplify this would be the case of Netflix which envisioned a digital future for entertainment despite others in the industry dismissing the idea. The empirical research done by Bligh, Kohles, and Yan (2018) points out how leaders can affect their followers' mindset. Specifically, the relationship among leadership styles and employee error-learning orientation was investigated. Evidence shows that employees were more willing to learn from their mistakes when their leaders adopt transformational leadership style. However, it was found that other types of leadership styles, for example, laissez-faire and aversive leadership, can be detrimental to employees' orientation towards error learning. It was also reported that the reason for laissez-faire and aversive leadership reduction in employees' error learning is partially because these two types of leadership styles would lead employees to develop a fixed, rather than growth mindset.

Hence, it is vital for leaders to adopt appropriate behaviors to promote growth mindset of employees. Indeed, employees in a growth mindset company are 47% more likely to say that their colleagues are trustworthy, 34% more likely to feel a strong sense of ownership and commitment to the firm, 65% more likely to say that the company promotes innovation, according to the research done by Carol Dweck (Harvard Business Review, 2014). Indeed, CEO of Microsoft, Nadella recognizes the value of growth mindset and engaged in fostering the company culture that emphasizes employee learning and development (Levine, 2019). This was reiterated by Gottfredson and Rajaram (2021) who advocated:

> The key is to focus on the central aspect of vertical development: make meaning in the most cognitively and emotionally sophisticated ways. Psychologists and neuroscientists have identified one factor foundational to one's meaning making: their mindsets. In fact, this is what Satya Nadella focused on to elevate Microsoft's culture leading to the dramatic growth they have experienced. His experience helps us identify the specific mindsets that should be focused on for upgrading leaders' operating

systems so that they can better navigate change, pressure, ambiguity, and uncertainty. When Nadella took over as CEO, he saw that Microsoft's culture socially incentivized leaders to be focused on looking good (fixed mindset), being right (closed mindset), avoiding problems (prevention mindset), and getting ahead (inward mindset). But he wanted and created a culture that socially incentivized leaders to be focused on learning and growing (growth mindset), finding truth and thinking optimally (open mindset), reaching goals (promotion mindset), and lifting others (outward mindset).

The company also explicitly rewarded risk-taking behaviors of managers, given the belief that employees could achieve rapid learning through mistakes and errors. There are several recommendations for promoting growth mindset – valuing hard work, encouraging employee learning and helping employees challenge difficult problems, promoting experimentation of new ideas, giving feedback to their performance, and emphasizing the importance of not being afraid of making mistakes and learning from them (Bansal, 2021).

Adopting a growth mindset is easier said than done. Actually, managers could misinterpret the meaning of it and practice it in less effective ways. For example, Dweck (2016) argued that sometimes people have a limited understanding about a growth mindset. People can sometimes confuse a growth mindset with other types of mindsets or attitudes, such as being flexible and/or open-minded. Also, Dweck argued that there is no such thing as a pure growth mindset, as everyone has a mixture of fixed and growth mindset. People could also sometimes misconstrue a growth mindset as simply praising and rewarding effort without putting outcomes aside. However, a growth mindset is not about ignoring the outcomes for the sake of appreciating the efforts people made, but rather it is about emphasizing the process that leads to positive organizational outcomes, for example, learning, seeking help from others, creating and implementing new, bold strategies, and feedback. Finally, a growth mindset is not something that people just need to adopt but those with the mindset must take actions based on that. Organizations that value a growth mindset also need to set expectations about employees' behaviors that are revolved around it. Encouraging employees to act on a growth mindset is particularly important, because as mentioned above, people can adopt a fixed mindset, especially when they receive criticism or experience setbacks and/or undesirable outcomes. When such negative incidents occur, people tend to become more rigid and inflexible, feel insecure, and become less willing to accept others' feedback for future growth. In order to practice a growth mindset, employees need to recognize these fixed-mindset triggers and understand that they actually thwart them from achieving growth and future progress.

As much as a growth mindset, a winning mindset also requires people to consistently work on and practice. There are five practical tips about building a winning mindset: (a) not relying on your talent; (b) building your GRIT (sustained passion and perseverance towards one's long-term goal or objective); (c) generating momentum with small steps; (d) trusting one's own vision; and (e) taking actions (Mahaffey, 2017). It is important for leaders who try to adopt a winning mindset to be not overly concerned about making mistakes or preventing problems. When people become prevention-focused, they will be less likely to set aspirational goals and might end up with limiting their own potential. Rather, leaders should be more promotion-oriented to pursue winning and gains (Gottfredson & Reina, 2020), and thereby, adopt a winning mindset. For both growth and winning mindset to be adopted and practiced among leaders, organizations could provide a technique called nudge (Güntner, Schaninger, & Sperling, 2018). Much like an organizational culture that requires persistent efforts and involvement from multiple stakeholders, the organization needs to encourage and motivate their leaders to adopt the right mindset. A nudge is a simple intervention that can influence people's mind and behaviors in an unconscious manner without limiting their autonomy. Research has shown that a nudge can change the waste tossing behavior of Chinese employees working in a garment factory (Wu & Paluck, 2021). Organizations can instill behaviors that are derived from growth and winning mindsets in employees by coming up with a nudge so that employees could acquire the new mindsets. A nudge is particularly effective to promote a certain mindset since it does not make people feel that they adopt the mindset on their own volition instead of being forced to do so by the organization.

1.8 Strategy 3: Pursue Two Separate Journeys at Once

Many firms that have attempted to transform but have failed before (Anthony & Schwartz, 2017). This is usually due to the leaders' approach towards change as one monolithic process. Instead, success necessitates repositioning the core business while actively investing in the new growth business. An example will be Apple where Steve Jobs renewed the core Macintosh franchise with the launch of the iMac and the iBook while concurrently releasing the device and content ecosystem with iPod and iTunes. Other companies such as Amazon and ThyssenKrupp have also successfully adopted this strategy. As the future of markets becomes more volatile, entering new growth markets becomes essential for a company to transform itself and remain competitive.

Firms often face a common dilemma of whether they should focus their investment on improving upon their products or operations by exploiting on their current capabilities or on developing new innovations through exploration (Levinthal & March, 1993). However, solely focusing on one while ignoring the other is not an ideal practice. When firms emphasize too much on continuing to enhance their existing competence, there is a risk that they would not become able to catch up with any changes or technological advancement in the industry. In contrast, if firms heavily seek for innovations even in the domains where their competence does not lie, firm performance and effectiveness would likely fluctuate. Researchers have thus suggested that it be best for firms to pursue two of them simultaneously (i.e., ambidexterity), so that firms can achieve optimal performance (He & Wong, 2004; March 1991; O'Reilly & Tushman, 2004).

Boumgarden, Nickerson, and Zenger (2012) explained that managers could take two different approaches to navigate firm with certain levels of exploitation and exploration – ambidexterity and vacillation. Ambidexterity refers to that mangers try to achieve exploitation and exploration simultaneously. For example, firms could have two divisions, one of which focuses on exploitation (for example, targeting the needs and demands of current customers) and the other focuses on exploration (for example, expanding its business into new sectors or industries). The other approach, vacillation, concerns that firms focus on either one type of strategies (exploitation or exploration) at one time, and then they switch to the other. This approach is more temporally dynamic and assumes that firms would develop some capability in exploitation (or exploration) during the time they focus on the strategy. The capability would stick to the firms for some time, even after they switch to the other strategy, and therefore, the firms can temporally achieve a good balance of these two strategies and reap the benefits from both.

Diversification in business also has a critical implication in firm performance. For example, strategic researchers have been extensively studying the relationship between diversification and accounting measures of performance, market-based measures of performance, and other performance indicators such as research and development (R&D), innovation, and riskiness (Ahuja & Novelli, 2017). Though the relationship between diversification and performance is intricate and often depends on contextual factors, diversification can be value-maximizing and synergy-making if firms can access certain assets that can be only accessible through newly entered markets, reduce transaction costs, coordinate with other organizations, and mitigate potential risks. Without careful deliberation, engaging in diversification or pursuing multiple goals at once definitely does have a potential for more harm than good. However, not diversifying at all is also risky and can be a potential impediment to organizations' future growth and development of competitive advantages to other companies. Fosfuri, Giarratana, and Roca (2016) also argued that diversification can lead to a competitive advantage of the organizations that follow both business and social logics (social business hybrids). Organizations can achieve diversification through various ways such as launching new products for different customers and markets from their core targets, opening up new sales and/or distribution channels, as well as allocating their investment to different areas of R&D (Markides, 1997). By effectively diversifying business, organizations can manage their risks by reducing reliance on specific customers and resources and integrating novel capabilities from other firms into their own existing ones. One notable example is Disney, and only 32% of their profits come from movies and parks like Disneyland and Disney World (lumen, n.d.).

Reddy, Kurdziel, and Sanfilippo (2019) illustrated various benefits of diversification. First, although sometimes considered to distract organizations' focus, diversification can help organizations protect their core business. Second, diversification can accelerate organizations' growth. Third, diversifying firms may be seen more attractive to investors compared to less diversifying firms. Fourth, diversification can bring potential benefits to firms by allowing them to leverage and create synergies with their core capabilities. Diversification can thus help organizations build new firm capabilities that can transform their main businesses, leading to a positive feedback loop. For instance, an organization could acquire new information and technology systems through merger and acquisitions when entering a new market, which can not only drive success in the new market but enhances the organization's overall technological competence and increases their repository of resources, thereby leading to the success in their core market. Such integration of new resources and technology can help firms improve other parts of their business as well, which results in the transformation of the organization's entire business. Also, diversification could produce more profits and adds greater value to organizations in emerging markets rather than in developed ones (Caudillo, Houben, & Noor, 2015). Organizations that diversify their business in the markets that are too similar to their existing, established ones may limit opportunities to learn and acquire new skills and experiences that can be fed back to their existing capabilities. In other words, less bold diversification strategies may not produce much profit, and they are unlikely to lead to transformation of organizations.

1.9 Strategy 4: Develop a Road Map Before the Disruption Occurs

Being merely responsive is not adequate for a leader to ensure that his or her company will successfully survive when a disruption occurs. A leader must also be proactive to comprehend the rapid changes and hence be agile in the consistent efforts to respond adequately to leverage the organization. Normally, transformations often cannot be fully addressed and completed within the average tenure of a CEO (Anthony & Schwartz, 2017). Hence, this suggests that a company need to be quick in responding to changes and has limited time to waste in getting started with their transformation initiatives and execution process. Many companies that were disrupted were rather slow to plan and respond, hence met with troubles a decade or more after the first warning symptoms of major disruption emerged. None of these organization's leaders had developed effective transformation plans on time to respond swiftly. One example of a leader who came up with a road map is Reed Hastings of Netflix who laid down the groundwork for transformation as far back as 2007. Given the difficulty of effectively making and implementing transformational changes within the organization, developing a concrete roadmap is critical. The research from McKinsey showed that 70% of transformations the organizations fail, and transformational changes would require much more time and investment than anticipated by business leaders. Without having solid plans, attempts of making transformational changes would likely go futile. For instance, many businesses were unprepared for digital transformation when the COVID-19 outbreak occurred (D'Auria & De Smet, 2020; BDO, 2020). This is despite that it had been a foresee-able future that organizations have to eventually move to digital platforms given the rapid and evolving technological advancements. This instance showcases that many business leaders had not put sufficient efforts and have not been seriously committed to the development of clear plans of responses and transformative changes for the future before the need arose (Crisis Communications, 2020). It is thus imperative for organizations to develop capable leaders who can effectively expect the need for changes and implement strategies accordingly. Leaders need to relate and identify these potential crises which could potentially happen in the future and hence have a long-term focus and vision in their business and its environment.

In more concrete terms, researchers have identified several key factors that are central in making transformation in organizations, namely (a) external environment; (b) mission and strategy; (c) leadership, organizational culture; and (d) individual and organizational performance (Burke & Litwin, 1992). Leadership is intricately associated with all these four factors. Leaders need to proactively assess the challenges that lie in the external environments and to engage in developing and implementing necessary strategies and organizational practice. Moreover, for leaders to guide effec-tive transformational changes, there are some other recommendations. For example, leaders must make their commitments to organizational changes clear and transpar-ent to their employees while open to expect resistance or pushbacks from employees against the organizational changes implemented. Leaders need to think of ways to convince their employees of the necessity and importance of the changes so that they could avoid any potential conflicts within the organization. Leaders' involvement and their commitment in making transformation is vital where it commences from laying out concrete plans for the changes that they want to see happens.

Understanding critical components that lead to successful transformation is thus vital for managers in developing a concrete roadmap and identifying a specific set of actions and strategies that need to be implemented by employees. Bucy, Fin-layson, Kelly, and Moye (2016) emphasized three essential aspects for transforma-tion: people, process, and skill. Concerning the people, organizations need to ensure an appropriate governance structure, or a *transformation office* (TO) is established. TO consists of "a few respected executives supported by analysts from the finance and HR functions" (Bucy et al., 2016). In the TO, there should be a chief transfor-mation officer (CTO) who regularly reports to the CEO about the progress about intraorganizational efforts and decisions concerning transformation. Thus, the role played by the CTO is critical, and the organization needs to entrust this position to someone who can orchestrate and guide the transformation. The second compo-nent necessary for effective transformation concerns the process. Bucy et al. (2016) specifically recommended to set up a weekly meeting to follow up on each of the organization's transformative efforts. This weekly meeting serves as a platform where line leaders update their progress and ask the CTO relating to questions and con-cerns about the transformative plans. Finally, it is imperative for the organization to develop robust tracking and reporting systems (i.e., tools). Such tools are necessary to monitor performance to understand the progress of transformative initiatives and to identify any problems being faced by managers who are in charge of implementing the initiatives. The top-down instruction from the CTO to line managers about the transformative plans is usually inadequate to get the managers stay motivated to achieve transformation. When planning to transform some areas of organizations, it is necessary for executives to consider the people who will be in charge of overseeing transformation, how the progress is monitored, and how the organization will address potential problems during the process of transformation.

Also, Argenti, Berman, Calsbeek, and Whitehouse (2021) examined 128 companies and identified six attributes that lead to successful company transformation. These attributes include (a) employee pay (employees in the organizations with successful transformation were compensated more highly); (b) employee stock options (employees receive more stock options); (c) employee satisfaction (employees in these companies reported greater satisfaction); (d) diversity and inclusivity (these companies emphasize equity in hiring practices); (e) women managers (these companies employee more women in managerial positions); and (f) women employees (these companies have a greater proportion of female employees). Their study provides important insights on how organizations can set up the environment that is more conducive to transformations. Microsoft rolled out their transformation initiatives about overhauling the company's vision and mission and shifting from a product focus to an inclusive one, to be people focus. One aspect they did was to revise their compensation policy to encourage more teamwork and collaboration among employees. Their transformative initiative yielded a great success, and Microsoft moved from a software company to a cloud-services company and gained $1.5 trillion market capitalization. Also, Anthony, Trotter, and Schwartz (2019) conducted a similar study and examined the companies that achieved the highest-impact business transformations over the past decade. The study found that these companies have a purpose-driven mission (for example, Netflix is not simply committed to distributing content digitally to their customers but becoming a leading producer of original content). To achieve successful transformation in organizations, executives need to take various factors into due consideration. Hence, it is crucial for the management to carefully consider how and what organizations need to do and develop a clear roadmap towards transformation.

1.10 Strategy 5: Make the Transformation Meaningful

For initiatives to succeed, a leader must be able to inspire others to work towards the intended outcomes. Employees must believe that change efforts would potentially make significant difference and impact between success and failure. By making the transformation personalized and openly engaging their employees, leaders can rally them and encourage action. Successful leaders are also known to refer to their own life experiences to exemplify their determination to overcome obstacles. This can both motivate and inspire employees to do the same for the company. Many of transformational changes in the organization ended up failing. According to Gleeson (2017), one of the reasons for such failures may be attributed to the fact that many organizational members become less motivated in making changes when they experience what Gleeson calls *change battle fatigue* stemming from "past failures plaguing the minds of employees and the sacrifices made during the arduous change process". In order to prevent employees from being exhausted, it is not simply enough to impose organizational changes upon employees but instead, leaders have to ensure that followers clearly understand the reasons and meanings behind the changes. In other words, leaders have to explain why certain organizational changes are necessary and important to both the entire organization and also individual employees by involving the employees throughout the process (The Limeade Team, n.d.). For example, when FMC Corporation, a manufacturing company in the United States, engaged in acquisition of DuPont's Crop Protection business, it was able to successfully navigate this change process by developing the "Nature of Next", an internal communication campaign whereby the managers clearly explained the vision and meaning for the acquisition (Galbraith, 2018). Indeed, research also shows that the way leaders communicate the values and meanings of the changes would affect the lasting transformation of the organization (Dalpiaz & Di Stefano, 2018). Clear top-down communication from management about changes also encourages employees to engage in bottom-up efforts and cross-functional core processes that link different activities and competencies (Dichter, Gagnon, & Alexander, 1993).

But how can organizations effectively tell employees about the significance of transformation? Ricks (2020) shared a four-step process of communicating organizational change, which involves (1) sharing a vision, (2) telling a story, (3) making those in the organization the heroes, and (4) charting the path. As reiterated already, followers will not be empowered and inspired unless leaders provide clear visions. Storytelling also plays a key role in order to effectively communicate the company's vision and goals for the change. For example, Scandinavian Airlines, when facing financial struggles, created a short handbook for employees that describes "how "storm clouds" and "bad weather" had struck the business and how it faced challenges in being profitable" (Ricks, 2020). Communicating changes in the form of a story is particularly valuable because it emphasizes that employees are not just part of the changes but actually the main characters or heroes who lead the changes, soliciting active participation and involvement on the part of employees. Finally, it is also important for the organization to help employees understand how they can actually achieve the changes. For example, Rakuten, a Japanese online retailer, changes the language of the company and asked 7,100 employees in Tokyo to conduct business in English, despite that the majority of the employees were native Japanese. Employees find this initiative personally challenging, and therefore, Rakuten helped employees chart the path to achieve the change through both words (for example, telling employees that the company is fully committed to the employees' learning of English) and actions (for example, funding for language programs). It is thus essential for organizations to provide resources for employees to handle the changes and transition so that employees will not feel overwhelmed by participating in the change process.

By simply telling employees about organizational changes is not sufficient to accomplish transformation (Galbraith, 2018). Almost one-third employees do not understand why specific organizational changes happen. Such lack of employees' understanding of the purpose of making organizational changes presents a barrier to eliciting motivation and commitment from employees to drive transformation. It is also plausible that those who do not see the value of certain changes might become more cynical about organizational changes, resulting in resistance or push-back from employees (DeCelles, Tesluk, & Taxman, 2013). As transformation can-not be achieved without employees, Galbraith (2018) emphasized the importance of articulating the value and significance of changes or explaining "What's in it for me?" to employees; in other words, employees need to be communicated about how the changes can be personally important or meaningful. There are four important ways to motivate employees to be committed to organizational changes: (a) inspiring employees by presenting a compelling vision for the future, (b) keeping employees informed by providing regular communications, (c) empowering leaders and man-agers to lead through change, and (d) finding creative ways to involve employees in the change. For the first point, the management needs to explain why transfor-mation is important as well as its positive impacts on employees and the organiza-tion. Second, the management needs to communicate to employees the information about transformation (for example, motive, value, progress) in a clear and consistent manner. Third, it is vital that leaders feel confident in leading through changes so that employees also feel assured of the value of transformation. Finally, the manage-ment needs to solicit feedback and involve the employees throughout the transfor-mation process so that employees feel more personally accountable and proactive for the changes that they are making.

Seeking involvement from employees is particularly critical in any kinds of change management in organizations. Involvement is not simply about assigning to employees specific tasks and knowledge necessary for transformation but rather "giv-ing people real ownership of an initiative or milestone that contributes to the trans-formation" (McKinsey & Company, 2021). To facilitate successful transformations, one-way communication from the management to tactical leaders and/or line manag-ers and/or employees is not sufficient, but the most successful organizations typically engage the employees in face-to-face communication and internal, organization-wide meetings such as town halls. As an example, Tabrizi, Lam, Girard, and Irvin (2019) explained how digital transformation should take place in organizations. They pro-vided two suggestions with regard to employee involvement. First, organizations need to leverage insiders and solicit insights from the staff who have in-depth knowledge and experiences about what really works and what does not in their daily work. Transformation can be more readily achieved if the management incorporates the feedback from employees; by doing so, employees would also feel that the digital transformation is more personally relevant and that they actually contribute to the large-scale changes made by the organization. Second, concerning digital transformation, the organization needs to recognize employees' fear of being replaced to avoid potential pushback from employees. The organization needs to be beware of whether employees positively or negatively view the changes and to send appropriate messages to them if they perceive the transformation as a threat. This requires the management to constantly and closely collect feedback from employees and continue to involve them throughout the process of transformation. Failing to do so would likely result in less active participation of employees in transformation initiatives or potential pushback from those with cynical attitudes towards the changes.

References

Ahuja, G., & Novelli, E. (2017). Redirecting research efforts on the diversification-performance linkage: The search for synergy. *Academy of Management Annals, 11*(1), 342–390.

Al-Amri, A. Y., Hassan, R., Isaac, O., & Masoud, Y. (2018). The effect of transformational leadership on organizational innovation in higher education: The case of developing countries. *International Journal of Management and Human Science, 2*(4), 25–37.

allAfrica. (2021, August 30). *President Akinwumi Adesina calls for transformational leadership in Africa, shares personal experiences with lecture audience.* https://allafrica.com/stories/202108300837.html

Andressen, P., Konradt, U., & Neck, C. P. (2011). The relation between self-leadership and transformational leadership. *Journal of Leadership & Organizational Studies, 19*(1), 68–82.

Anthony, S. D., & Schwartz, E. I. (2017, September 20). What the best transformational leaders do. *Harvard Business Review.* https://hbr.org/2017/05/what-the-best-transformational-leaders-do

Anthony, S. D., Trotter, A., & Schwartz, E. I. (2019, September 24). The top 20 business transformations of the last decade. *Harvard Business Review.* https://hbr.org/2019/09/the-top-20-business-transformations-of-the-last-decade

Argenti, P. A., Berman, J., Calsbeek, R., & Whitehouse, A. (2021, September 14). The secrete behind successful corporate transformations. *Harvard Business Review.* https://hbr.org/2021/09/the-secret-behind-successful-corporate-transformations

Asher, E. (2016). *Elon Musk: A case for transformational leadership.* https://doi.org/10.13140/RG.2.1.2353.9609

Avolio, B. J., & Bass, B. M. (1995). Individual consideration viewed at multiple levels of analysis: A multi-level framework for examining the diffusion of leadership. *The Leadership Quarterly, 6*(2), 199–218.

Bansal, V. (2021, May 6). How to promote a growth mindset in the workplace. *TechTello.* https://www.techtello.com/how-to-promote-growth-mindset-in-workplace/

Bass, B. M., & Avolio, B. J. (1994). *Improving organizational effectiveness through transformational leadership.* Sage.

BDO. (2020). *COVID-19 is accelerating the rise of the digital economy.* https://www.bdo.com/insights/business-financial-advisory/strategy,-technology-transformation/covid-19-is-accelerating-the-rise-of-the-digital-e

Bligh, M. C., Kohles, J. C., & Yan, Q. (2018). Leading and learning to change: The role of leadership style and mindset in error learning and organizational change. *Journal of Change Management, 18*(2), 116–141.

Boumgarden, P., Nickerson, J., & Zenger, T. R. (2012). Sailing into the wind: Exploring the relationships among ambidexterity, vacillation, and organizational performance. *Strategic Management Journal, 33*, 587–610.

Brower, T. (2020, May 3). Creating the future of work: 10 leadership strategies for the greatest impact. *Forbes.* https://www.forbes.com/sites/tracybrower/2020/05/03/creating-the-future-of-work-10-leadership-strategies-for-the-greatest-impact/?sh=47e1e19f5a7a

Bucy, M., Finlayson, A., Kelly, G., & Moye, C. (2016, May 9). The 'how' of transformation. *Harvard Business Review.* https://www.mckinsey.com/industries/retail/our-insights/the-how-of-transformation

Burke, W. W., & Litwin, G. H. (1992). A causal model of organizational performance and change. *Journal of Management, 18*(3), 523–545.

Business Daily. (2021, August 2). *Ngozi Okonjo-Iweala set to make history as first woman and African to head WTO.* https://www.france24.com/en/tv-shows/business-daily/20210208-ngozi-okonjo-iweala-set-to-make-history-as-first-woman-and-african-to-head-wto

Business & Leadership. (2021, November 3). *Lee Kuan Yew – The Warren Buffet of Singapore – Leadership transformed Singapore into world powerhouse.* https://www.businessandleadership.com/leadership/item/lee-kuan-yew-leadership-transformed-singapore/

Caldwell, C., Dixon, R. D., Floyd, L. A., Chaudoin, J., Post, J., & Cheokas, G. (2011). Transformative leadership: Achieving unparalleled excellence. *Journal of Business Ethics, 109*(2), 175–187.

Caudillo, F., Houben, S., Noor, J. (2015, August 1). Mapping the value of diversification. *McKinsey & Company.* https://www.mckinsey.com/business-functions/strategy-and-corporate-finance/our-insights/mapping-the-value-of-diversification

Cohen, J., Schrimper, M., & Taylor, E. (2019, July 29). Elephant in the room: Making a culture transformation stick with symbolic actions. *McKinsey & Company.* https://www.mckinsey.com/business-functions/people-and-organizational-performance/our-insights/the-organization-blog/elephant-in-the-room-making-a-culture-transformation-stick-with-symbolic-actions

Crisis Communications. (2020, June 22). 6 key steps that will help your company respond to any crisis situation. *RepTrak.* https://www.reptrak.com/blog/6-key-steps-that-will-help-your-company-respond-to-any-crisis-situation/

Crowne, K. A. (2019). Investigating antecedents of transformational leadership in students. *Journal of International Education in Business, 12*(1), 80–94. https://doi.org/10.1108/JIEB-07-2018-0029

Dalpiaz, E., & Di Stefano, G. (2018). A universe of stories: Mobilizing narrative practices during transformative change. *Strategic Management Journal, 39*, 664–696.

D'Auria, G., & De Smet, A. (2020, March 16). Leadership in a crisis: Responding to the coronavirus outbreak and future challenges. *McKinsey & Company.* https://www.mckinsey.com/business-functions/organization/our-insights/leadership-in-a-crisis-responding-to-the-coronavirus-outbreak-and-future-challenges

DeCelles, K. A., Tesluk, P. E., & Taxman, F. S. (2013). A field investigation of multilevel cynicism toward change. *Organizational Science, 24*(1), 154–171.

Delaney, H., & Spoelstra, S. (2015). Case study: Steve Jobs as a transformational leader. In B. Carroll, J. Ford, & S. Taylor (Eds.), *Leadership: Contemporary critical perspectives* (pp. 81–83). Sage.

Deloitte. (n.d.). *Future of work.* https://www2.deloitte.com/us/en/insights/focus/technology-and-the-future-of-work.html

Dichter, S. F., Gagnon, C., & Alexander, A. (1993, February 1). Leading organizational transformations. *McKinsey & Company.* https://www.mckinsey.com/business-functions/organization/our-insights/leading-organizational-transformations

Dosik, D., Bhalla, V., & Bailey, A. (2020, July 31). A lot will change—So must leadership. *BCG.* https://www.bcg.com/publications/2020/importance-of-transformative-leadership-post-coronavirus

Dweck, C. (2016, January 13). What having a "growth mindset" actually means. *Harvard Business Review.* https://hbr.org/2016/01/what-having-a-growth-mindset-actually-means

Fosfuri, A., Giarratana, M. S., & Roca, E. (2016). Social business hybrids: Demand externalities, competitive advantage, and growth through diversification. *Organization Science*, *27*(5), 1275–1289.

Galbraith, M. (2018, October 5). Don't just tell employees organizational changes are coming—Explain why. *Harvard Business Review.* https://hbr.org/2018/10/dont-just-tell-employees-organizational-changes-are-coming-explain-why

Gartner. (n.d.). *Future of work reinvented.* https://www.gartner.com/en/insights/future-of-work

Getsmarter. (2020, September 28). *How to respond to the future of work: The importance of upskilling.* https://www.getsmarter.com/blog/market-trends/how-to-respond-to-the-future-of-work-the-importance-of-upskilling/

Gottfredson, R., & Rajaram, K. (2021). *Elevate leaders' operating systems to navigate disruptive conditions.* Association for Talent Development, United States.

Gottfredson, R., & Reina, C. (2020, January 17). To be a great leader, you need the right mindset. *Harvard Business Review.* https://hbr.org/2020/01/to-be-a-great-leader-you-need-the-right-mindset

Groysberg, B., Lee, J., Price, J., & Cheng, J. Y-J. (2018). The leader's guide to corporate culture. *Harvard Business Review.* https://hbr.org/2018/01/the-leaders-guide-to-corporate-culture

Güntner, A., Schaninger, B., & Sperling, J. (2018, July 16). Changing mindsets and behavior, one "nudge" at a time. *McKinsey & Company.* https://www.mckinsey.com/business-functions/people-and-organizational-performance/our-insights/the-organization-blog/how-to-change-mindset-and-behavior

Hancock, B., Lazaroff-Puck, K., & Rutherford, S. (2020, January 30). Getting practical about the future of work. *McKinsey Quarterly.* https://www.mckinsey.com/business-functions/organization/our-insights/getting-practical-about-the-future-of-work

Harari, M. B., Williams, E. A., Castro, S. L., & Brant, K. K. (2021). Self-leadership: A meta-analysis of over two decades of research. *Journal of Occupational and Organizational Psychology*, *94*(4), 890–923.

Hartnell, C. A., & Walumbwa, F. O. (2011). Transformational leadership and organizational culture. In N. M. Ashkanasy, C. P. M. Wilderom, & M. F. Peterson (Eds.), *Handbook of organizational culture and climate* (2nd ed., pp. 225–248). Sage.

Harvard Business Review. (2014). *How companies can profit from a "Growth Mindset".* https://hbr.org/2014/11/how-companies-can-profit-from-a-growth-mindset

He, Z. L., & Wong, P. K. (2004). Exploration vs. exploitation: An empirical test of the ambidexterity hypothesis. *Organization Science*, *15*(4), 481–494.

Kets de Vries, M. F. R. (2016, October 5). Lessons in destructive leadership from Africa. *INSEAD Knowledge.* https://knowledge.insead.edu/leadership-organisations/lessons-in-destructive-leadership-from-africa-4965

Kets de Vries, M. F. R., Sexton, J. C., & Ellen III, B. P. (2016). Destructive and transformational leadership in Africa. *Africa Journal of Management, 2*(2), 166–187.

Kumar S. (2014). Establishing linkages between emotional intelligence and transformational leadership. *Industrial Psychiatry Journal, 23*(1), 1–3. https://doi.org/10.4103/0972-6748.144934

Lagosums. (2021, March 1). *10 leadership lessons we can learn from Dr. Ngozi Okonjo-Iweala.* https://lagosmums.com/10-leadership-lessons-dr-okonjo-iweala/

Lancefield, D., & Rangen, C. (2021, May 5). 4 actions transformational leaders take. *Harvard Business Review.* https://hbr.org/2021/05/4-actions-transformational-leaders-take

Lancefield, D. (2020, November 6). How to be a visionary leader and still have a personal life. *Harvard Business Review.* https://hbr.org/2020/11/how-to-be-a-visionary-leader-and-still-have-a-personal-life

Levine, S. R. (2019, February 26). Outperform with a growth mindset culture. *Forbes.* https://www.forbes.com/sites/forbesinsights/2019/02/26/outperform-with-a-growth-mindset-culture/?sh=46ab4b8d3c2c

Levinthal, D. A., & March, J. G. (1993). The myopia of learning. *Strategic Management Journal, 14*, 95–112.

lumen. (n.d.). *Reading: Diversification example.* https://courses.lumenlearning.com/cochise-marketing/chapter/reading-diversification-example/#footnote-1185-1

Mahaffey, D. (2017, September 22). Five ways to develop a winning mindset. *Forbes.* https://www.forbes.com/sites/forbescoachescouncil/2017/09/22/five-ways-to-develop-a-winning-mindset/?sh=3c1129524ca2

Manyika, J., Lund, S., Chui, M., Bughin, J., Woetzel, J., Batra, P., Ko, R., & Sanghvi, S. (2017, November 28). Jobs lost, jobs gained: What the future of work will mean for jobs, skills, and wages. *McKinsey Global Institute.* https://www.mckinsey.com/featured-insights/future-of-work/jobs-lost-jobs-gained-what-the-future-of-work-will-mean-for-jobs-skills-and-wages

Manz, C. C. (1986). Self-leadership: Toward an expanded theory of self-influence processes in organizations. *Academy of Management Review, 11*(3), 585–600.

Manz, C. C., & Sims, Jr. H. P. (1980). Self-management as a substitute for leadership: A social learning theory perspective. *Academy of Management Review, 5*(3), 361–367.

March, J. G. (1991). Exploration and exploitation in organizational learning. *Organization Science, 2*(1), 71–87.

Markides, C. C. (1997). To diversify or not to diversify. *Harvard Business Review.* https://hbr.org/1997/11/to-diversify-or-not-to-diversify

Marques-Quinteiro, P., Vargas, R., Eifler, N., & Curral, L. (2018). Employee adaptive performance and job satisfaction during organizational crisis: The role of self-leadership. *European Journal of Work and Organizational Psychology, 28*(1), 85–100.

McKinsey & Company. (2020, October 28). *The path to true transformation.* https://www.mckinsey.com/business-functions/transformation/our-insights/the-path-to-true-transformation

McKinsey & Company. (2021, December 7). *Losing from day one: Why even successful transformations fall short.* https://www.mckinsey.com/business-functions/people-and-organizational-performance/our-insights/successful-transformations

Montuori, A., & Donnelly, G. (2017). Transformative leadership. In *Handbook of personal and organizational transformation* (pp. 1–33). https://doi.org/10.1007/978-3-319-29587-9_59-1

Negishi, M. (2014). How SoftBank's Masayoshi Son gets what he wants. *The Wall Street Journal.* https://www.wsj.com/articles/BL-JRTB-16336

Office of the United States Trade Representative. (2021, February 5). *Office of the United States Trade Representative Statement on the Director General of the World Trade Organization*. https://ustr.gov/about-us/policy-offices/press-office/press-releases/2021/february/office-united-states-trade-representative-statement-director-general-world-trade-organization

Okonjo-Iweala, N. (2021, February 13). *Statement of Director-General Elect Dr. Ngozi Okonjo-Iweala to the Special Session of the WTO General Council*. https://www.wto.org/english/news_e/news21_e/dgno_15feb21_e.pdf

O'Reilly, C. A., & Tushman, M. L. (2004). The ambidexterous organization. *Harvard Business Review*. https://hbr.org/2004/04/the-ambidextrous-organization

Pasztor, A., & Martin, A. (2016). SoftBank and OneWeb CEOs diverge in leadership styles. *The Wall Street Journal*. https://www.wsj.com/articles/softbank-and-oneweb-ceos-diverge-in-leadership-styles-1482172686

Peng, J., Li, M., Wang, Z., & Lin, Y. (2021). Transformational leadership and employees' reactions to organizational change: Evidence from a meta-analysis. *The Journal of Applied Behavioral Science, 57*(3), 369–397. https://doi.org/10.1177/0021886320920366

Premium Times. (2015, April 9). *Okonjo-Iweala listed among 50 greatest world leaders*. https://www.premiumtimesng.com/news/top-news/180832-okonjo-iweala-listed-among-50-greatest-world-leaders.html

Prussia, G. E., Anderson, J. S., & Manz, C. C. (1998). Self-leadership and performance outcomes: The mediating influence of self-efficacy. *Journal of Organizational Behavior, 19*, 523–538.

Reddy, P., Kurdziel, A., & Sanfilippo, L. (2019, August 9). Transformative healthcare growth through diversification. *McKinsey & Company*. https://www.mckinsey.com/industries/healthcare-systems-and-services/our-insights/transformative-healthcare-growth-through-diversification

Renner, B., Betts, K., & Cook, J. (2021, July 26). Future of work: The state of the food industry. *Deloitte*. https://www2.deloitte.com/us/en/insights/industry/retail-distribution/future-of-food-retail-workforce.html

Ricks, A. F. (2020, June 26). How to communicate organizational change: 4 steps. *Harvard Business School Online*. https://online.hbs.edu/blog/post/how-to-communicate-organizational-change

Sarros, J. C., Cooper, B. K., & Santora, J. C. (2008). Building a climate for innovation through transformational leadership and organizational culture. *Journal of Leadership & Organizational Studies, 15*(2), 145–158.

SoftBank Group. (n.d.). *Vision & strategy: SoftBank's next 30-year vision*. https://group.softbank/en/philosophy/vision/next30

Stewart, G. L., Courtright, S. H., & Manz, C. C. (2011). Self-leadership: A multilevel review. *Journal of Management, 37*(1), 185–222.

Sun, J., Chen, X., & Zhang, S. (2017). A review of research evidence on the antecedents of transformational leadership. *Education Sciences, 7*(1), 15.

Tabrizi, B., Lam, E., Girard, K., & Irvin, V. (2019, March 13). Digital transformation is not about technology. *Harvard Business Review*. https://hbr.org/2019/03/digital-transformation-is-not-about-technology

The Limeade Team. (n.d.). *How to communicate change in the workplace in 8 steps*. https://www.limeade.com/resources/blog/8-ways-to-communicate-change-to-employees/

Trapp, R. (2021, September 29). How to build a transformational culture in the workplace. *Forbes*. https://www.forbes.com/sites/rogertrapp/2021/09/29/how-to-build-a-transformational-culture-in-the-workplace/?sh=3d9e60183465

University of Massachusetts Global. (2020, February 12). *What is transformational leadership? Understanding the impact of inspirational guidance.* https://www.umassglobal.edu/news-and-events/blog/what-is-transformational-leadership

Wilson, G. (2020, May 19). Top 10 influential business leaders in Africa. *Business Chief.* https://businesschief.eu/leadership-and-strategy/top-10-influential-business-leaders-africa

Wu, S. J., & Paluck, E. L. (2021). Designing nudges for the context: Golden coin decals nudge workplace behavior in China. *Organizational Behavior and Human Decision Processes, 163*, 43–50. https://doi.org/10.1016/j.obhdp.2018.10.002

Yohn, D. L. (2021, February 8). Company culture is everyone's responsibility. *Harvard Business Review.* https://hbr.org/2021/02/company-culture-is-everyones-responsibility

Zhytkova, L. (2021, March 12). Women and leadership: A conversation with Julia Gillard and Ngozi Okonjo-Iweala. *Brookings.* https://www.brookings.edu/events/women-and-leadership-a-conversation-with-julia-gillard-and-ngozi-okonjo-iweala/

Chapter 2

Value Creation Innovative Culture

Organizations must advocate, and ingrain values that shapes an innovative culture with an outcome-based approach. They need to recruit talents that have such intrinsic motivation and values, but beyond that to comprehend the nuances to create the eco system and operational structure that inspires them to create the recurring value-creation effect.

Kumaran Rajaram, PhD

2.1 Introduction

Organizations pursue varying different forms and types of innovations. These innovations could be with regard to their products or services, internal processes, and business models, among other aspects (Purcell, 2019). Innovations remain essential for organizations today that exist in highly volatile environments. If companies do not embrace innovation and change, they will struggle to stay afloat with the rapidly changing and VUCA (volatility, uncertainty, complexity, and ambiguity) external environments. Convincingly, innovation brings plenty of benefits to the organization. The innovations serve as a means of growth, keep organizations relevant, and provide ways for them to differentiate themselves. Hence, an innovatively rooted culture is vital for organizations to build on. Innovation culture is defined as a multi-dimensional context that includes the intention to be innovative, the infrastructure to support innovation, operational level behaviors necessary

DOI: 10.4324/9781003286288-3

to influence a market and value orientation, and the environment to implement innovation (Dobni, 2008). Successful organizations have the capacity to incorporate innovation, its practices into the organizational culture and management processes of the organization. In a nutshell, an innovation culture could potentially bring about varying benefits for an organization.

2.2 Innovative Culture

Further to that, an innovative culture drives an outcome-based approach to value creation. An outcome-based approach focuses on deliverables of products such as quality and service, instead of simply selling the products one-off. To create value, an outcome-based approach highlights to organizations the specific needs of consumers and subsequently builds upon them. Hence, an outcome-based approach to value creation combined with an innovative culture can assist an organization in transforming themselves and creating competitive edges. Despite the evident advantages entailed in an innovative organizational culture, fostering such culture is easier said than done. Jassawalla and Sashittal (2002) addressed this point and illustrated what distinguishes organizations with a highly innovation-supportive culture from those with a low innovation-supportive culture. Specifically, seven aspects of the organizations could foster the innovation-supportive culture, namely (a) stories; (b) social rituals; (c) physical symbols; (d) leadership; (e) interactions; (f) tacit and explicit knowledge; and (g) frame of reference. For instance, when it comes to stories, organizations with a highly innovative culture would emphasize risk taking, developing and promoting shared understanding, as well as cooperation across different divisions within the organizations. Such stories, when consistently repeated by the management, have a bearing on employees' attitudes and behaviors towards innovation. Also, the role of leadership plays a vital role, and when employees do not feel safe to share their own radical ideas in their teams because a leader and other members censor their ideas heavily, i.e., low psychological safety (Edmondson, 1999), the notions of creativity and innovation are likely curtailed. Hence, the management should not only emphasize an innovative culture but also implements policies and organizational practice that are consistent with such culture so that employees can freely express their ideas and opinions. Goryunova (2015) recognized that organizations are a complex system whereby organizational foci, goals, business innovations, and performance need to be well aligned. She proposed four types of organizational cultures: (a) economic bureaucratic culture; (b) paternalistic hierarchical culture; (c) individualistic competitive culture; and (d) ethical learning culture. The first two types are rather conservative and do not foster much creativity among employees, and therefore, innovations are less likely to be radical and novel. The latter two are geared more towards implementation of innovations. However, the individualistic competitive culture might not be very sustainable due to an extreme competitive pressure. This might potentially cause inefficient resource allocation among employees for innovations or push employees to take unethical behaviors. Organizations with an ethical learning culture is supposedly most conducive to innovations among the four, and this can be fostered by ethical leadership whereby leaders provide fair treatment to their employees and motivate them to pursue the common good. This culture promotes a long-term orientation and a forward-looking perspective, and organizations provide their employees with the opportunities for individual learning and voice behaviors. As noted above, organizations also need to focus on innovations that create values. As Priem (2007) put, "Consumers are arbiters of value" (p. 219), organizations need to develop products or services that provide values to their customers, in line with a *consumer benefit experienced* (CBE) perspective. In other words, organizations need to put their consumers in their mind when producing innovations, as value creation eventually conduces to increased revenues and firm profits. Value creation heavily depends on organizations' ability to leverage employee knowledge, and therefore, the role of human resource management and practices play a central role (Lepak, Smith, & Taylor, 2007). As such, promoting a right organizational culture is critical to enable the development of innovations and to achieve value creation for customers.

2.3 Organizations That Adopt Innovative Culture

Pixar is an example of a company with an innovative culture. Pixar has produced many critically acclaimed feature films. While all of them are unique from the norms in their own rights, they still somehow manage to reach their target audience. They do not constantly create films out of already successful franchises and often diversify their film offerings. This is possible due to their culture that promotes creativity and innovation among their employees. At Pixar, creativity is not the job of a single individual but a team. The company encourages employees to regularly share unfinished work, break down silos, feel empowered, and embrace constraints (Schroeder, 2020). Pixar built an innovative team environment that promoted risk taking and creativity and imperatively also respected deadlines that ensure deliverables to be attained as committed. On top of that, Pixar understands their target audience and their specific needs. Their films have a deep emotional core that is often based on real life, and this is the value-proposition that makes them so engaging to audiences of all ages. They understand and was able to connect the most crucial aspects in their stories to their audience that resonate well with many regardless of their stories being seen through the eyes of a fictional animated character. By understanding their audience, Pixar is creating value by leaving an impact on them to help shape them in positive and lasting ways. Google is another company that has famously displayed a culture of innovation. Google excels in relatively unusual forms of innovation such as information technology and business architecture, analytical decision making and participative product development (Iyer & Davenport, 2008). They balance chaotic ideation with data-driven methods for assessing ideas. Google's ability to challenge the status quo and think outside the box is not just a culture booster but also related to value creation (Schneider, 2018). A study published in MIT Sloan Management Review identified a substantial positive correlation between an organization's capacity to innovate and come up with new ideas, and its profitability. The ways in which google encourages their employees to be innovative are described on their rework website. Some of these aspects include communicating a clear vision, giving employees autonomy, hiring those who are highly intrinsically motivated, providing a sense of psychological safety by encouraging risk taking, and promoting connectivity.

In the airline industry, the Lufthansa Group launched Lufthansa Innovation Hub (LIH) in Berlin in 2014 to create innovative business models by leveraging their technological capability and expertise. The LIH's value mission is "to expand the Lufthansa Group's footprint along the travel chain to systematically create and capture the value beyond flying" (Lufthansa Innovation Hub, n.d.-a). The LIH opened a new office in Singapore and China in 2019, respectively. It focuses on analyzing recent developments in the travel and mobility tech ecosystems, develops business model innovations, makes partnerships with business units within the Lufthansa Group as well as travel tech startups, and encourages the Group for further investment in innovations (Future Travel Experience, 2019; Lufthansa Innovation Hub, n.d.-b). Put differently, the LIH can fuel the Group's consistent innovations based on the evidence and data amassed from their research. Organizations can develop and maintain its creative and innovative capabilities by investing their resources into such unit being solely dedicated to innovations and technology within organizations, thereby developing competitive advantages over other firms as well as creating values to customers. The other example concerns a hospitality industry. Nordic Choice Hotels, one of the largest hotel corporates with a total of 16,000 employees working in 200 hotels located in Scandinavia, Finland, and the Baltics, is known for their creative and innovative business models and ranked top 10 most innovative companies in 2017 (Hospitality Net, 2018). Nordic Choice Hotels invested in innovations, such that they started a company, eBerry that is specifically responsible for technological and digital aspects of the company's operation such as maintaining websites, apps platforms, loyalty programs, as well as customer service. Furthermore, Head of Business, Christian Lundén, remarked in an interview that they consulted with NASA about space tourism to "find out how our popular world of hospitality can be a really big player in space" (Alice, n.d.). This demonstrates how ambitious and forward-looking the organization is. In summary, Nordic Choice Hotels not only promotes an innovative mindset and culture internally but also invests organizational resources into building a branch that solely focuses on the organization's digitalization, so that they can keep pace with this rapidly changing industry.

While the strategies highlighted by Pixar and Google are just some tips to facilitate an innovative culture, there are other radical and innovative strategies that an organization may adopt to do so. We have advocated five key strategies to shape a company's culture, its innovation and value creation through outcome-based deliverables. Figure 2.1 presents a visual representation of these recommended five key strategies.

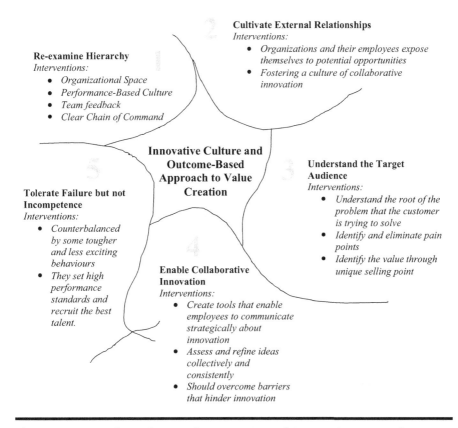

Cultivate External Relationships
Interventions:
- *Organizations and their employees expose themselves to potential opportunities*
- *Fostering a culture of collaborative innovation*

Re-examine Hierarchy
Interventions:
- *Organizational Space*
- *Performance-Based Culture*
- *Team feedback*
- *Clear Chain of Command*

Innovative Culture and Outcome-Based Approach to Value Creation

Understand the Target Audience
Interventions:
- *Understand the root of the problem that the customer is trying to solve*
- *Identify and eliminate pain points*
- *Identify the value through unique selling point*

Tolerate Failure but not Incompetence
Interventions:
- *Counterbalanced by some tougher and less exciting behaviours*
- *They set high performance standards and recruit the best talent.*

Enable Collaborative Innovation
Interventions:
- *Create tools that enable employees to communicate strategically about innovation*
- *Assess and refine ideas collectively and consistently*
- *Should overcome barriers that hinder innovation*

Figure 2.1 Innovative Culture and Outcome-Based Approach Framework

2.4 Strategy 1: Re-examine Hierarchy

One strategy is to promote an innovative culture is by opening up organizational space which enables innovators to overcome barriers and hierarchies (Ishak, 2017). Organizations with a flatter structure tend to be more innovative. Similarly, a top-down structure can hinder employees from being engaging and participating in the innovation process. Primarily, because employees may feel intimidated or fearful of being judged or being told off for their ideas. The strategy then should be flattening the organization and removing hierarchical barriers. Innovation is driven by a more collaborative workplace where transparency and creative freedom are prioritized over structure and inflexibility. While many hold similar views about hierarchy and innovative culture, Sanner and Bunderson (2017) provide an alternative perspective. They emphasized that a growing body of research adopts the right kind of hierarchy that help teams become better innovators and learners. Their argument against insisting for a flat hierarchy is that many teams often become unfocused, tumultuous, and inefficient. Hence, they suggest three things leaders can do to take advantage of the power of hierarchy. First is to have a clear chain of command. Here, we recommend leaders need to lay out the reporting structure and examine the efficacy of why that is the way it is designed. Second is to create a performance-based culture. This enables employees to be motivated and assist them to drive their performance which is tied to their deliverables. Last is to make use of team feedback. This enables one to reflect, aligns the team members' expectations and enhance their weakness and/or align to the address the issues from varying perceived dimensional perspectives. In a nutshell, hierarchies do sometimes suppress innovation though the pros can outweigh the cons given the right structure. Ultimately, what is best for a particular organization is dependent on their own specific situation. It is vital for organizations to first analyze their internal and external environment before committing to change.

The implementation and success of innovations greatly depend on organizational structures. Damanpour and Aravind (2012) summarized how different types of organizational structures conduce to employee creativity, firm innovation, and by implication the downstream consequence of organizational changes. Innovations can occur at various domains of firm business: (a) technological product and process innovations, (b) service innovations, administrative innovations, as well as (c) radical and incremental innovations. It is believed that an organic firm structure (versus mechanistic structure) leads to greater innovative performance, for example, centralization and formalization are negatively related to innovative behavior, whereas integration is positively associated with innovation (Dedahanov, Rhee, & Yoon, 2017). An ambidextrous structure, firms engage in both exploitations, (i.e., building on firm's existing knowledge and capability to produce new products) and exploration (i.e., exploring and developing new capabilities that used to be outside the firm's dominant areas of competitive advantage) approaches to innovations, which has recently gained more prominence (Boumgarden, Nickerson, & Zenger 2012; He & Wong, 2004; March 1991). In particular, Boumgarden et al. (2012) highlight that the same organizational structure is unlikely to consistently yield firm profits over time, but firms need to maintain a good balance of exploitation and exploration. This is because, for example, when firms are completely organic and flat, it becomes increasingly difficult for the management to facilitate internal control and structure, potentially disrupting the communication among employees and failing to implement successful innovations.

Another useful perspective upon considering how to design the firm structure is to reap innovative benefits is structural co-alignment. In other words, firms that invest highly in R&D and technological capability may not be successful in innovations if firms do not adopt the structure that leverages such investment or vice versa. For instance, Marín-Idárrage and Cuartas-Marín (2013) found the evidence that structural co-alignment among different types of organizational structure (differentiation, centralization, and formalization) produced a synergistic effect and led to greater firm performance. Also, Raymond and St-Pierre (2010) reported that small and medium enterprises (SMEs) with high co-alignment in strategic capabilities in terms of R&D and technology were more successful in product innovations compared to the Small Medium Enterprises (SMEs) that are low on these capabilities. These studies point to the importance of having a gestalt picture of firm business to effectively facilitate innovations. In other words, when firms attempt to implement an organic structure to promote innovations, they also have to focus on developing and investing in the domains relevant to innovations so that they can achieve correspondence between the firm structure and capabilities.

2.5 Strategy 2: Cultivate External Relationships

An innovative culture could be created and built on by developing relationships that extend beyond the boundaries of the organization (Ishak, 2017). By doing so, organizations and their employees expose themselves to potential opportunities to acquire and share, disseminate knowledge. This enables co-innovation or joint-development agreements, benefiting the contributing parties. These relationships facilitate to understand who will produce leads in emerging technologies such as virtual and augmented reality. Tesla has also embraced open innovation by removing patent walls for any other companies who want to use their technology. The significance of a collaborative approach was re-iterated and emphasized during the period COVID-19 pandemic where companies turned to open innovation to adapt to the struggles and challenges brought upon by the pandemic situation (Dahlander & Wallin, 2020). By opening up and accepting help from others, organizations are fostering a culture of collaborative innovation both within their own company and the industry they operate in. This can help them create and capture even more value.

Firms that aim to enhance their innovations are thus encouraged to build partnership with other firms. Through strategic alliances, firms can leverage novel expertise and resources that could be utilized to develop new products and services. In particular, the literature of strategic alliances indicates that diversity in alliance portfolio plays a crucial role in facilitating firm innovations and performance. For example, Cui and O'Connor (2012) found the evidence that resource diversity in alliance portfolio contributes to firm innovations when resources and information are shared between a focal firm and its partners. Lucena and Roper (2016) also supported the view that alliance diversity leads to innovative performance, and specifically, technology alliance diversity enhances firms' capabilities in combining knowledge (i.e., absorptive capacity and ambidexterity in R&D), which then conduces to firm innovations. However, extant research also introduces a caveat to arbitrarily increasing the diversity of an alliance portfolio. Sampson (2007) found that R&D alliances with a moderate level (versus low or high levels) led to greater firm innovations, because firms cannot effectively leverage the capabilities that are too distant from their own. Similarly, Hagedoorn, Lokshin, and Zobel (2018) considered two disparate dimensions of partner type diversity – variety and relevance – and reported that, analogous to the findings from Sampson (2007), neither too low nor high level on these dimensions of alliances may not conduce to firm innovation. Partnering with startups might also provide established firms with novel opportunities for growth and innovations. Sopra Steria Scale up is one such example. The organization focuses on building partnerships with startups with certain innovative ideas to address clients' issues so that the organization can meet the clients' needs, while the startups can launch them in the market. Head of Sopra Steria Scale up, Tobias Studer Andersson, called what the company is doing "connecting the dot" (Tandsæther-Andersen, 2019). Drawing on the example of Sopra Steria, Shipilov, Furr, and Andersson (2020) illustrated four steps for firms to establish effective partnership with startups: (a) identify the most valuable problem to solve; (b) make potential partners aware of the problem; (c) match with partners ready to cross the divide; and (d) contract for success. What is particularly impressive about Sopra Steria is that the organization itself does not have capabilities to internally devise solutions for their clients; however, their competence in identifying appropriate startups enables the development of innovations, showcasing the importance of expanding firms' networks and leveraging their external relationships.

2.6 Strategy 3: Understand the Market Segment

An organization must seek to understand its consumers deeply to truly deliver a product or service that they want and need. By being curious about customer problems, embedded issues, and desires, an organization can nurture and shape a culture of innovation that aims to cater to consumer wants and needs. Insights as such can lead to disruptive solutions (Brochu, 2018). For instance, Lego had once struggled to reach out to female children who were a large and crucial part of the market. The company had tried to launch products specifically targeting the segment but failed multiple times. They did a large-scale study with both male and female children to better comprehend these specific market segments. From the analysis of the study, Lego subsequently launched "Lego Friends" that enables success by being able to relate to both boys and girls. By examining and responding to the needs of their market segment, Lego managed to revive and attain profitable growth. To formulate innovative and customer-centric ideas, companies are required to follow these three steps (Gupta, 2020). Firstly, companies must understand the root of the problem that the customer is trying to solve. Secondly, they should identify and eliminate pain points, so that more resources and help could be rendered to address them respectively. Lastly, they should look beyond their products, where they need to identify the value through unique selling point that enables its sustainability in the market. Overall, an organization should duly consider consumers' perspectives and come up with innovative solutions that bring value to both the customers and the company.

Desouza and colleagues (2008) emphasized the value of customer-driven innovation for organizational survival. They proposed three ways in which organizations can leverage their customers to produce innovations. Specifically, organizations need to identify, analyze, and communicate with their customers. Segmentation plays a key role in identifying customers in order to tailor their products to specific customer needs. Then, organizations need to analyze customer information, and therefore, information and communication technologies are vital to process and correctly interpret customer data. It is also important to constantly communicate with customers to ensure that organizations indeed address crucial customer needs. Furthermore, they emphasize that organizations need to integrate customers into their innovation process to improve existing products and services. When it comes to having customers involved in organizations' innovation processes, Gustafsson, Kristensson, and Witell (2012) examined four dimensions of customer communication (i.e., frequency, direction, modality, and content). They found that frequent, two-way communication in which organizations ask for customers' feedback contributes to product success. To effectively leverage customer communication, organizations need to have managerial relationship capability and marketing innovations that are critical for effective value creation (Sánchez-Gutiérrez, Cabanelas, Lampón, & González-Alvarado, 2019). Moreover, organizations need to be able to not only identify current customer needs but also project *future* customer needs (Stanko & Bonner, 2013). The firms' capability of creating values *with* customers, rather than *for* customers, is becoming increasingly more vital.

In reality, even when companies fail to incorporate customers' opinions and feedback, they would be still able to develop something new, but their products would not be likely to be well received by customers. One such example is concerned with the case whereby Microsoft launched Windows 8 during their intense competition in the industry (Korst & Whitler, 2020). Windows 8, despite the Microsoft's unrivalled competitive edge in technology, was referred as the "epic fail of the decade" in the *Harvard Business Review*, and this failure happened mainly because Microsoft focused on developing products that would be functionally better than the products from their competitors such as Apple and Google but failed to focus on their customer needs. Put differently, Microsoft developed what they believed valuable from their own perspective without taking customers' perspectives into account – an approach referred to as inside-out. However, organizations should adopt an outside-in approach whereby organizations listen to customers instead of overly sticking to their internal beliefs. Hence, it is critical to lead innovation processes by making external investments to identify and analyze customer needs. Microsoft, however, learned from their mistakes when they developed Windows 10. Specifically, they invited marketing and business development leaders during their product strategy meetings and seek constant feedback from customers and markets. This helped Microsoft define target customers and identify what kinds of features would be needed for their new product. In conclusion, customer perspectives cannot be more emphasized to yield successful firm innovation outcomes.

2.7 Strategy 4: Enable Collaborative Innovation

Collaborative innovation can help an organization innovate at a much more efficient and effective rate compared to relying on individual innovators. This is because working in groups can facilitate fresh ideas and different perspectives. Isaacs and Ancona (2019) provide three suggestions on how to build a culture of collaborative innovation. Firstly, the organization must create tools that enable employees to communicate strategically about innovation. By allowing their colleagues to propose new ideas and challenge existing ones, innovators can develop a stronger strategic argument. Secondly, organizations should assess and refine ideas collectively and consistently. Innovation ideas should be reviewed and refined constantly, not just once or twice a year. Lastly, organizations should overcome barriers that hinder innovation. In a nimble organization, leaders should do whatever they can to clear the way for promising innovation initiatives and help innovation teams gain access to the resources they require. In a nutshell, these three practices can help an organization facilitate effective collaborative innovation and consequently create a more innovative organization culture.

Furthermore, there are several approaches to enhancing collaborative innovations in organizations. A review conducted by An, Deng, Chao, and Bai (2014) identified a holistic approach to managing collaborative innovations. Specifically, there are three kinds of demands to foster what they call *collaborative innovation community capacity building* (CICCB). The first kind of such demands is trust building among employees for enhancing the organizational effectiveness. Second, sustainability building is critical to achieve organizational efficiency. Put differently, employees need to have a consensus around how innovative processes take place. Third, they emphasized the importance of building extensive networks among employees and promoting communication and connectivity for increased organizational competitiveness. Enhanced communication based on organization-wide networks would promote sharing and exchange of information, knowledge, and resources, which should, in turn, conduce to more effective collaborations among employees. Further, Jarvenpaa and Välkangas (2020) investigated two important factors influencing collaborative creativity: (a) inner time (a temporal resource that people need to generate creative ideas on their own) and (b) social time (a temporal resource for people to "share and integrate ideas by engaging with others" (p. 568). For a successful collaborative innovation, it is critical for employees to have both inner time and social time, where the lack of either one of them leads to suboptimal collaborative creativity. At the same time, Jarvenpaa and Välkangas (2020) presented a caveat that advanced technology might potentially reduce both inner time and social time, leading to the end of collaborative creativity. It is thus imperative for organizations to consider appropriate use of advanced technology so that the time for employees to generate creative ideas and have them discussed with their colleagues will not be significantly lost.

To achieve collaborative innovations, collaborative climate in organizations is undoubtedly important. Research shows that collaborative climate promotes positive impacts of cognitive diversity in work groups on creativity (Younis, 2019). Specifically, cognitive diversity has greater influence on creativity when organizational culture supports collaborative climate, immediate supervisors support collaboration, and employees and work groups have favorable attitudes towards collaboration. However, the core question is to reflect on "how can organizations promote such a climate?". Gino (2019) illustrates six training techniques by which organizations can adopt to foster sustained collaboration among employees: (a) teach people to listen, not talk; (b) train people to practice empathy; (c) make people more comfortable with feedback; (d) teach people to lead and follow; (e) speak with clarity and avoid abstractions; and (f) train people to have win-win interactions. These techniques promote harmonious interactions among employees which are critical for a collaborative climate to be shaped within a work team and organization. Furthermore, these interventions also promote positive interpersonal relationships, which encourage employees' novel ideas without them being concerned about criticism from others. Creating an environment that promotes employees' communication is thus critical for building a collaborative climate.

2.8 Strategy 5: Tolerate Failure but Not Incompetence

Although innovative cultures are desirable and leaders claim to understand what it comprises, many find it challenging to create and sustain (Pisano, 2019). This is largely because innovative cultures are very much misunderstood. The favorable behaviors that are associated with innovative cultures are only one side of the coin. They must be counterbalanced by tougher and less exciting behaviors. One example will be balancing a tolerance for failure with an intolerance for incompetence. Since innovation involves exploring the uncertain and unknown, a tolerance for failure is often emphasized for organizations that aspire to develop an innovative culture. Without it, employees may be fearful to challenge the status quo for fear of being reprimanded and penalized. Generally, highly innovative organizations embrace and tolerates failures to a certain extent but many are usually intolerant of incompetence. They set high performance standards and recruit the best talent. While failure may be tolerated, mediocre technical skills, sloppy thinking, bad work habits, and poor management are not. Hence, it is vital that organizations ensure that failure is not the result of incompetence. An innovative culture should also ensure that employees work on innovation initiatives to the best of their ability.

It is thus essential for managers to ensure that any poor performance due to incompetence needs to be swiftly addressed by the organization. However, managers might not want to be overly harsh and criticize their employees for poor performance. Nonetheless, they are encouraged to comprehend all potential causes of poor performance, manage physical and psychological distances with their employees, engage in active listening, provide effective but non-threatening feedback, and develop a learning mindset (Moss & Sanchez, 2004). It is critical to fully understand why employees failed to perform successfully. Managers need to carefully assess whether the cause of the failure was employees' bad working habits or instead employees had good intention to be creative and innovative. Incompetence should not be tolerated, but managers must identify the cause of poor performance accurately and explicitly. Otherwise, employees might feel that they are punished for being risk-taking and perceive their organization to be intolerant for any kinds of failures, that might reduce poor performance due to incompetence but also potentially hinder innovations (Kriegesmann, Kley, & Schwering, 2005). In other words, organizations should reward risk-taking behaviors (Tushman & Nadler, 1986), but they also need to articulate that the failures due to risk-taking behaviors are not equated with the failures due to incompetence.

Concurrently, managers need to be able to give critical feedback to their employees. This is helpful as employees might sometimes not meet the standards set by organizations and they may require to make changes and re-align their behaviors. Some managers find it difficult to give such feedback because they do not want to hurt employees' feelings. In a recent *Harvard Business Review* article, Jensen and Baumgartner (2021) explained some strategies that managers can use when providing tough feedback to their employees. They recommended managers to describe the behavior that they want to reinforce or correct. When managers give difficult feedback, they should avoid interpreting their employees' behaviors in their own ways and using evaluative languages. But instead, they should base their feedback on observable facts and employees' tangible behaviors and use more descriptive languages. Second, managers need to explain the impact of employees' poor performance and why it needs to be addressed. The main purpose is to make the employees aware of what is at stake. Third, managers should clearly outline what they want their employees to do in the future and provide direct instruction. Such feedback-giving should reinforce the employees' belief that the organization *does* tolerate risk-taking behaviors and potential failures but does not accept any poor performance stemming from their sloppy work attitudes. For organizations to effectively foster an innovative culture and elicit more creativity and innovation from employees, frequent communication between managers and employees is essential. This aspect should never be overlooked or less emphasized that would only possibly create negative ripple effects and impact to the deliverables.

References

Alice. (n.d.). *How Nordic Choice's brand of innovation is transforming hospitality – Newsletter 61.* https://www.aliceplatform.com/blog/learning-hospitality-innovation-from-nordic-choice-hotels

An, X., Deng, H., Chao, L., & Bai, W. (2014). Knowledge management in supporting collaborative innovation community capacity building. *Journal of Knowledge Management, 18*(3), 574–590. https://doi.org/10.1108/JKM-10-2013-0413

Boumgarden, P., Nickerson, J., & Zenger, T. R. (2012). Sailing into the wind: Exploring the relationships among ambidexterity, vacillation, and organizational performance. *Strategic Management Journal, 33*(6), 587–610. https://doi.org/10.1002/smj.1972

Brochu, B. (2018). Six lessons from corporations with the best innovation culture. *RocketSpace*. https://www.rocketspace.com/corporate-innovation/six-lessons-from-corporations-with-the-best-innovation-culture

Cui, A. S., & O'Connor, G. (2012). Alliance portfolio resource diversity and firm innovation. *Journal of Marketing, 76*(4), 24–43.

Dahlander, L., & Wallin, M. (2020, June 5). Why now is the time for "open innovation". *Harvard Business Review*. https://hbr.org/2020/06/why-now-is-the-time-for-open-innovation

Damanpour, F., & Aravind, D. (2012). Organizational structure and innovation revisited: From organic to ambidextrous structure. Michael, D. Mumford (Eds.), In *Handbook of organizational creativity* (pp. 483–513). Elsevier.

Dedahanov, A. T., Rhee, C., & Yoon, J. (2017). Organizational structure and innovation performance. *Career Development International, 22*(4), 334–350. https://doi.org/10.1108/CDI-12-2016-0234.

Desouza, K. C., Awazu, Y., Jha, S., Dombrowski, C., Papagari, S., Baloh, P., & Kim, J. Y. (2008). Customer-driven innovation. *Research-Technology Management, 51*(3), 35–44.

Dobni, C. B. (2008). Measuring innovation culture in organizations. *European Journal of Innovation Management, 11*(4), 539–559. https://doi.org/10.1108/14601060810911156

Edmondson, A. (1999). Psychological safety and learning behavior in work teams. *Administrative Science Quarterly, 44*(2), 350–383.

Future Travel Experience. (2019, February). *Exclusive interview: Lufthansa Innovation Hub reveals the true scale of its ambitions in Asia.* https://www.futuretravelexperience.com/2019/02/lufthansa-innovation-hub-reveals-true-scale-ambitions-asia/

Gino, F. (2019). Cracking the code of sustained collaboration. *Harvard Business Review*. https://hbr.org/2019/11/cracking-the-code-of-sustained-collaboration

Goryunova, E. (2015). Creating organizational culture for radical sustainable innovation: A complexity science approach. *Academy of management annual meeting proceedings*. https://doi.org/10.5465/AMBPP.2015.158

Gupta, S. (2020, October 1). Are you really innovating around your customers' needs? *Harvard Business Review*. https://hbr.org/2020/10/are-you-really-innovating-around-your-customers-needs

Gustafsson, A., Kristensson, P., & Witell, L. (2012). Customer co-creation in service innovation: A matter of communication? *Journal of Service Management, 23*(3), 311–327. https://doi.org/10.1108/09564231211248426

Hagedoorn, J., Lokshin, B., & Zobel, A. K. (2018). Partner type diversity in alliance portfolios: Multiple dimensions, boundary conditions and firm innovation performance. *Journal of Management Studies, 55*(5), 809–836.

He, Z.-L., & Wong, P.-K. (2004). Exploration vs. exploitation: An empirical test of the ambidexterity hypothesis. *Organization Science, 15*(4), 481–494. https://doi.org/10.1287/orsc.1040.0078

Hospitality Net. (2018, July 30). *Discover how Nordic Choice Hotels became one of the most innovative brands in Norway.* https://www.hospitalitynet.org/news/4089435.html

Isaacs, K., & Ancona, D. (2019, August 12). 3 ways to build a culture of collaborative innovation. *Harvard Business Review*. https://hbr.org/2019/08/3-ways-to-build-a-culture-of-collaborative-innovation

Ishak, W. (2017, September 28). *Creating an innovation culture.* McKinsey & Company. https://www.mckinsey.com/business-functions/strategy-and-corporate-finance/our-insights/creating-an-innovation-culture

Iyer, B., & Davenport, T. H. (2008, April). Reverse engineering Google's innovation machine. *Harvard Business Review*. https://hbr.org/2008/04/reverse-engineering-googles-innovation-machine

Jarvenpaa, S. L., & Välikangas, L. (2020). Advanced technology and end-time in organizations: A Doomsday for Collaborative Creativity? *Academy of Management Perspectives, 34*(4), 566–584. https://doi.org/10.5465/amp.2019.0040

Jassawalla, A. R. & Sashittal, H. C. (2002) Cultures that support product-innovation processes, *Academy of Management Perspectives, 16*(3), 42–54.

Jensen, D., & Baumgartner, P. (2021). Stop softening tough feedback. *Harvard Business Review.* https://hbr.org/2021/02/stop-softening-tough-feedback

Korst, J., & Whitler, K. A. (2020, January 10). Why the best tech firms keep customers front-of-mind. *Harvard Business Review.* https://hbr.org/2020/01/why-the-best-developers-keep-customers-front-of-mind.

Kriegesmann, B., Kley, T., & Schwering, M. G. (2005). Creative errors and heroic failures: Capturing their innovative potential. *Journal of Business Strategy, 26*(3), 57–64. https://doi.org/10.1108/02756660510597119

Lepak, D. P., Smith, K. G., & Taylor, M. S. (2007). Value creation and value capture: A multilevel perspective. *Academy of Management Review, 32*(1), 180–194.

Lucena, A., & Roper, S. (2016). Absorptive capacity and ambidexterity in R&D: Linking technology alliance diversity and firm innovation. *European Management Review, 13*(3), 159–178.

Lufthansa Innovation Hub. (n.d.-a). *About the Lufthansa Innovation Hub (LIH).* https://lh-innovationhub.de/wp-content/uploads/2019/02/LIH_Faktsheet_EN.pdf

Lufthansa Innovation Hub. (n.d.-b). *About us.* https://lh-innovationhub.de/en/about-us/

March, J. G. (1991). Exploration and exploitation in organizational learning. *Organization Science, 2*(1), 71–87.

Marín-Idárraga, D. A., & Cuartas-Marín, J. C. (2013). Structural co-alignment influence on SMEs performance. *International Journal of Business and Management, 8*(22), 76.

Moss, S. E., & Sanchez, J. I. (2004). Are your employees avoiding you? Managerial strategies for closing the feedback gap. *Academy of Management Perspectives, 18*(1), 32–44.

Priem, R. L. (2007). A consumer perspective on value creation. *Academy of Management Review, 32*(1), 219–235.

Pisano, G. P. (2019). The hard truth about innovative cultures. *Harvard Business Review.* https://hbr.org/2019/01/the-hard-truth-about-innovative-cultures

Purcell, W. (2019, October 31). The importance of innovation in business. *Northeastern University.* https://www.northeastern.edu/graduate/blog/importance-of-innovation/

Raymond, L., & St-Pierre, J. (2010). Strategic capabilities for product innovation in SMEs: A gestalts perspective. *The International Journal of Entrepreneurship and Innovation, 11*(3), 209–220. https://doi.org/10.5367/000000010792217236

Sampson, R. C. (2007). R&D alliances and firm performance: The impact of technological diversity and alliance organization on innovation. *Academy of Management Journal, 50*(2), 364–386.

Sánchez-Gutiérrez, J., Cabanelas, P., Lampón, J. F., & González-Alvarado, T. E. (2019). The impact on competitiveness of customer value creation through relationship capabilities and marketing innovation. *Journal of Business & Industrial Marketing, 34*(3), 618–627.

Sanner, B., & Bunderson, J. S. (2017, December 11). The truth about hierarchy. *MIT Sloan Management Review.* https://sloanreview.mit.edu/article/the-truth-about-hierarchy/

Schneider, M. (2018, October 23). *How Google built a culture that inspires new ideas every day.* Inc.Com.

Schroeder, B. (2020). *Pixar purposely embeds creativity into their culture, and it drives their success: Three things you can do to bring creativity into your culture or team. Forbes.* https://www.forbes.com/sites/bernhardschroeder/2020/01/02/pixar-purposely-embeds-creativity-into-their-culture-and-it-drives-their-success--three-things-you-can-do-to-bring-creativity-into-your-culture-or-team/?sh=39f41751358a

Shipilov, A., Furr, N., & Andersson, T. S. (2020, May 27). Looking to boost innovation? Partner with a startup. *Harvard Business Review.* https://hbr.org/2020/05/looking-to-boost-innovation-partner-with-a-startup

Stanko, M., & Bonner, J. (2013). Projective customer competence: Projecting future customer needs that drive innovation performance. *Industrial Marketing Management, 42.* https://doi.org/10.1016/j.indmarman.2013.05.016

Tandsæther-Andersen, B. H. (2019, May 24). Sopra Steria Scale up's Tobias Studer Andersson on going into the 'battlefield' with clients and startups: It's really all about connecting the dots. *Medium.* https://medium.com/startup-norway/sopra-steria-scale-ups-tobias-studer-andersson-on-going-into-the-battlefield-with-clients-and-4c58479799c6

Tushman, M., & Nadler, D. (1986). Organizing for innovation. *California Management Review, 28*(3), 74–92. https://doi.org/10.2307/41165203

Younis, R. (2019). Cognitive diversity and creativity: The moderating effect of collaborative climate. *International Journal of Business and Management, 14*(1), 159–168.

Chapter 3

Re-strategizing with Re-value Proposition

Companies need to re-think on how to re-position themselves continuously
to ensure they are able to offer the competitive edge and facilitate value-
add to their stakeholders.

Kumaran Rajaram, PhD

3.1 Introduction

Competitive advantages no longer last as long as before. With constant advancements in new technology, organizations find themselves, their products and services
being threatened with irrelevance or potentially to be outdated. Further to this, the
COVID-19 pandemic has shown us how fragile organizational strategies can be that
requires leaders to be agile in having them improvised or changed to sustain business
deliverables. Hence, we could clearly acknowledge that with changes in the competitive environment come the changes in organizational strategies. Stagnant organizations will not be able to compete effectively with other players in the market that
makes them not to survive or sustain in the long run. Companies also make essential
improvisations and/or changes to their business model when they enter new markets
by adjusting to local expectations and requirements (The Economist Intelligence
Unit & KPMG International, 2006). As such, business models must be continuously reviewed, improvised, or adapted by meeting the evolving rapid changes. On
top of battling with the evolving changes in business strategy, organizations must
also find new ways to differentiate themselves to maintain a competitive edge. New

DOI: 10.4324/9781003286288-4

sources of value propositions are needed to gain a larger share of the market. Unfortunately, the aspect of value has a life-span inline to currency and relevance that does not often last for prolonged period without any changes or improvisations. It is rare for companies nowadays to sustain a lasting competitive advantage and more so they often last for only a short phase, for instance under a year. It can then be concluded that stability, not change is most dangerous in highly dynamic competitive environments. Stability leads to inertia and habits which while comfortable can largely impede on a company's innovative and proactive efforts. Hence, companies must constantly re-assess, re-strategize, and create new, unique, and at times even radical (if required) value propositions that will allow them to stand out from competitors.

3.2 Re-strategizing Value Proposition

In order to remain competitive, organizations need to constantly go back to their own value propositions and try to update and improve them so as to keep pace with any changes happening to external environments. Value propositions are "the value a company promises to deliver to customers should they choose to buy their product" (Twin, 2020). Value propositions are critical because they navigate companies' strategies and products that they offer (Bojanowski, 2019). As described above, value propositions often reflect only the current values, beliefs, and knowledge (Deanhouston+, 2021), which may be outdated as time progresses. Companies thus need to re-evaluate their value propositions so that they can create and sustain their competitive advantages, identify new competency, and effectively respond to the changes in consumer preferences, industry, technology, and even political and societal systems. Business and organizational leaders can ask themselves on the daily basis (Otlowski, 2019) – though provoking questions such as (a) "What are the problems our customers have?", (b) "What problems do we need to solve?", and (c) "What are the recent changes that are happening in the industry?". For example, digital transformation is one of the strongest drivers that push organizations to engage in re-strategizing their value propositions, and one exemplar is Uber (Gorsht, 2014). Building on the taxi business that mainly focuses on the value of taking a passenger from Point A to Point B, Uber started offering a variety of options in price and style (for example, selecting the options from SUV to Carpooling, choosing drivers based on safety and efficiency), which allowed the company to create additional and individualized values for customers by capitalizing on their service and technology. Also, re-evaluation of value propositions has implications in management of talents within the organization. In response to the COVID-19 pandemic, Gilmore (2021) argues that foreign direct investment (FDI) organizations need to reconsider their employee value propositions, that can be defined as a strategic statement that communicates an organization's mission, goals, values, workplace culture, and employer branding. Due to the radical shift in employees' working mode in response to the COVID-19 pandemic, organizations are now required to re-assess what values they are providing employees (for example, in terms of reward, work benefits, culture, and growth) and whether such values correspond to what employees currently wish to attain in the organizations.

3.3 Strategic Interventions to Re-evaluate and Enhance Value Propositions

There are varying strategic manners in which companies can re-evaluate and improve their value propositions. For instance, business leaders need to (a) research target customers in detail, (b) understand the company's strengths, (c) articulate the values that the company's products or services offer, (d) pay attention to the competitors and current business trends, (e) quantify the value to track whether the strategies aligned with current value propositions are effective, and (f) communicate the companies' value propositions amongst employees and customers (Rockcontent, 2020). It is vital to objectively assess both positive and negative aspects of the values and always tailor or individualized the values from the customers' perspective. Also, in terms of advocating and sharing value propositions, organizations are encouraged to do so creatively that the audience could easily understand and digest the key messages contained in the new value propositions (Bouzine, Molloy, & Monteleone, n.d.). Concerning the customer-centric perspectives, re-assessing the value propositions is crucial to tailor the company's offerings and products to their customers' needs. Whenever companies re-design their value propositions, they should consider how their new values contribute to the improvement of the customer experience. Indeed, Maynes and Rawson (2016) emphasized the importance of linking the customer experience to organizational values. Bough, Breuer, Maechler, and Ungerman (2020) also described that there are three building blocks of customer-experience transformation. The first one is to build aspiration and purpose. In other words, organizations should develop customer-centric vision and aspiration, establish link to value, and translate into roadmap. Whenever re-strategizing value propositions, companies should start from considering how they create more values to their customers. The other two blocks will be more relevant once companies consider and develop new values that are closely linked to customers, as these blocks pertain to what the companies can do to transform their businesses based on their new value propositions. The second building block for improved customer experience is to enable the transformation. This entails transforming mindsets and building capabilities, updating technology, establishing cross-functional governance and agile operating model, and implementing appropriate measurement and performance-management systems. The third building block is to transform the business through discovering customer needs, designing solutions, and delivering impact. As such, the first building block is most pertinent to the idea of re-strategizing value propositions, and it is fundamental to any transformational efforts and changes in which companies engage subsequently. Failing to assess the value propositions will likely amount to not only reduced quality in customer experience but also suboptimal firm performance.

3.4 How to Do Re-value Propositions?

When re-strategizing with re-value propositions, the management should not take a completely top-down approach. Employees are to be encouraged to be involved and participate when the organization revises and refines their value propositions rather than imposing the values on the employees. Coleman (2022) provided four useful tips with regard to this point. First, leaders should engage organizational employees more comprehensively. The management can formally and publicly communicate employees with the process of refreshing value propositions so that the employees are given the opportunities to reflect on the company's visions and purposes. Second, organizational leaders are also encouraged to listen to employees' voice more extensively and authentically. Leaders can both formally and informally encourage employee feedback. For example, the management can set up a focus group to connect with employees and obtain feedback from the employees concerning the organizational values, missions, culture, and purposes. Third, once the organization revises value propositions, they need to communicate the new values consistently and widely to employees. This process is critical to internalize the new values among employees. Lastly, Coleman proposed that the organization should recognize the employees who live the company's purpose and values (for example, rewarding the employees, sharing the stories of the employees). Role models are to be acknowledged to encourage other organizational members to demonstrate the values and behave accordingly. Bingham (2020) also recommended to make the company values foundational. Refreshing value propositions in itself are not sufficient to drive changes in employees' behaviors. Equally crucial is what can be done to stick the values to the organization through consistent efforts in communicating them to their employees.

3.5 Organizations That Re-strategize with Re-valuation

Netflix is a prime example of an organization that changed their business model and brought new value to their consumers. Customers of Netflix have access to numerous movies and TV shows, where one could watch their desired shows anytime and anywhere. Their flexibility schemes enable their clients to easily cancel their subscription and change to their preference as deemed appropriate. Initially starting out as a DVD rental delivery service, Netflix recognized the opportunities coming from video content streaming. They adapted and changed their business model despite attaining tremendous success with their initial one. Today, Netflix is pushing to bring more value by aiming to become a leading producer of original content (Anthony, Trotter, & Schwartz, 2019). Their CEO has managed to adopt and maintain tireless re-invention, going beyond their original core capabilities (Cohan, 2013). As a whole, Netflix shows that an organization should never assume that their successful business model will last forever for prolonged period, thus should be agile by continuously capturing new value. If Netflix had held on with a rigid and fixated mindset to their DVD rental service model, they would not be here today.

Another example of an organization that managed to successfully adapt their strategy and find new value is Fujifilm. In the book *The End of Competitive Advantage* McGrath (2013a, 2013b) describes the story of how Fujifilm managed to successfully navigate the varying changes in the external environment and sustain itself as a global player. When CEO Minoru Ohnishi realized film would become less relevant in the industry with Sony releasing the first filmless camera, he quickly sprang into action. The company heavily invested in digital technologies to prepare for the change. Despite outsiders criticizing the company's move as "single-minded", employees were determined and had faith in the company and the strategy. By the end of 2003, Fujifilm had around 5,000 digital processing labs in chain stores within the United States while its competitor, Kodak, had less than a hundred. The company also diversified their offerings by capturing opportunities outside the photography industry. The company continued doing so and by the end of 2011, Fujifilm achieved $25 billion in revenue. To conclude, the case study of Fujifilm proves that having quality products alone is not adequate to sustain the company in the long run to deal with a competitive market. Unlike Kodak, Fujifilm changed their strategy and captured new opportunities as it came their way.

A variety of industries and businesses have been severely impacted by the COVID-19 pandemic, and one of them is retail industry (Atmar et al., 2020). Because people's movement was greatly restricted and they were refrained from shopping onsite unless it is for essentials (for example, food, medication, toiletries), many of the non-essential retails had to shut down their businesses temporarily or even permanently. The changes in external environments, consumer behaviors, and product demands present the very situation where business leaders had to reconsider their value propositions to sustain their businesses. Under the COVID-19 pandemic, retail organizations needed to heavily invest in digital technology so that they could offer their services and products without requiring face-to-face interactions with consumers. According to Enriquez (2020), Audio House, electronics retailer in Singapore, was able to ramp up its online business and also had their employees go through Facebook live sessions during the time of the circuit breaker (i.e., lockdown in Singapore that restricted people's movements and imposed the preventive measures such as mask wearing and working from home). This training provided employees with opportunities to learn about how they can present their products via the web and helped the organization to effectively adapt and shift to a digital environment. Another example is Zalora, fashion retail platform (Enriquez, 2020). Zalora used its data analytics to understand consumers' purchasing behaviors. During one business quarter in 2020 amid the COVID-19 pandemic, Zalora recently observed nearly 2 million downloads of its application. Although the company's primary sellers are such categories as sports, personal care, and beauty, the company quickly responded to this rising demand and added essentials like masks and sanitizers on its platform. These cases from retail companies reflect the importance of re-assessing its business based on external changes and crises so that they can use their resources most optimally.

Xiaomi is a relevant example that successfully re-defined digital platform-based ecosystems and became one of the leading companies in the industry. The company reached $15 billion in revenue within seven years after they entered the smartphone market and became one of the largest IoT companies (Yang, Ma, & Chattopadhyay, 2021). As there is fierce competition in the platform-business industry, it is necessary for the companies to constantly reflect on their business models and strategies so that they could continue to survive for a long term. Xiaomi adapted a distinct strategy

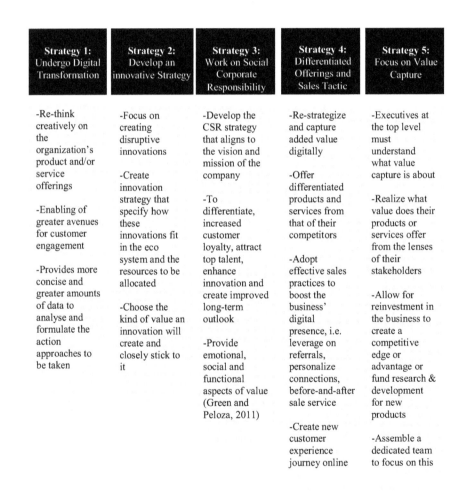

Strategy 1: Undergo Digital Transformation	Strategy 2: Develop an innovative Strategy	Strategy 3: Work on Social Corporate Responsibility	Strategy 4: Differentiated Offerings and Sales Tactic	Strategy 5: Focus on Value Capture
-Re-think creatively on the organization's product and/or service offerings -Enabling of greater avenues for customer engagement -Provides more concise and greater amounts of data to analyse and formulate the action approaches to be taken	-Focus on creating disruptive innovations -Create innovation strategy that specify how these innovations fit in the eco system and the resources to be allocated -Choose the kind of value an innovation will create and closely stick to it	-Develop the CSR strategy that aligns to the vision and mission of the company -To differentiate, increased customer loyalty, attract top talent, enhance innovation and create improved long-term outlook -Provide emotional, social and functional aspects of value (Green and Peloza, 2011)	-Re-strategize and capture added value digitally -Offer differentiated products and services from that of their competitors -Adopt effective sales practices to boost the business' digital presence, i.e. leverage on referrals, personalize connections, before-and-after sale service -Create new customer experience journey online	-Executives at the top level must understand what value capture is about -Realize what value does their products or services offer from the lenses of their stakeholders -Allow for reinvestment in the business to create a competitive edge or advantage or fund research & development for new products -Assemble a dedicated team to focus on this

Figure 3.1 Re-strategizing with Re-value Proposition Framework

that combines the Corporate Venture Capital (CVC) approach and the ecosystem approach (Tong, Guo, & Chen, 2021). The CVC approach can be viewed as an established company invests in start-ups in the hope of future pay-off. The ecosystem approach requires the ecosystem leader to create a network of complementary companies using their own technologies and resources as a leverage. What Xiaomi has done was the combination of these two approaches and it now has a mobile platform where more than 300 million connected IoT devices that are supported worldwide from 400 partner companies. Xiaomi is not just an ecosystem leader but also proactively engages in the CVC and invests in their partner companies. Hence, Xiaomi's value does not just lie in their smartphone business but is also derived from collaborative value creation process with other stakeholders or its co-value creation. If the company simply focused on smartphone business, they would not have grown into a one of the global internet and software companies. Xiaomi thus redefines the company's value as a provider of technological ecosystem, through which they gained competitive advantages in an extremely competitive industry.

With an adequate scholarly in-depth analysis as well as validated real-life experiences, five vital strategies are recommended, with appropriate illustrations of how businesses could potentially leverage on to offer value-add beyond their already good stead currently. These will be presented and elaborated in Figure 3.1.

3.6 Strategy 1: Undergo Digital Transformation

The undertaking of the digital transformation process is a strategic decision that requires many existing processes within the organization to be refurbished. As a result, some organizations may feel hesitant to engage in this vital futurist aspect of digital transformation. Digitization is crucial for a business to remain relevant, aligned to clients' needs and contemporary in their product, service offerings. Leveraging on the global digital transformation movement allows both B2B and B2C businesses to enhance their performance across key operational areas as well as creating new value for their customers concurrently (Krach, 2016). The primary question to ask is how digitalization adds value to an organization? First, it helps to refocus the attention to customer service. Online reviews, forums, and rating systems significantly influence whether or not a customer purchases an organization's product or service. Hence, digitization has pushed many companies to be more mindful and cautious in their analysis of customer experience. This facilitates improvement and to re-think creatively on the organization's product and/or services offerings, which will benefit them in the long run. Another benefit is the enabling of greater avenues for customer engagement. Increased connectivity brought about by social media can assist companies reach out to both current and potential customers. Additionally, digitization provides added convenience for both the business and consumers, while it provides more concise and greater amounts of data for the company to analyze and formulate the required action approaches to be taken. Today, organizations are spending millions of dollars for digital transformation initiatives. However, before investing into these technologies or digitalization support systems, an organization must first understand how this change to be incorporated fits into the overall business strategy and the impact it has on the business deliverables. Otherwise, organizations will find themselves failing to reach their intended goals (Tabrizi, Lam, Girard, & Irvin, 2019), although the underlying intentions are for the betterment of the company's growth. Digital transformation provides possibilities for efficiency gains and customer intimacy but without the correct growth mindset to change and adapt, in contrary continuing with flawed organizational practices, digital transformation will only magnify those issues.

3.6.1 Benefits of Digitalization for the Organization and Employees

Digital transformation not only provides increased quality of customer experiences but also has a variety of impacts on organizations and employees. For instance, Pratt (2021) explained that digital technologies such as automation and artificial intelligence can increase efficiency and productivity, improve the management of organization's resources, and enable the organization to become more resilient and adaptive to social and economic upheavals. Digitalization also improves employees' work experiences. Employees working in the organization where digital transformation is promoted would be able to have more seamless collaboration with colleagues, as digital platforms facilitate information sharing and communication among them (Newman, 2018). Such efficient communication based on technology helps employees save their time and work in a more productive and effective manner (Pardo, 2018). Additionally, digital communication channels make teamwork easier even among employees coming from different departments or divisions. Pardo (2018) also pointed out how digitalization leads to better decision-making because of the application and usage of big data available to the organizations.

Further to this, due to the advancement of digitalization, an increasing number of employees are not required to work in traditional manners but are allowed to work more flexibly in terms of their work location and schedule, which enabled them to maintain a better work-life balance. Another benefit concerning digitalization includes increased innovation (Tacke, 2018). Digitalization would enhance employees' awareness of new technologies and recent trends and enable them to capitalize on them so that companies can engage in greater innovation (Thompson, 2021). Finally, employees feel more engaged when organizations promote digitalization. To effectively undertake digitalization process, organizations need to allocate their resources to employees' training so that they are sufficiently exposed to and capable of using new technology. Such investment and training would enhance employees' perception of being valued by the organizations, conducing to greater motivation and engagement at work.

3.6.2 Difficulties Surrounding Digitalization

However, digital transformation is not always easy to achieve, where some organizations experience barriers in implementing digitalization. For instance, some organizations lack in competencies and might not have the information technology (IT) teams that possess sufficient skills and knowledge in facilitating digitalization. Also, even if organizations want to buttress their digitalization initiatives, unless they have a defined strategy, their investments would likely go futile. Another important issue is employees' pushback against the introduction of changes in work procedures and flows due to digitalization. Digitalization invariably requires changes and transformation in work structure and procedures, which could induce the resistance from employees (Plutora, 2020). Organizations thus need to carefully plan and design change management so that digital transformation can be effectively conducted.

To overcome these challenges and make digital transformation successful, there are important points for the management to take note of (McKinsey & Company, 2018). Specifically, organizations need to (a) have the right, digital-savvy leaders in place, (b) build capabilities for the workforce of the future, (c) empower people to work in new ways, (d) give day-to-day tools a digital upgrade, and (e) communicate frequently via traditional and digital methods. Concerning the first point, when organizations start engaging in digital transformation, it is critical to identify the leaders who can manage the initiatives effectively and have them dedicate to the change effort on the full-time basis. When companies have certain digital-savvy individuals in the leadership role, they are more likely to achieve a successful digital transformation. Second, digital transformation requires the organization to build talent and skills that are conducive to the initiative. For example, organizations can redefine the roles and responsibilities of their employees to align them with the transformation's goals. Also, organizations are encouraged to engage technology-innovation managers who can help bridge potential gaps between the traditional and digital parts of their business so that employees can better learn about new technology and tools, facilitating the goal of digital transformation. Additionally, organizations should recruit right talents for digital transformation, in other words, hiring and recruitment practices should also be revolved around specific needs required for digital transformation.

Third, organizations should encourage employees to work in new ways to increase the likelihood of successful digital transformation. Digital transformation requires changes at the individual employee level embedded with behavioral and attitudinal shifts. To empower employees to work in new ways, new technological changes can be adopted through telecommuting or open work environments. Also, organizations can seek for employees' feedback about where certain digital changes can be adopted, so that employees feel more accountable for the changes that happen in the organization. Fourth, providing upgraded digital tools with employees is also critical. One way to do so is to integrate new technology with the standard operating procedures. Digitalizing employees' daily work routines and procedures should promote employees' receptiveness of digital transformation. Finally, communicating about digital transformation should help employees understand a big picture about what the organization is trying to achieve. Without frequent and consistent communication, it may be unclear to employees why digital transformation is happening and why it is important for the future of the organization as well as of employees. It is also necessary that organizations set clear targets and goals concerning digital transformation and frequently update employees with their progress. These five points are critical for organizations to succeed in digital transformation. BCG reported that only 30% of digital transformations are successful (Forth, Reichert, de Laubier, & Chakraborty, 2020). Aside from the five points suggested by McKinsey, BCG emphasized the value of an agile governance mindset in order to implement behavioral changes towards successful digital transformations. Agile mindsets among the management and employees should be able to pick up new changes more quickly and effectively. Thus, fostering such mindset and organizational culture is another important factor for the successful digital transformations.

3.7 Strategy 2: Develop an Innovation and Disruptive Strategy

On top of digitization, organizations should also focus on creating disruptive innovations that potentially will bring further enhanced value to the organization. Although many companies invest heavily in innovation, they often find their innovation initiatives failing. Further to this, successful innovators themselves have a hard time sustaining their performance. Well established Companies like Polaroid, Nokia, Yahoo, and many others have met with varying challenges when it comes to innovation (Pisano, 2015). The core problem is primarily caused by the lack of an innovation strategy. Without one, a company will not be able to make trade-off decisions and choose the elements of the innovation system. Further to that, different parts of the organization might end up pursuing conflicting priorities. While there is no one standard system for every organization, a clear innovation strategy can help an organization design a system to match their specific competitive needs. An innovation strategy should specify how the various types of innovation fit into the business strategy as well as the resources that should be allocated respectively. Additionally, innovation creates value for both current and potential customers. For example, innovation can make a product perform better in terms of efficiency and effectiveness, enhance the level of convenience, enable higher durability, reduce cost by having the selling price lower, and many more. A company should choose the kind of value their innovation will create and closely stick to it, primarily because the necessary skills, capabilities, and resources required will be different given the varying goals, and thus will take time to build up. Apple, for example, focuses its innovation in making its products easier, convenient to use, and creating a seamless experience across all of them.

Innovations can be broken down into two dimensions (market and technology), each of which has two levels (existing and new), creating four different types of innovations (Lopez, 2015). The first type of innovation has been discussed, i.e. disruptive innovation. Organizations develop new technology but implement it in their current markets. A good example is Apple's introduction of iPhone in the mobile phone market. Apple's iPhone disrupted the mobile phone market by introducing novel features and functions that customers would have never imagined the mobile phones to have. The second type is incremental innovation, which is the most common form whereby organizations take advantage of their existing technology within their existing markets so that they could provide greater values to their customers. Such innovations mainly entail small updates to their products or services. The third type architectural innovation in which organizations use their existing technology but introduce the innovations in new markets, in other words, organizations experiment whether their current competency might give them another competitive advantage in different markets. This will be effective if the new market is receptive to what companies would offer because they do not have to make too much investment in terms of developing new technology from scratch. The fourth form of innovation is radical innovation, which is done by developing new technology and implementing it in new markets. This type of innovation is usually considered revolutionary, and a good example is Netflix, as the company completely transformed the way people watch and enjoy movies and TV shows through providing online streaming services.

What promotes these organizational innovations then? There are a variety of practical and empirical recommendations. For example, de Jong, Marston, and Roth (2015) offer the eight essentials of innovation – aspire, choose, discover, evolve, accelerate, scale, extend, and mobilize. In a nutshell, they recommended organizations to strategically plan out what kinds of opportunities they have, what innovations they can create to seize the opportunities in existing and new markets for the company's future growth, and how they can sustain their innovations in the long term. Some of the other practical recommendations are defining the company's value proposition and assessing and developing companies; core capabilities (Kylliäinen, 2018). From the research scholars' perspectives, there are other important considerations organizations need to be aware of when it comes to innovations (Lam, 2011). For instance, organizational structures have huge implications in organizations' innovative behaviors. In particular, organizations can have either mechanistic (more rigid and hierarchical) or organic structure (more fluid and adaptive to changes). Usually, organizations with an organic structure would perform better in the industry characterized by rapid, frequent changes and therefore tend to be more competent in developing innovations, compared to those with a mechanistic structure. Also, some researchers focused on the role of appropriate contexts in facilitating organizational knowledge creation (Nonaka, 1994; Nonaka & Takeuchi, 1995). In order to generate new ideas and knowledge, it is critical for organizations to offer the contexts where their employees can interact and exchange their perspectives with each other.

Christensen, Raynor, and McDonald (2015) provided a detailed explanation about what disruptive innovation is. First, they explained that disruption describes a process whereby a smaller company with fewer resources is able to successfully challenge established incumbent business. By focusing on most profitable customers, incumbents often ignore the needs of others, creating a certain degree of overlooked customer segments. Disruptive innovators usually identify these overlooked segments and create the products with better functionality (and frequently at a lower price) than those offered by the incumbents. Specifically, disruptive innovations originate in two different ways. First, organizations can engage in disruptive innovations by gaining low-end footholds. This can be achieved by focusing on the customers who are seen less profitable and demanding in the market. Second, disruptive innovations can be achieved by gaining new-market footholds. This strategy is essentially concerned about turning non-consumers into consumers by creating a new market where nobody exists, and therefore, no competition is happening. This is exemplified by the case of Xerox; though the company started off by targeting large corporations in the early days of photocopying, they created a new market by switching to the strategy of offering affordable services to individuals and small organizations (for example, school librarians, bowling-league operators). Thus, organizations need to either identify overlooked, low-end customers or create a completely new market, to simply develop and launch innovations are not sufficient to be called disruptive innovations.

An example of disruptive innovation is iPhone (Sampere, 2016). When the product came out in 2007, it was not disruptive in the sense that it did not target the low-end customers or create a new market. However, its subsequent development was a disruption to the laptop, i.e., specifically, the iPhone became a primary access point to the Internet and started to replace the laptop (Christensen et al., 2015). As exemplified by the iPhone, disruptive innovations are very effective in many cases, since the incumbents would not usually expect the disruption in the market, and therefore, their responses tend to be suboptimal. King and Baatartogtokh (2015) provided three recommendations to managers concerning the application of the theory of disruptive innovations. First, the managers need to calculate the value of winning. Although one criterion for innovations to be considered as disruptive is to create a new market, managers adopt this strategy based on a deliberate consideration of the potential for profits there. If the entry barrier is too low or the product is easily substitutable, competition in the new market can become cutthroat very easily. Second, managers should make a careful evaluation about the existing resources and competence of their organization before making moves. It is critical to leverage their own capabilities to be successful in new businesses. Leveraging existing capabilities could be done by reconfiguring organizations' resources in novel ways as well. Organizations' disruptive innovations could come from not only building completely new products but also re-thinking how the existing resources can be combined to develop innovations. Lastly, managers should consider collaborating with other companies and working with new entrants. Disney collaborated with (and acquired) Pixar to leverage the strengths of Pixar as a content developer, instead of fiercely competing with them. Collaboration with start-ups with unique strengths often results in acquiring new resources and competence, which could contribute to the development of novel or even disruptive innovations subsequently.

3.8 Strategy 3: Work on Corporate Social Responsibility

In recent times, more emphasis and attention has been paid to the corporate social responsibility (CSR) policies of businesses. Ethical issues such as fair trade, sustainability, and diversity have been increasingly scrutinized by the public. Organizations that do not have the appropriate CSR strategies in place may face backlash from consumers, resulting in boycotts and a tarnished reputation. Hence, organizations should develop their CSR strategy to the best of their ability. Other equally important reasons why companies should integrate CSR methods into their core values include (a) greater innovation, (b) brand differentiation, (c) attracting top talent, (d) increased customer loyalty, and (e) better long-term outlook. On top of that, CSR can generate value for an organization's consumers. It can provide three forms of value to consumers: emotional, social, and functional (Green and Peloza, 2011). CSR does not only enable organizations to meet current consumer support but it also provides them with varying benefits.

A variety of factors influence organizations' engagement in CSR. In their review, Aguinis and Glavas (2012) have summarized various predictors of CSR, some of which include institutional and stakeholder pressures (for example, shareholder activism, media pressure, local community pressure), regulation and standards (for example, standards and certification, perceived CSR by consumers), third-party evaluation, context, and climate (for example, country-specific corporate governance structure, country context, sociocultural environment), organizations' missions and values, shareholders/ownership, firm motives, as well as structure and governance of the organizations. Recently, Gupta, Briscoe, and Hambrick (2017) demonstrated that CSR is not only determined by external influence or only the firm leaders and executives but is also shaped by the ideology shared among organizational members. They found that liberal organizational political ideology was positively associated with the following three types of CSR activities: (1) omnibus CSR including such categories as employee relations, environment, human rights, (2) representation of women in top management, and (3) domestic partner benefits.

As mentioned above, CSR has, by and large, a positive influence on organizations and enhances their reputation, consumer loyalty and firm evaluations, financial performance, employee engagement and commitment, organizational citizenship behaviors (Aguinis & Glavas, 2012; Bouraoui, Bensemmane, Ohana, & Russo, 2019). Also, it can be geared towards either internal or external aspects of organizations. Farooq, Rupp, and Farooq (2017) have shown that external CSR is positively associated with loyalty and boosterism, whereas internal CSR can increase employees' interpersonal helping. One of the key mechanisms underlying the positive effects of CSR is organizational identification, such that employees feel more motivated to integrate their personal identity with organizational one, increasing their efforts and commitment to the organization.

Levi Strauss & Co., a leading apparel company on the globe, has been known for its commitment to CSR. According to their sustainability report in 2019, the company engaged in various programs that facilitate the operation of its business in environmentally friendly manner. For example, Levi was able to save more than 3.5 billion liters of water in its finishing process since its introduction in 2011. Also, the company tries to reduce carbon emission by 90% in its facilities and 40% across the global supply chain by 2025. The company is also aiming to shift to 100% renewable electricity in its facilities and have reached 72% as of 2018 (Levi Strauss & Co., 2020). Additionally, they developed a comprehensive worker well-being initiative worldwide, which ensures the rights of employees, including the prohibition of child labor and forced or trafficked labor, ethical standards, working hours, and wages and benefits (Levi Strauss & Co., 2017).

Upshaw (2021) argued that organizations need to be careful about developing a corporate social responsibility strategy that is seen authentic to their customers. Sometimes, organizations might engage in CSR strategies that are not much aligned with their own businesses, values, cultures, and brands. If the organizations' CSR efforts are seen inauthentic, their public trust and credibility will be likely put in jeopardy. Upshaw (2021) provided six tips when it comes to developing CSR strategies. First of all, it is critical to get buy-in from company's executives. The support from executives will be vital in order to communicate the value of CSR to employees and other relevant stakeholders. To get buy-in from the executives, a key is to demonstrate the business value of CSR strategies and the positive impacts made by the CSR on the company's performance and long-term value for their stakeholders. The second tip is to identify material issues or the areas of CSR issues where companies can best address. The areas of CSR which each company should focus on would likely vary depending on the company's business. For example, a technology company would focus on data privacy rather than sustainable agriculture which is more likely to be taken up as an issue by a food company. Organizations can identify the material issues either internally or through consulting their stakeholders. Also, they can review the United Nation's Sustainable Development Goals as a starting point and link most relevant issues to their CSR efforts and strategies.

Third, once the material issues are determined, companies need to consider how they address the issues in a way that is aligned with their values and culture. As mentioned above, the strategies that are not well aligned with the organization's identity could backfire and may not be sustainable. The fourth step is to establish a goal framework so that organizations can effectively organize and manage the goals of their CSR initiatives. For example, organizations can organize their goals around areas and scopes of impacts, difficulty, and importance. Fifth, creating a system of implementation and accountability is necessary for effective execution of the CSR strategies and goals. Creating a governance system within the organizations helps employees and executives accountable for their CSR initiatives. Lastly, it is critical to communicate about CSR strategy and goals with honesty, transparency, and repetition. Organizations should decide how frequently and in what ways they will update their progress with their employees and stakeholders. These six points would help organizations design their CSR strategies that are not only more authentic to their organizational core values and identities but also more goal-driven, thereby increasing the chance of achieving their goals. One thing that organizational leaders should bear in mind when developing CSR strategies is that they should not consider them as another tool to increase firm performance and profitability. The experiments conducted by Meier and Cassar (2018) showed that the intentions behind CSR initiatives matter. When employees could perceive their organization's CSR not to be genuinely designed to contribute to society, they may likely react negatively, which would make it difficult to elicit commitment from them. It is thus necessary for organizations to communicate their intentions in creating positive impacts on societal issues clearly and frequently to their employees and stakeholders to ensure their engagement to achieve the CSR goals.

3.9 Strategy 4: Differentiated Offerings and Contemporary, Updated Sales Tactic

With e-commerce becoming increasingly popular, it is vital for businesses to duly consider how they can re-strategize and capture added value digitally. Business must offer consumer products and services that are differentiated from that of their competitors. This is especially so in the digital marketplace, where one search result can lead to hundreds of potential options. Once the offering is differentiated, the sales tactic an organization adopts becomes the key to success. Virtual selling is much less forgiving and easily reachable than in-person selling. Hence, organizations must adopt effective sales practices online as this could make or break the business. Companies must boost the business' digital presence, leverage on referrals, personalize connections, add value through before- and after-sale service, and leverage on advocates inside the buying organization. Primarily, organizations should work on creating new customer-experience journey online to boost sales and create further value for consumers.

Although diversification of products and services is critical in firm performance, their effects are also contingent on other factors. For example, Su and Tsang (2015) found that product diversification leads to better financial performance for the firms that maintain relationships with a broad range of secondary stakeholders than those with a narrow scope. They also demonstrated that such positive relationship between diversification and firm performance for the firms with more diverse secondary stakeholders is particularly stronger when firms engaged in unrelated diversification (versus related diversification). Also, service differentiation was found to strengthen the positive effect of customer centricity on business performance and to have a direct positive influence on firm innovativeness (Gebauer, Gustafsson, & Witell, 2011). Other researchers argue that differentiation can take two different forms – horizontal differentiation and vertical differentiation, each of which would differentially affect such variables as firms' profit, competitive advantages, rivalry restraint (Makadok & Ross, 2013). However, apparently, differentiation has only upsides, and Hamilton and Richards (2009) proposed that it would have an inverted U-sharped relation with the depth of product assortment, such that the deepest assortment of products would occur when the level of product differentiation is intermediate, while the assortment would be shallow when the levels of firms' engagement in product differentiation are at the tails. Also, extreme diversification can be detrimental to firms when it is not perceived as appropriate by firms' stakeholders (Greenwood, Li, Prakash, & Deephouse, 2005).

In practice, IKEA's business success is often attributed to its product differentiation strategy by offering a wide range of home furnishing products at as low cost as possible, while maintaining the products' quality (Jarrett & Huy, 2018). For example, IKEA designed their own stores in a quite distinctive way so that it can differentiate itself from other home furniture brands. They have also opened their stores in more than 50 countries, which allows the company to reach the customers worldwide. Also, concerning service differentiation, IKEA also offers unique customer experiences through taking advantage of social media, one of which is its YouTube channel. The contents of the videos offered by IKEA's YouTube channel are quite diverse and broad, and they are not only about the information on its products and assembly instructions but also about things such as some ideas and tips on how to design one's home space (for example, designing bathroom, making a microgreens garden). Their videos even contain the themes of social entrepreneurship and business ethics. IKEA utilizes other social media platforms (for example, Twitter, Facebook, and Instagram) too, which also help the company provide unique service and experiences to both current and potential customers.

Leinwand and Mainardi (2016) argued that differentiation is not just about developing one or two isolated products that are distinct from others. Such differentiation is not very sustainable and does not produce long-term profits, as the popularity of a single product usually does not last for a long time, especially in the industries where a fierce competition exists. As in the case of IKEA, companies can differentiate themselves from others when they could build distinctive organizational capabilities and constantly develop and offer an entire line of products, services, customer experiences, as well as brand images that are truly unique to them. Leinwand and Mainardi (2016) listed several recommendations for companies to set apart themselves from their competitors: being skeptical of benchmarking and not blindly following the common practices in the industry; working backward by setting goals first and identifying the capabilities that organizations currently possess and the capabilities that the organizations will need for differentiation; developing the practices that are unique to the company; when acquiring other companies, looking for those that can complement the capabilities and resources that are missing in the organizations and being mindful about the management after the integration; having different teams and divisions to work cross-functionally; and explicitly codify implicit knowledge and understanding in the organizations. Organizations are thus encouraged to achieve differentiation and develop a unique identity based on their capabilities instead of a single product or service. Differentiation through capabilities is not easily imitated by other competitors and therefore likely provides a more long-lasting competitive advantage in given industries.

Lindecrantz, Gi, and Zerbi (2020) emphasized that personalizing customer experiences is a critical component of companies' differentiation strategies. A good example of the personalized customer experience is Amazon; when customers do online shopping on Amazon.com, they are recommended various items based on their purchase history and searches. Customers also receive emails from Amazon for personalized recommended items. Furthermore, Amazon started a personal shopping service called Amazon Prime Wardrobe. This is exclusive for Prime members, and customers complete a survey about their preferences for fashion; a team of stylists then provide personalized recommendations from various brands. Sephora, an international beauty-product retailer, is another exemplary case that focuses on providing highly personalized experiences to their customers. The company offers a mobile application in which customers can book in-store makeovers and fashion consultation. When customers have their make-ups done in stores, their make-up artists can input each item and product they used for the make-ups in customers' personal profiles. Sephora's loyalty program called Beauty Insider also offers customized products based on their profiles. Sephora now has 25 million members for their loyalty program, and 80% of their total transactions come from the members of the program. In order to have such successful personalization strategies, Lindecrantz et al. (2020) described eight core elements that are required to succeed in personalization: (a) Data Foundation: *data management: Develop a multidimensional view of the customer to serve as the backbone of analytics. Quality should take precedence over quantity; having the right data is more important than having extensive data)*; (b) Decisioning: *(i) customer segmentation and analytics (Segment customers, identify value triggers and score customers accordingly; (ii) playbook (Create library of campaigns and content that can be matched with customers); (iii) decisioning engine (campaign coordination): Develop a multichannel decision engine to prevent conflicting messages and drive maximum value per touchpoint;* (c) Design (i) cross-functional teams: Assemble a cross-functional, co-located team to manage weekly deployment in a test-and-learn culture for faster results; (ii) talents, capabilities, and culture: secure the right capabilities and talent, often begun by setting the right ambition in leadership; d) Distribution: (i) technology enablement: An optimized technology platform can be complex; start with existing technology and squeeze value from it first; and (ii) test and learn: Don't wait for perfection; get started and improve over time with analytics. Achieving highly personalized customer service would help organizations become differentiated from others and obtain a source of long-lasting competitive advantage, as their competitors cannot easily imitate it.

3.10 Strategy 5: Focus on Value Capture

Executives at the top level must understand what vale capture is about. Organizations need to realize what value does their products or services offer from the lenses of their stakeholders. That value needs to be identified and explicitly captured so that necessary resources could be pumped in to improvise or make it relevant to the customers' changing needs. Value capture is a vital process for ongoing survival and sustainability as it allows for reinvestment in the business to create a competitive edge or advantage or fund research & development (R&D) for new products. Value is captured from clients through for example superior customer value that leads to satisfied customers, customer loyalty and retention, higher current and future sales, higher market share and customer equity and profits. From a company's value chain aspect, value capture could be appreciated from the increased value in supply chain, in other words in consumer's dollar. Vertical integration, direct marketing, producer alliances, and cooperatives are often directed towards capturing more of the end-use value.

Often times, innovators assume that once value is created, rewards will follow but this is simply not the case all the times (Michel, 2014), organizations must also ensure that they capture the value and invest in it appropriately in order to reap the full benefits which is crucial for managers to be conscious of it. Senior leaders must emphasize the importance of value capture and that it should be integral to every strategy and innovation exercise in the firm. Leaders must assemble a dedicated team to focus on value capture as well.

Value capture is determined by varying factors. Value capture is defined as the realization of exchange value and argued that it would be contingent on several factors (Bowman and Ambrosini, 2000). For instance, organizations cannot fully capture values from their own products and innovations when customers' bargaining power is enhanced. Also, Chatain (2010) found that expertise advantage relative to the relevant competitors (as opposed to all competitors) and the level and intensity of the client relationship would matter to value capture. Research has also pointed that firms need to be cautious about others appropriating the values they create. Kim (2016) reported that isolating mechanisms based on geographic scope of knowledge acquisition can prevent value capture of other firms. As a result, the focal firms that create certain value can fully capture this value, which then translates into better firm performance. Moreover, some firms might form alliance with other firms and engage in value capture, which may require the repositioning of their value proposition. In the context of alliance, firms can engage in value creation through forming relationships with other firms, and it is also important for them to consider how they achieve value capture or split the gains with their partners. In the context of alliance, value capture might be affected by factors as the (a) partners' complementary resources, (b) development and/or acquisition of value-creating resources, and (c) relation-specific investments (Dyer, Singh, & Hesterly, 2018). The relative bargaining power of partners in the alliance limits firms' ability to capture value (Lavie, 2007). Furthermore, evidence shows that there are much more multilevel perspectives on value capture (Lepak, Smith, & Taylor, 2007). For example, Call and Ployhart (2021) recently proposed that factors such as employees' psychological states concerning their jobs, their task behaviors, and job characteristics can affect the extent to which firms can create and capture values.

Michel (2014) has emphasized the importance of value capture and introduced how some of the contemporary companies engage in it. For instance, when Netflix was competing Blockbuster, the company introduced a subscription model as opposed to the revenue model based on late fees. One of the concerns will be changing the price-setting mechanism. Instead of setting prices based on production costs and/or prices set by competitors, companies can charge customers based on the value of the offerings to them (for example, Bossard's ecosyn-lubric). Google has implemented a different strategy for value capture called auctioning. As Google gains revenue from advertisers' payments to crop up on its search engine, the company makes advertisers bid for the certain keywords that they want to be associated with – or how much money they are willing to pay for a click on their ads – and allows the top bidder to be highlighted in the search engine.

Concerning customer data, Brown et al. (2017) provided three potential avenues for organizations to capture more value. First, organizations should tease out critical patterns from the information such as customer purchase and transaction histories. The important consideration here is that though most companies analyze and use customer records to their own advantages, the inferences derived from the data are often used in an isolated manner. For example, a bank can pool various types of customer information and analyze it to obtain insights that could address different kinds of issues such as churn, fraud, and default risk. Second, optimal use of customer data would help organizations exponentially improve their performance and productivity. By fully capturing value from customer data, organizations would be able to, for example, identify the areas of business where they are lacking expertise or the areas where they have excessive resources. They could optimize their use of resources and thereby reduce inefficiency across organizational functions. Third, value capture from customer data would enable breakthrough solutions and services. Some leading companies use various types of customer data to develop novel services. For example, Ginger.io uses the customer data about sleep, mobility, and communication patterns that are obtained through smartphones and fitness devices for clinical assessments and diagnosis for patients with mental illness. As such, there may be lots of hidden insights embedded in customer data, which could potentially help to improve organizational productivity and innovation. Towards these ends, organizations should put efforts into enriching their customer data and investing in IT teams to enhance the organizational capability in analyzing the data. Also, if the data can be made sharable and accessible, it is also possible to collaborate with the third parties to generate important insights from the data.

Also, Busellato, Dretin, and Kishore (2021) argued that there would be many opportunities for value capture in procurement and operation management. For example, digitalization can be facilitated in procurement to enhance optimization. It is important for organizations to track spending for each supplier over time and identify the gap between actual and expected spending, so that they can understand the areas where they could make potential improvements. As digitalization is a critical part for value capture in procurement, organizations should help the members of the procurement team develop digital capabilities and encourage them to use more digital solutions. Digitalization does not occur in a single day. Organizations thus need to provide a training program that extensively covers new digital tools so that their procurement teams can become more effective in developing optimal solutions. Organizations need to be stable but adaptable enough to respond to threats and opportunities where organizations might have to reorganize themselves to capture maximum values as quickly as possible (Keller, 2018). In all, value capture is not an isolated strategy that can be done solely by executives or a team of the organization. Rather, it would often require a long-term perspective as well as substantive, organizational-scale interventions and efforts to achieve. It is thus critical for organizational leaders to think through the areas where they could potentially capture greater value than now and specific changes that organizations need to go through (for example, digitalization, re-designing of the organization) to achieve value capture.

References

Aguinis, H., & Glavas, A. (2012). What we know and don't know about corporate social responsibility: A review and research agenda. *Journal of Management, 38*(4), 932–968. https://doi.org/10.1177/0149206311436079

Anthony, S. D., Trotter, A., & Schwartz, E. I. (2019, September 24). The top 20 business transformations of the last decade. *Harvard Business Review.*

Atmar, H., Begley, S., Fuerst, J., Rickert, S., Sleatt, R., & Tjon Pian Gi, M. (2020, April 24). The next normal: Retail M&A and partnerships after COVID-19. *McKinsey & Company.* https://www.mckinsey.com/business-functions/m-and-a/our-insights/the-next-normal-retail-m-and-a-and-partnerships-after-covid-19

Bingham, S. (2020, August 4). How HR leaders can adapt to uncertain times. *Harvard Business Review.* https://hbr.org/2020/08/how-hr-leaders-can-adapt-to-uncertain-times

Bojanowski, C. (2019, December 4). Why you need to refresh your B2B value proposition. *SmarkLabs.* https://www.smarklabs.com/blog/why-you-need-to-refresh-your-b2b-value-proposition/

Bough, V., Breuer, R., Maechler, N., & Ungerman, K. (2020, October 27). The three building blocks of successful customer-experience transformations. *McKinsey & Company.* https://www.mckinsey.com/business-functions/marketing-and-sales/our-insights/the-three-building-blocks-of-successful-customer-experience-transformations

Bouraoui, K., Bensemmane, S., Ohana, M., & Russo, M. (2019). Corporate social responsibility and employees' affective commitment. *Management Decision, 57*(1), 152–167. https://doi.org/10.1108/MD-10-2017-1015

Bouzine, S., Molloy, M., & Monteleone, C. (n.d.). Storytelling in times of crisis: How to reevaluate your business value proposition. *evolveMKD.* https://www.evolvemkd.com/storytelling-in-times-of-crisis/

Bowman, C., & Ambrosini, V. (2000). Value creation versus value capture: Towards a coherent definition of value in strategy. *British Journal of Management, 11*(1), 1–15. https://doi.org/10.1111/1467-8551.00147

Brown, B., Kanagasabai, K., Pant, P., & Pinto, G. S. (2017, March 15). Capturing value from your customer data. *McKinsey & Company.* https://www.mckinsey.com/business-functions/mckinsey-analytics/our-insights/capturing-value-from-your-customer-data

Busellato, N., Dretin, R., & Kishore, S. (2021, February 25). Now is the time for procurement to lead value capture. *McKinsey & Company.* https://www.mckinsey.com/business-functions/operations/our-insights/now-is-the-time-for-procurement-to-lead-value-capture

Call, M. L., & Ployhart, R. E. (2021). A theory of firm value capture from employee job performance: A multidisciplinary perspective. *Academy of Management Review, 46*(3), 572–590. https://doi.org/10.5465/amr.2018.0103

Chatain, O. (2010). Value creation, competition, and performance in buyer-supplier relationships. *Strategic Management Journal, 32*(1), 76–102. https://doi.org/10.1002/smj.864

Christensen, C. M., Raynor, M. E., & McDonald, R. (2015). What is disruptive innovation? *Harvard Business Review.* https://hbr.org/2015/12/what-is-disruptive-innovation

Cohan, P. (2013, October 22). Netflix's reed Hastings is the master of adaptation. *Forbes.*

Coleman, J. (2022, May 28). It's time to take a fresh look at your company's values. *Harvard Business Review.* https://hbr.org/2022/03/its-time-to-take-a-fresh-look-at-your-companys-values

Deanhouston+. (2021, February 25). *Is there value in revisiting a brand's value proposition?* https://www.deanhouston.com/inspire/is-there-value-in-revisiting-a-brands-value-proposition/

De Jong, M., Marston, N., & Roth, E. (2015, April 1). The eight essentials of innovation. *McKinsey Quarterly.* https://www.mckinsey.com/business-functions/strategy-and-corporate-finance/our-insights/the-eight-essentials-of-innovation

Dyer, J. H., Singh, H., & Hesterly, W. S. (2018). The relational view revisited: A dynamic perspective on value creation and value capture. *Strategic Management Journal, 39*(12), 3140–3162. https://doi.org/10.1002/smj.2785

Enriquez, M. (2020, August 31). The future of retail after COVID-19. *CNA.* https://www.channelnewsasia.com/business/the-future-of-retail-in-a-covid-19-era-money-mind-638331

Farooq, O., Rupp, D. E., & Farooq, M. (2017). The multiple pathways through which internal and external corporate social responsibility influence organizational identification and multifoci outcomes: The moderating role of cultural and social orientations. *Academy of Management Journal, 60*(3), 954–985. https://doi.org/10.5465/amj.2014.0849

Forth, P., Reicher, T., de Laubier, R., & Chakraborty, S. (2020, October 29). Flipping the odds of digital transformation success. *BCG.* https://www.bcg.com/publications/2020/increasing-odds-of-success-in-digital-transformation.

Gebauer, H., Gustafsson, A., & Witell, L. (2011). Competitive advantage through service differentiation by manufacturing companies. *Journal of Business Research, 64*(12), 1270–1280. https://doi.org/10.1016/j.jbusres.2011.01.015

Gilmore, J. (2021, July 21). Why now is the time for FDI businesses to re-evaluate their Employee Value Propositions. *EY.* https://www.ey.com/en_ie/workforce/why-now-is-the-time-for-fdi-businesses-to-re-evaluate-their-employee-value-propositions

Gorsht, R. (2014, August 20). Why it's time to rethink the value proposition. *Forbes.* https://www.forbes.com/sites/sap/2014/08/20/why-its-time-to-rethink-the-value-proposition/?sh=663f5df04b3d

Green, T., & Peloza, J. (2011). How does corporate social responsibility create value for consumers? *Journal of Consumer Marketing, 28*(1), 48–56.

Greenwood, R., Li, S. X., Prakash, R., & Deephouse, D. L. (2005). Reputation, diversification, and organizational explanations of performance in professional service firms. *Organization Science, 16*(6), 661–673. https://doi.org/10.1287/orsc.1050.0159

Gupta, A., Briscoe, F., & Hambrick, D. C. (2017). Red, blue, and purple firms: Organizational political ideology and corporate social responsibility. *Strategic Management Journal, 38*(5), 1018–1040. https://doi.org/10.1002/smj.2550

Hamilton, S. F., & Richards, T. J. (2009). Product differentiation, store differentiation, and assortment depth. *Management Science, 55*(8), 1368–1376. https://doi.org/10.1287/mnsc.1090.1032

Jarrett, M., & Huy, Q. (2018, February 2). IKEA's success can't be attributed to one charismatic leader. *Harvard Business Review.* https://hbr.org/2018/02/ikeas-success-cant-be-attributed-to-one-charismatic-leader

Keller, S. (2018, February 20). Reorganizing to capture maximum value quickly. *McKinsey & Company.* https://www.mckinsey.com/business-functions/people-and-organizational-performance/our-insights/reorganizing-to-capture-maximum-value-quickly

Kim, M. (2016). Geographic scope, isolating mechanisms, and value appropriation. *Strategic Management Journal, 37*(4), 695–713. https://doi.org/10.1002/smj.2356

King, A. A., & Baatartogtokh, B. (2015, September 15). How useful is the theory of disruptive innovation? *Harvard Business Review.* https://sloanreview.mit.edu.remotexs.ntu.edu.sg/article/how-useful-is-the-theory-of-disruptive-innovation/

Krach, K. (2016, August 25). 5 ways digitization can add value to your company. *LinkedIn.* https://www.linkedin.com/pulse/5-ways-digitization-can-add-value-your-company-keith-krach/

Kylliäinen, J. (2018, December 28). Innovation strategy – What is it and how to develop one? *Viima.* https://www.viima.com/blog/innovation-strategy

Lam, A. (2011). Innovative organizations: Structure, learning and adaptation. In *Innovation. Perspectives for the 21st Century.* Madrid, Spain: BBVA.

Lavie, D. (2007). Alliance portfolios and firm performance: A study of value creation and appropriation in the U.S. software industry. *Strategic Management Journal, 28*(12), 1187–1212. https://doi.org/10.1002/smj.637

Leinwand, P., & Mainardi, C. (2016, May 19). Your whole company needs to be distinctive, not just your product. *Harvard Business Review.* https://hbr.org/2016/05/your-whole-company-needs-to-be-distinctive-not-just-your-product

Lepak, D. P., Smith, K. G., & Taylor, M. S. (2007). Value creation and value capture: A multilevel perspective. *Academy of Management Review, 32*(1), 180–194. https://doi.org/10.5465/amr.2007.23464011

Levi Strauss & Co. (2017, December). *Labor standards – Terms of engagement.* https://www.levistrauss.com/wp-content/uploads/2019/02/TOE_Feb2019.pdf

Levi Strauss & Co. (2020, July). *2019 sustainability review.* https://www.levistrauss.com/wp-content/uploads/2020/07/LSCo.-2019-Sustainability-Review.pdf

Lindecrantz, E., Gi, M. T. P., & Zerbi, S. (2020, April 28). Personalizing the customer experience: Driving differentiation in retail. *McKinsey & Company.* https://www.mckinsey.com/industries/retail/our-insights/personalizing-the-customer-experience-driving-differentiation-in-retail

Lopez, J. (2015, June 29). Types of innovation. *Constant Contact.* https://techblog.constantcontact.com/software-development/types-of-innovation/

Makadok, R., & Ross, D. G. (2013). Taking industry structuring seriously: A strategic perspective on product differentiation. *Strategic Management Journal, 34*(5), 509–532. https://doi.org/10.1002/smj.2033

Maynes, J., & Rawson, A. (2016, March 4). Linking the customer experience to value. *McKinsey & Company.* https://www.mckinsey.com/business-functions/marketing-and-sales/our-insights/linking-the-customer-experience-to-value.

McGrath, R. G. (2013a). *The end of competitive advantage: How to keep your strategy moving as fast as your business.* Harvard Business Review Press.

McGrath, R. G. (2013b, June). Transient advantage. *Harvard Business Review.* https://hbr.org/2013/06/transient-advantage

McKinsey & Company. (2018, October 29). *Unlocking success in digital transformations.* https://www.mckinsey.com/business-functions/people-and-organizational-performance/our-insights/unlocking-success-in-digital-transformations

Meier, S., & Cassar, L. (2018, January 31). Stop talking about how CSR helps your bottom line. *Harvard Business Review.* https://hbr.org/2018/01/stop-talking-about-how-csr-helps-your-bottom-line.

Michel, S. (2014, October). Capture more value. *Harvard Business Review.* https://hbr.org/2014/10/capture-more-value

Newman, D. (2018, February 8). Communication changes in the digital transformation. *Future of Work.* https://fowmedia.com/communication-changes-in-the-digital-transformation/

Nonaka, I. (1994). A dynamic theory of organizational knowledge creation. *Organization Science, 5*(1), 14–37.

Nonaka, I., & Takeuchi, H. (1995). *The knowledge creating company.* Oxford University Press.

Otlowski, A. (2019, March 21). How to define/redefine your value proposition for better business outcomes. *HIPB2B.* https://www.hipb2b.com/blog/how-to-define-redefine-your-value-proposition-for-better-business-outcomes

Pardo, D. (2018, June 12). 8 advantages of digitalization of business. *Ehorus.* https://ehorus.com/digitalization-of-business/

Pisano, G. P. (2015, June). You need an innovation strategy. *Harvard Business Review.* https://hbr.org/2015/06/you-need-an-innovation-strategy

Plutora. (2020, November 12). *Top 4 digital transformation challenges (and how to solve them).* https://www.plutora.com/blog/digital-transformation-challenges

Pratt, M. K. (2021, March 10). 10 digital transformation benefits for business. *SeachCIO.* https://searchcio.techtarget.com/tip/Top-10-digital-transformation-benefits-for-business

Rockcontent. (2020, November 20). *6 ways to improve your value proposition.* https://rockcontent.com/blog/how-to-improve-value-proposition/

Sampere, J. P. V. (2016, February 2). Apple's shrinking impact in the smartphone industry. *Harvard Business Review.* https://hbr.org/2016/02/apples-shrinking-impact-in-the-smartphone-industry

Su, W., & Tsang, E. W. K. (2015). Product diversification and financial performance: The moderating role of secondary stakeholders. *Academy of Management Journal, 58*(4), 1128–1148. https://doi.org/10.5465/amj.2013.0454

Tabrizi, B., Lam, E., Girard, K., & Irvin, V. (2019, March 13). Digital transformation is not about technology. *Harvard Business Review*. https://hbr.org/2019/03/digital-transformation-is-not-about-technology

Tacke, G. (2018, October 16). 5 ways digitalization is changing innovation. *Simon Kucher*. https://www.simon-kucher.com/en-sg/blog/5-ways-digitalization-changing-innovation

The Economist Intelligence Unit & KPMG International. (2006). *Rethinking the business model*. http://www.in.kpmg.com/pdf/Rethinking_business_model06.pdf

Thompson, N. (2021, May 24). 8 benefits of digital transformation for your employees. *Conosco*. https://www.conosco.com/blog/8-benefits-of-digital-transformation-for-your-employees-2021/

Tong, T. W., Guo, Y., & Chen, L. (2021, September 9). How Xiaomi redefined what it means to be a platform. *Harvard Business Review*. https://hbr.org/2021/09/how-xiaomi-redefined-what-it-means-to-be-a-platform

Twin, A. (2020, July 5). Value proposition. *Investopedia*. https://www.investopedia.com/terms/v/valueproposition.asp

Upshaw, T. (2021, September 17). Your CSR strategy needs to be goal driven, achievable, and authentic. *Harvard Business Review*. https://hbr.org/2021/09/your-csr-strategy-needs-to-be-goal-driven-achievable-and-authentic

Yang, H., Ma, J., & Chattopadhyay, A. (2021, April 26). How Xiaomi became an Internet-of-Things powerhouse. *Harvard Business Review*. https://hbr.org/2021/04/how-xiaomi-became-an-internet-of-things-powerhouse

BUSINESS SUSTAINABILITY AND FUTURE MARKETS

2

Chapter 4

Re-assessing and Re-innovating Business Strategy

Organizations should have the eco-system that enables them to re-evaluate and re-innovate their business strategies in a formalized as well as on an adhoc basis to continuously sense pulse by relating to the external and internal environments by responding in an agile manner.

Kumaran Rajaram, PhD

4.1 Introduction

The COVID-19 pandemic reiterates clearly that organizations need to be agile by continuously re-assessing and re-innovating their business strategy to respond quickly and deal with the evolving rapid changes in the competitive landscape. This enables them to align, improve, and sustain themselves in the long run. The future entails varying unforeseen and unprecedented circumstances that are bound to occur, be it from shifts in demand to the development of revolutionary technology. Business strategies must be consistently reviewed and adjusted to integrate information from the operations process aspects and the changing external market situations (Edmondson and Verdin, 2017). They highlighted a common pattern that has emerged in many cases of strategic failure across industries,

DOI: 10.4324/9781003286288-6

ranging from small gaps in execution to the point of business failure when initial strategies were not aligned, modified based on evolving market research information and experienced insights provided. Such issues occur largely due to how top executives believed that their strategies are full-proof and wrongly shift the blame to the performance gaps during execution. In reality, a strategy should be viewed as a hypothesis rather than a concrete, rigid plan. In an uncertain and volatile world, accentuated by the pandemic-stricken world that we live in today, it is ever-imperative that business strategies have to be consistently reviewed with agility and growth mindset, validated and calibrated to suit the ever-evolving situational circumstances.

4.2 Re-assessing Business Strategy

Hence, strategy should be viewed as a dynamic activity that goes through cycles of reviewing, testing, and adjusting. All hypotheses do commence with a thorough situational assessment and analysis. As such, to re-assess a business strategy means to re-examine it honestly, while surveying the internal and external environments the organization exists in. Aside from ensuring a strategy's consistency with its environment, there are other vital criteria to take into due consideration when evaluating an organization's strategy. These elements include: (a) internal consistency (b) availability of essential resources, (c) adequate level of risk but within the safe operating zone, apt time horizon, and workability (Tilles, 1963). Upon re-assessment, the next phase would be re-transformation, re-innovation, or improvisation of the business strategy. This means to adjust, improve, and change the strategy in a way that enables the organization to not only keep afloat or survive but the space and momentum to thrive in its present climate. There are targeted ways in which an organization can do this.

4.3 Interventions to Re-assess and Re-innovate Business Strategy

Research evidence provides useful frameworks that can be used by practitioners to re-assess business strategy. For example, the most classic one is the five forces model developed by Michael E. Porter (1979). Porter's five forces model encompasses five important factors that govern competition in an industry – namely, threat of new entrants, bargaining power of customers, bargaining power of suppliers, threat of alternative/substitute products or services, and bargaining power of customers. The stronger the forces that exist within an industry, the more intense the competition in the industry would be. Thus, organizations can reap the greatest profits by weakening these forces and shifting the industry to the state of being perfectly competitive. The framework is useful for designing firms' global, general strategies, but researchers have proposed other frameworks that are geared towards the assessment of specific strategies implemented by firms. For example, Savage, Nix, Whitehead, and Blair (1991) illustrated how firms should manage their stakeholders. They developed a framework that helps firm analyze different types of stakeholders. Specifically, the framework consists of two dimensions – stakeholders' potential for (a) cooperation with organization and (b) threat to organization. Based on these two dimensions, Savage et al. (1991) identified four types of stakeholders: (a) marginal – low on both dimensions; (b) supportive – high on cooperation but low on threat; (c) nonsupportive – low on cooperation but high on threat; and (d) mixed blessing – high on both. They also advocated a strategy for each type of stakeholders. The recommended framework thus sheds light on how firms reconsider their strategies concerning stakeholders and how to allocate their resources appropriately. Gatignon, Tushman, Smith, and Anderson (2002) assessed organizational innovations on three different dimensions. The first dimension concerns the locus of innovation in a product's hierarchy. Gatignon et al. (2002) viewed products as "composed of hierarchically ordered subsystems or modules" (p. 1105) and explained that some of the innovation would serve as the core and tightly coupled with other subsystems, and others would play a more peripheral role and be less interdependent with other subsystems. In other words, some innovations make greater impacts on the entire products of the similar kinds than do others. The second dimension is types, and some innovations are considered architectural ones that would change how existing subsystems are linked with each other. The other type is called generational innovation that entails changes in the subsystems. The third dimension is characteristics, whereby innovations can be either radical or incremental and competence-enhancing or competence-destroying. Such framework can guide practitioners to evaluate what types of innovations firms are currently engaging in as well as which areas of innovations they might have to pursue in the future.

Finally, Vorhies and Morgan (2003) discuss how organizations can manage their marketing strategies. Based on a configurational approach, they emphasized the importance of fit between organizational marketing characteristics and strategic types in the success of marketing strategies. They argued that organizations need to engage in specific marketing strategies that are aligned with their business strategies. For example, firms that implement the analyzer marketing strategy, balancing "a focus on securing their position in existing core markets with incremental moves into new product markets" (p. 102), need to have high levels of specialization and teamwork to effectively implement various types of marketing strategies in a coordinated manner. When re-assessing firms' business plans and making changes to them, it is thus imperative to reflect on marketing strategies so that an entire flow of business is efficiently and effectively executed.

Trevor and Varcoe (2016) explained how executives can test their company's strategic alignment. There are two primary questions for the executives to consider. The first question is how well the business strategy supports the fulfillment of the company's purpose. In other words, the executives are encouraged to think about whether the strategy is aligned with what the company is trying to achieve. The second question is how well the company supports the achievement of the business strategy. The company is required to possess varying types of resources and capabilities to effectively execute their strategy. When the company is lacking them, the executives might have to consider either revising their strategies or coming up with other strategies to obtain the resources and capabilities to achieve their purpose and goals. It is also vital to regularly review, validate, and test the strength of company strategies (Bradley, Hirt, and Smit, 2011). Specifically, they proposed ten tests in the form of questions to identify the strategies that are effective. Specifically, the ten tests include: (a) Will your strategy beat the market?; (b) Does your strategy tap a true source of advantage; (c) Is your strategy granular about where to compete?; (d) Does your strategy put you ahead of trends?; (e) Does your strategy rest on privileged insights?; (f) Does your strategy embrace uncertainty?; (g) Does your strategy balance commitment and flexibility?; (h) Is your strategy contaminated by bias?; (i) Is there conviction to act on your strategy?; and (j) Have you translated your strategy into an action plan? Although these questions mostly seem to be common sense to executives, a McKinsey Quarterly survey revealed that many executives actually passed only three or fewer among the ten tests (Bradley et al., 2011). Executives are expected to constantly reflect on their company's strategies and develop a formal and informal system that makes them examine the appropriateness and effectiveness of their strategies.

4.4 GE-McKinsey Nine-Box Matrix

McKinsey has also provided a useful tool to assess company's business portfolio planning called the GE-McKinsey nine-box matrix (McKinsey, 2008). This tool allows the company to systematically evaluate and determine in which business unit they should invest their cash. Specifically, the matrix consists of two dimensions: (a) the attractiveness of the relevant industry and (b) the unit's competitive strength within that industry. Each dimension is assessed on three levels – low, medium, and high. Depending on the levels of two dimensions, the company can take one of three strategies: hold, harvest/sell, or invest/grow. When the level of the market attractiveness is greater than that of the competitive strength of business unit, the company is recommended to invest in the unit, as the unit has high growth potential and is expected to generate massive returns. However, when the level of the market attractiveness is lower than that of the competitive strength of business unit, the company should divest the unit because it is likely unattractive to the market. Finally, when the levels of the market attractiveness and the competitive strength of business unit match, the company can keep investing in the unit. The framework serves as a useful diagnostic tool for executives to identify which business units they should focus on based on the analyses of their industries.

4.5 Applied Case Studies: Organizations That Have Re-evaluated and Re-innovated Their Business Strategies

Let us examine a case study of an organization to illustrate this notion. The Walt Disney has re-evaluated and adapted its strategy to be future-ready. Despite Disney's massive initial success in the early 2000s with famous animated films releases such as *The Lion King* and *Aladdin*, regrettably its appeal began to dwindle. While they had some well performing releases, they had an equal share of many other less memorable ones. To revitalize the brand, Bob Iger, former CEO of the company, led the company to acquire Pixar, Marvel, Lucasfilm, and 20th Century Fox. The first three acquisitions by themselves have earned Disney more than $33.8 billion at the global box office. Overall, the company's net income increased 404% under Iger, who had rightfully recognized the urgent need for the company to diversify their assets and seek new growth opportunities. Their most recent and prominent venture, Disney+, a streaming service aiming to compete with the likes of Netflix, Hulu, and Amazon Video, is another prime example of how Disney is constantly re-assessing its strategy to sustain relevance in the current rapid evolving business environment. Disney's unmatched collection of Intellectual Property (IP), unique brand, and good content monetization abilities give it a noteworthy competitive advantage over Netflix (Trainer, 2019). We could appreciate from the above illustration of how Disney has transformed to move with the changing times that enabled it to quickly align and shifted its strategy accordingly.

Another example, Twitter has been successful in re-assessing its own business and strategies. Due to intense competitions with other companies in the same industry that offer social network services like Facebook and Snapchat, Twitter was facing challenges in increasing its revenues and experienced a net loss of $521 million in 2015. The company was also suffering from identifying the core visions of the company's business. It struggles in financial performance and lack of clarity in company's goals and purposes in terms of how the company can serve its customers. Jack Dorsey, when he re-assumed the role of CEO in 2015, decided to adopt an approach called "jobs to be done" or focusing its business on what really matters to customers whom the company is offering its services to, i.e. jobs or problems that the company needs to solve for customers (Duncan & Hindo, 2021). In order to clarify strategic visions for Twitter, Dorsey took three steps. First, the company tried to understand what customers really need Twitter for and how they use it by conducting interviews with customers and gathering data from website usage. This helped the company identify what specific jobs the company was doing for customers, which sharpened the company's strategic focus. Second, the company determined the priorities among the jobs that they identified. The company conducted workshops where company leaders evaluated the jobs and problems to determine their importance and whether Twitter can provide effective, yet differentiating solutions compared to other companies. Third, the jobs identified to be priority in the preceding stage were shared and communicated in the company. Based on the priority, the company reviewed and assessed the existing services to tailor to the customers' needs. The jobs to be done approach were shown to be very effective, as demonstrated by Twitter's growth in the number of active users and the increase in shares by 170% in past five years.

Japan Airlines (JAL) is another example. The company has decided to launch a low-cost airline in Asia where there were increasing demands of budget airlines (Rosen, 2018). JAL had not previously focused on investing in low-cost carriers, as their primary focus was on offering a full-service airline model to their customers. Especially, in Japan, low-cost carriers were not quite successful in the domestic aviation market, as Japanese travelers often chose to travel using high-speed rail network which is more efficient and affordable in many cases. However, the market for low-cost carriers overseas has been expanding, especially in the Asia-Pacific region, and the needs and demands of the customers from the international market would vary to a greater extent than the Japanese-domestic customers. Some customers might rather purchase a flight ticket at a more reasonable price even if they sacrifice the quality and quantity of services to some extent. In particular, the Asia-Pacific region has some large international markets, for example, in China and India, and offering more low-cost carriers would help JAL diversify their services and offerings, which should help them capture more various types of customers. JAL thus re-assessed their strategic focus and decided to incorporate low-cost carrier into their primary business to acquire a new customer base. This case illustrates the critical value of carefully observing and examining the needs in the current and future market and making drastic shifts in organization's strategies when necessary.

On the flip side, organizations that fail to constantly practice agility by re-assessing, re-improvising, and re-innovating their business strategies are highly in the potential trajectory to fail. Take for example the case of Woolworths that was a large-sized retail chain in the United Kingdom with over 800 stores across the country. Despite their significant presence, their final store closed in early 2009. Part of their failure had to do with their poor financial position due to the increasing cost of rental which rose from £70m to £160m within a short span of ten years. However, this was not the only contributing reason. Woolworths' outdated business model had also contributed to the company's demise (Rigby, 2008). They sold the similar products people could easily pick out at a supermarket or a value store, making it highly vulnerable to competition. While other similar businesses in the industry caught on and adjusted their strategy, Woolworths continued their low-margin business. As a result, their operating margin had dropped to a meagre 0.2% by 2007, after falling into operating losses the previous year. Further to their disconnected business model, Woolworths also failed to embrace the increasingly digital nature and changing trends of consumers (Burgess, 2013). As a whole, Woolworths shows how failing to acknowledge and acclimatize to changes in the environment can lead to failure. With today's increasingly volatile environment, organizations need to adopt strategies that can both sustain their business and equip them with the required capacity to embrace future markets. The proposed recommended strategies below are the important ones that can assist an organization to do so (Figure 4.1).

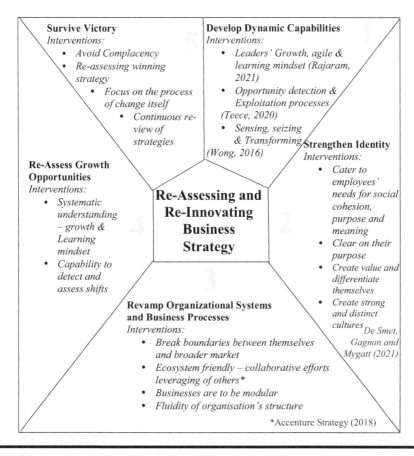

Figure 4.1 Re-assessment and Re-innovation Business Strategy Framework

4.6 Strategy 1: Develop Dynamic Capabilities

Dynamic capability refers to the organization's ability is defined as the firm's ability to integrate, build, and reconfigure internal and external competences to address rapidly changing environments (Teece, Pisano, & Shuen, 1997). Rajaram (2021) advocates the adoption of a growth, agile, and learning mindset for leaders to navigate the rapidly evolving situational context. In this process, leaders must unlearn and relearn while being responsive and quick to embrace the changes and have the business acumen to incorporate them seamlessly, even though it's challenging in the initial phases. According to Teece (2020), the dynamic capabilities framework is concerned with both the opportunity detection and exploitation processes that managers chase to create advantage. In the new global context, the dynamic capabilities framework is designed to analyze what enables firms to strategize successfully in environments signalized by high levels of uncertainty. A firm can develop its dynamic capabilities through three organizational activities (Wong, 2016). First is "sensing", which refers to the assessment of opportunities and consumer needs which exist outside of the organization in order for the organization to understand the market. The second is "seizing", which involves designing innovative business models and gaining access to capital and resources. The last activity is "transforming", which necessitates that an organization constantly streamline, improve, and modify organizational practices. From a holistic perspective, the framework reminds managers to organize internal and external resources to recognize opportunities and threats as well as to seize and neutralize them respectively. It also reminds managers to revamp the internal systems, culture, and business model to tackle the external changes.

In contrast to the view that dynamic capabilities are partly embedded in individuals in the top management (Teece, 2012), Eisenhardt and Martin (2000) stressed that dynamic capabilities can be considered as part of organizational routines. Specifically, Eisenhardt and Martin (2000) elaborated on dynamic capabilities and emphasized the importance of simple rules, as they wrote,

> Effective dynamic capabilities in high-velocity markets are simple, not complicated as they are in moderately dynamic markets. Simple routines keep managers focused on broadly important issues without locking them into specific behaviors or the use of past experiences that may be inappropriate given the actions required in a particular situation.
>
> (p. 1111)

Simplicity in routines and decision-making rules (for example, two-rule routines adopted in Yahoo!) can help firms flexibly respond to external changes while preventing any potential disruption in coordination and communication in organizations under rapidly changing environments (Eisenhardt & Sull, 2001). In other words, organizations can develop dynamic capabilities by (a) focusing on developing dynamic capabilities as part of their routines and/or (b) encouraging executives and managers of the organization to engage in the activities presented by Teece et al. (1997) and Wong (2016) – i.e., sensing, seizing, and transforming.

Let us now examine with some examples on how organizations foster their dynamic capabilities. IBM implemented several different strategies to engage in sensing and seizing, respectively (Harreld, O'Reilly, & Tushman, 2007). For sensing, the firm engaged in four different initiatives. First, IBM had its technology team meet every month to discuss the potential of emerging technologies as well as to assess the market so that firms can identify new opportunities. Also, the firm had its strategy team to meet monthly as well to make strategic decisions. Their strategy team consists of individuals from different functions including general managers, strategy executives, and other key functional leaders. Third, the firm adopted the initiatives called *Winning Plays* where a group of 300 leaders were selected by the CEO and senior leaders annually and engaged in resolving the issues that would require cross-organization interdependence. Finally, IBM conducted a *Deep Dive* which is a highly structured, intensive problem-solving process whereby a general manager would request to carry out to thoroughly analyze and discuss business problems to identify solutions with the operating unit and the strategy group. With respect to seizing, IBM implemented three strategies: emerging business opportunities (EBO), strategic leadership forums (SLFs), and corporate investment fund (CIF). These strategies are all geared towards improving strategic execution by appropriately real-locating and reconfiguring their resources to respond to market and technological changes.

Cyfert, Chwilkowska-Kubala, Szumowski, and Miśkiewicz (2020) described the process of developing dynamic capabilities, which consists of five factors. First, they recommended organizations to search for opportunities. For example, organizations can conduct an analysis about their environment to identify and create new customer needs and to anticipate competitors' strategies and actions. The second factor involves knowledge management and learning. Specifically, organizations need to acquire new knowledge, engage in knowledge transfer within the organization so that everyone in the organization who is involved in organizational change has necessary information, and encourage employees to experiment for new, breakthrough ideas to emerge. The third factor is coordination. Resource management is a critical component for organizations to develop dynamic capabilities and can be achieved through coordination among employees. Organizations need to create a vision that integrates stakeholders, articulate the values of their actions and strategies implemented to these stakeholders, build stakeholder loyalty, integrate activities in the supply chain, enhance the employee commitment by increasing their involvement in organizational activities, and integrate and coordinate business processes. Fourth, dynamic capabilities can be developed through configuration and reconfiguration. Specifically, organizations need to acquire and create resources and skills and integrate them to leverage the synergistic effects as well as eliminate redundant and unnecessary resources and skills. Finally, organizations need to be able to adapt to changes in the external environment in an agile manner. What they can do includes transforming the business models and enhancing flexibility of the organizational structure. It is critical for managers to pay close attention to these five factors that contribute to the development of organization's dynamic capabilities.

Apple is a good example that illustrates how organizations can foster dynamic capabilities (Helfat, 2013). Apple used to have a conventional structure that was not conducive to innovations (Padolny & Hansen, 2020). When Jobs came back to Apple, he decided to combine the disparate departments and business units into one functional organization. Also, there are three leadership characteristics in Apple that Padolny and Hansen (2020) highlighted. The first one is deep expertise. Apple does not have the general managers who oversee their employees; rather, in Apple, experts lead other experts, and a manager is trained to become an expert too. Apple does not have somebody who can just manage others, but managers also need to possess critical skills and knowledge in their respective fields. In other words, all leaders in Apple are expected to have deep expertise, which should foster the organization's ability to solve issues and generate novel ideas. Second, Apple focuses on immersion in the details. In Apple, there is a principle: "Leaders should know the details of their organization three levels down". Such level of attention to details can be only achieved when leaders have deep expertise in what they do. Finally, Apple values leaders' willingness to collaboratively debate with others. This promotes cross-functional collaboration among the leaders and employees who have expertise in different domains. Apple's emphasis on deep expertise, attention to details, and collaboration among employees with different expertise showcases how organizations can develop dynamic capabilities to achieve more innovations.

4.7 Strategy 2: Strengthen Identity

Organizational imperatives can enable an organization to become future-ready, and one of the aspects relates to an organization's identity (De Smet, Gagnon, & Mygatt, 2021). Companies that focus only on profits will fall behind those that create a strong identity that caters to their employees' needs for social cohesion, purpose, and meaning. Three ways in which future-ready organizations could accomplish this: (a) To be clear on their purpose, (b) To create value and differentiate themselves, and (c) Create strong and distinct cultures that help attract and retain the best people. Purpose is vital as it helps employees navigate uncertainty, encourages commitment, and exposes untapped market potential. A value agenda helps the organization more easily achieve its strategic priorities and provides them with insight on how to shift resources when priorities change. Culture is vital to create a cohesive and long-lasting organization. Hence, companies with deep rooted and strong cultures attain up to three times higher total returns to shareholders compared to those without them. Overall, an organization needs a secure identity in order to achieve longevity and success in the long run. As such, primary aspects of identity must be incorporated into an organization's strategy in a purposeful manner.

Organizational identity at the organizational level is defined as "those features of an organization that in the eyes of its members are central to the organization's character or self-image, make the organization distinctive from other similar organizations, and are viewed as having continuity over time" (Gioia, Patvardhan, Hamilton, & Corley, 2013, p. 125). DiLeonardo, Jurisic, and Schaninger (2021) presented three ways to strengthen organizational identity, which focus on (a) setting an actional purpose to find organizations' 'why'; (b) connecting the purpose to organizations' value agenda; and (c) defining behaviors for culture that enable the value agenda. Two of these propositions are linked to the ones presented by De Smet et al. (2021), but DiLeonardo et al. (2021) also emphasized the importance of behaviors. Once organizations identify key purposes and values, the specific action plans at both organizational and individual levels need to be laid out. Also, Ravasi and Schultz (2006) developed a theoretical framework about how organizational culture can be a useful resource to respond to identity threats. They argued that organizational cultures can help the processes of sense-making and sense giving about organizational identity when organizational identity is challenged by external changes. Specifically, organizational culture helps organizational members (a) clarify the purpose and objectives of organizations and (b) construct meaning and desired projected images of organizations to the public. Gioia et al. (2013) also argued that organizational identity is strengthened through the interactions with organizations' external stakeholders. Scott and Lane (2000), by developing a model of organizational identity construction (OIC), also proposed that organizational identity is developed by not only desired organizational images held by organization's top managers but also reflected stakeholder appraisals. Stakeholders play a critical role in shaping organizational identity, as they are the ones who perceive and construe organizational images presented to them by organizations. Therefore, organizations need to be mindful about how they communicate their images to stakeholders and how they can increase stakeholders' perceptions of affiliations with the organization. Also, organizations' efforts in interacting with external stakeholders constitute a critical ground for fostering organizational identification (Scott & Lane, 2000). Depending on the importance and urgency of stakeholders' claims, organizations might have to prioritize some stakeholders than others and focus on constructing specific identity that would address the stakeholders' concerns and needs. Indeed, Gioia, Price, Hamilton, and Thomas (2010) provided eight different themes concerning how organizations can forge an organizational identity, one of which focused on the importance of organizations achieving legitimacy by gaining affirmations from stakeholders. Taken together, for organizations to strengthen their identity, they should not focus on establishing and gaining consensus among internal organizational stakeholders but also need to seek approvals from external stakeholders.

Having a strong identity does help organizations to thrive in rapidly changing world. However, there should also be due consideration on the kinds of organizational identity that managers should strive to foster. There is some organizational identity that is conducive to become future-ready and capable of effectively responding to external changes in the environment. The first one is agility. Organizational agility is particularly crucial to organizations in the times of unprecedented crises. Those who fail to spot external changes that significantly impact them and to make necessary changes would not be able to continue to thrive. Organizations can become agile by implementing the system of testing, learning, and adapting and by enhancing the speed of innovations (Rigby, Elk, & Berez, 2020). Wade, Joshi, and Teracino (2021) also described six principles for organizations to develop their strategic agility, including: (a) prioritizing speed over perfection, (b) prioritizing flexibility over planning, (c) prioritizing diversification and efficient slack over optimization, (d) prioritizing empowerment over hierarchy, (e) prioritizing learning over blaming, and (f) prioritizing resource modularity and mobility over resource lock-in. In a nutshell, to foster agility, organizations need to be flexible and have diverse types of resources and skills so that they can make adaptation when necessary. Organizations need to foster the culture of learning instead of blaming employees when they make mistakes, so that employees would remain motivated and become more proactive in terms of continuous reflection and learning.

The other potential identity that contributes to the organizations is concerned with a flat organizational structure (Vaara, Harju, Leppälä, & Buffart, 2021). Flat organizational structures often involve minimal hierarchy, self-management, and empowerment, which are all critical factors for organizations to achieve speedy decision making, learning, as well as resilience. Vaara and colleagues (2021) highlighted factors that are vital in building a flat structure such as achieving transparency, using AI to enhance knowledge sharing, and encouraging agile learning. On a related note, McKinsey consultants proposed that organizations move from complex matrix structures to the helix structures (De Smet, Kleinman, & Weerda, 2019). In a helix structure, organizations disaggregate the traditional hierarchy into two lines of accountability – one focusing on supervising day-to-day work (value-creation leader) and the other on developing people and capabilities (capability leader). As such, the helix structure allows leaders to feel more empowered because those who are more suited to managing employees about skills and knowledge become free from the burden of overseeing their daily work. De Smet et al. (2019) described two main benefits of the helix structure: (a) making resource allocation more dynamic within the organization and (b) enhancing entrepreneurship and flexibility of the organizations. Both flat and helix structures should be effective particularly in a rapidly changing world where organizations need to constantly adapt to changes. Developing such identity is thus crucial to help organization's capability of revamping their business strategies constantly.

4.8 Strategy 3: Revamp Organizational Systems and Business Processes

Organizations that want to sustain their business and prepare themselves for the future market conditions need to break the boundaries between themselves and the broader market. Accenture Strategy (2018) advocated that a future-ready business will have three transformative characteristics embedded in their operational ecosystem and structure. Firstly, they are ecosystem friendly, where they value-add by contributing as well as take advantage of the network of participating companies. This enables them to productively share their knowledge with each other allowing them to accomplish much more than they would if they have worked alone. Secondly, future-ready businesses are modular, meaning that they enable diverse business models to make use of central capabilities while also allowing external organizations to access their assets. This allows them to speed up the development and implementation of new business ideas. Lastly, an organization's structure should be fluid. They should be able to source, identify, and manage their workforces effectively by being able to access the most suitable talent at the appropriate time. Altogether, a future-ready company must embrace a growth (learning and growing) and promotion (reaching goals) mindset by being willing to open up their organizational structure and work on strategic partnerships and collaborative efforts. How can organizations develop a network and ecosystem that conduce to their business success and survival under rapidly changing environments? With regard to this point, research evidence provides important caveats. Bakker (2016) highlighted the importance of strategic alliance partner reconfiguration, which refers to "structural changes in the set of firms that is jointly involved in an alliance over time" (p. 1920). He found that partner reconfiguration would entail the risk of unplanned project termination because it could cause disruption in alliance coordination. Such risk is especially salient when organizations reconfigure their alliance by exiting from current partnerships than entering new ones. Interestingly, Bakker did not find the evidence showing that alliance reconfiguration served as a means of adaptation – demonstrating the potential risk of disruption entailed in alliance reconfiguration when it is done inadvertently. Firms thus need to be especially mindful of keeping alliance partners that provide critical resources to them. Similarly, Van den Oever and Martin (2019) have demonstrated how organizational politics ("the use of influence to pursue goals other than those agreed among all partners", p. 583) and procedural rationality (collecting and analyzing information extensively during decision-making processes) would influence value creation and value appropriation from partnerships. Specifically, they reported that firms can generate higher total value from partnerships by using procedural rationality, but value appropriation from partnerships occurs when firms engage in organizational politics. Also, organizations with different decision-making procedures would likely get less appropriation values from their partners. These findings highlight the importance for managers to pay close attention to the decision-making strategies and internal processes adopted by other firms that they are in partnerships.

It is also crucial for organizations to design and develop internal systems and processes that enable effective knowledge sharing among employees but what can organizations do? Concerning these points, Al-Alawi, Al-Marzooqi, and Mohammed (2007) demonstrated that trust, communication, information systems, rewards, and organizational structures (for example, participative decision making, ease of information flow) were conducive to knowledge sharing. However, despite the evidence suggesting the value of internal practice supporting knowledge sharing, organizations seem to have not been up to speed on this (Volini et al., 2020). To facilitate knowledge sharing, Schaninger and Lauricella (2020) emphasized the importance of assessing organizational culture and identify the reasons why employees are not engaging in knowledge sharing behaviors at an optimal level. For example, managers can conduct one-on-one interviews to engage and ask employees about the relevant circumstances or situations. They could also check in to know whether employees prefer to keep or share the knowledge, particularly their motivation to do so. Once employees' attitudes and mindsets about knowledge sharing become explicit, organizations can design and implement apt interventions that are specifically geared towards addressing the constraints of knowledge sharing behaviors amongst employees. For instance, managers can take some time at the beginning of group meetings for employees to share new best practices, incorporate knowledge sharing into formal performance review process and reward employees who engage in the behavior, and integrate knowledge sharing as part of onboarding practices, and so on. By promoting knowledge sharing, organizations will be able to better leverage employees' unique insights and develop a shared mental model among employees.

4.9 Strategy 4: Re-assess Growth Opportunities

When re-evaluating an organization's strategy, a vital area to look at is on its new growth opportunities. Changes in the global environment can significantly impact this aspect. The COVID-19 pandemic has disrupted global consumption and forced people to ditch old habits and pick up new ones (Jacobides and Reeves, 2020). Organizations that wish to emerge stronger from the crisis must develop an agile (ability to respond and adapt) and growth (learning and growing) mindsets with a systematic understanding of rapidly changing habits. This applies to any other major disruptions or changes as well. By having the capability to detect and assess shifts, organizations will be able to identify opportunities to shape markets in a speedily and effective manner. One of the vital factors that enable firms to identify and leverage new business opportunities is absorptive capacity, defined as "an ability to recognize the value of new information, assimilate it, and apply it to commercial ends" (Cohen & Levinthal, 1990, p. 128). The firms with absorptive capacity are likely to adopt organizational processes and practices that facilitate external knowledge acquisition and intrafirm knowledge dissemination, leading to effective adaptation and responses to dynamic environments (Liao, Welsch, & Stoica, 2003). Even when organizations are exposed to the influence of rapidly changing environments, consumers' needs are required to modify their business strategies, those with absorptive capacity should be able to identify growth opportunities and leverage them to their own advantages. Firms can develop absorptive capacity through varying methods. For example, managerial efforts in providing information across organizations are imperative in facilitating the development of absorptive capacity; however, the value of the information provision within firms can be reduced with increasing levels of information from previous adopters of the information and past events that potential adopters experienced (Lenox & King, 2004). To make accurate evaluations of growth opportunities and effectively take advantage of them, organizations need to emphasize that managers focus on actively communicating novel information and opportunities. Furthermore, firms can develop their absorptive capacity through their R&D investments (Cohen & Levinthal, 1990). This is because absorptive capacity is path-dependent and cumulative, suggesting that firms that fail to develop relevant prior knowledge might not be able to take advantage of available opportunities in a given environment. Research and Development (R&D) investments thus enable the development of new knowledge as well as the capability of appropriating technological opportunities.

Digital competency is crucial in identifying and seizing available growth opportunities. In particular, COVID-19 pandemic changed how the business is conducted in retail industries, and e-commerce became a primary channel for customers to purchase products and services. Indeed, according to the EY Future Consumer Index, about 80% of United States (US) customers were changing their shopping styles (Gramling, Orschell, & Chernoff, 2021). Without having digital and technological competency, firms cannot stay resilient against such a large-scale shift in business operation but likely fail to leverage it to their own advantages. Briedis, Kronschnabl, Rodriguez, and Ungerman (2020) described several key ideas that help improve firms' agility and responsiveness to meet new customer experiences. For example, they emphasized the importance of injecting innovation into omnichannel. Retailers are encouraged to review their distribution channels available for customers and implement innovations through such means as bringing an in-store feel to the digital experience and diversifying delivery mechanisms. Organizations' efforts in adopting and utilizing new technology are crucial in fostering their absorptive capacity as well, given that those lacking necessary digital capacity are not able to identify opportunities in the first place. It is thus crucial for firms to continue to invest in organizational processes and structures to develop their technological competence so that they can keep up to date in any changes taking place in external environments.

4.10 Strategy 5: Survive Victory

While the initial successes should be celebrated, it is vital that it does not lead to complacency. A winning strategy should still be consistently re-assessed and revamped as the business environment is constantly changing. Without doing so, a winning strategy can easily turn into a losing one and may even be one of the contributing causes for the downfall of the organization. The highly risky part of any transformation effort is when the initial goals have been met (Satell, 2019). Hence, leaders must focus not only on immediate goals but also on the process of change itself which enables them to address key aspects required for sustainability. Overall, organizations should not stop by being easily satisfied but continue building on their strategies to navigate unprecedented and rapid changing situational contexts. How can organizational leaders stay motivated in seizing new opportunities, adopting growth and learning mindsets after initial successes? Typically, as outlined by behavioral theory of the firm, organizations become more risk-seeking as their performance becomes further away their aspiration levels (for example, Baum, Rowley, Shipilov, & Chuang, 2005; Park, 2007). In other words, firms' decision makers tend to become complacent and risk-averse once they meet their performance objectives. Firms that perform above their aspiration levels tend to conduct less search and exploration, limiting their opportunities for future innovations. These studies suggest that business leaders need to maintain their aspiration at the high level to stay vigilant for potential new opportunities, even when their performance feedback indicates that their companies perform satisfactorily. Relatedly, some researchers suggest the value of leaders' humility in restricting such leaders' complacency and building organizational competitive advantages. In the firms led by humble CEOs, top management teams are more likely to collaborate and share their visions, and to adopt an ambidextrous strategic orientation (Ou, Waldman, & Peterson, 2015). Vera and Rodriguez-Lopez (2004) also argue that a humble leader has characteristics such as being open to new possibilities and accepting success with simplicity, which leads to more active organizational learning, service, and resilience. These characteristics possessed by humble leaders conduces to several beneficial organizational outcomes such as innovation, productivity, low employee turnover, and continuous adaptation and renewal. Thus, CEO humility is a factor that would enable firms to achieve further success even after meeting their initial performance goals and objectives.

Given the importance of humble leadership, a natural question to ask next is how organizations can foster this leadership trait. Organizations can develop humbleness in leaders by explicitly embedding this element in hiring and recruiting practices as well as performance reviews, as in the remark from the CEO of eBay, "We hire people who aren't focused on me, me, me" (Vera & Rodriguez-Lopez, 2004, p. 406). Also, Morris, Brotheridge, and Urbanski (2005) proposed several potential individual-level enablers of humility in leaders, which include narcissism, machiavellianism (i.e., "the degree to which an individual is pragmatic, keeps emotional distance, and believes that ends can justify means", p.1335), self-esteem, and emotional intelligence. Aside from incorporating the considerations in these personality characteristics and individual attributes, organizations can design and administer leadership training initiatives that would foster the characteristics conducing to humility. For example, organizations can design training programs and performance reviews revolving around several important characteristics of humble leadership such as embracing a spirit of service and having the mindset of knowing what one does not know about (Dame & Gedmin, 2013). Integrating leadership humility into formal training programs and onboarding processes would develop firms' capability of re-evaluating and further revamping the strategies that have already yielded successes.

References

Accenture Strategy. (2018, May 18). How to become a future-ready business. *Harvard Business Review*.

Al-Alawi, A., Al-Marzooqi, N., & Mohammed, Y. (2007). Organizational culture and knowledge sharing: Critical success factors. *Journal of Knowledge Management, 11*, 22–42. https://doi.org/10.1108/13673270710738898

Bakker, R. M. (2016). Stepping in and stepping out: Strategic alliance partner reconfiguration and the unplanned termination of complex projects. *Strategic Management Journal, 37*(9), 1919–1941. https://doi.org/10.1002/smj.2429

Baum, J. A. C., Rowley, T. J., Shipilov, A. V., & Chuang, Y.-T. (2005). Dancing with strangers: Aspiration performance and the search for underwriting syndicate partners. *Administrative Science Quarterly*, *50*(4), 536–575. http://www.jstor.org/stable/30037221

Bradley, C., Hirt, M., & Smit, S. (2011, January 1). Have you tested your strategy lately? *McKinsey Quarterly*. https://www.mckinsey.com/business-functions/strategy-and-corporate-finance/our-insights/have-you-tested-your-strategy-lately

Briedis, H., Kronschnabl, A., Rodriguez, A., & Ungerman, K. (2020, May 14). Adapting to the next normal in retail: The customer experience imperative. *McKinsey & Company*. https://www.mckinsey.com/industries/retail/our-insights/adapting-to-the-next-normal-in-retail-the-customer-experience-imperative

Burgess, M. (2013, January 17). *Woolworths warned high street chains to adapt to digital four years ago*. HuffPost UK.

Cohen, W. M., & Levinthal, D. A. (1990). Absorptive capacity: A new perspective on learning and innovation. *Administrative Science Quarterly*, *35*(1), 128–152. https://doi.org/10.2307/2393553

Cyfert, S., Chwilkowska-Kubala, A., Szumowski, W., & Miśkiewicz, R. (2020). The process of developing dynamic capabilities: The conceptualization attempt and the results of empirical studies. *PLoS ONE*, *16*(4), e0249724. https://doi.org/10.1371/journal.pone.0249724

Dame, J., & Gedmin, J. (2013, September 9). Six principles for developing humility as a leader. *Harvard Business Review*. https://hbr.org/2013/09/six-principles-for-developing

De Smet, A., Gagnon, C., & Mygatt, E. (2021, February 18). Organizing for the future: Nine keys to becoming a future-ready company. *McKinsey & Company*.

De Smet, A., Kleinman, S., & Weerda, K. (2019, October 3). The helix organization. *McKinsey Quarterly*. https://www.mckinsey.com/business-functions/people-and-organizational-performance/our-insights/the-helix-organization

DiLeonardo, A., Jurisic, N., & Schaninger, B. (2021, February). Build your organizational identity. *McKinsey & Company*.

Duncan, D. S., & Hindo, B. (2021, October). How Twitter applied the "Jobs to Be Done" approach to strategy. *Harvard Business Review*.

Edmondson, A. C., & Verdin, P. J. (2017, November 9). Your strategy should be a hypothesis you constantly adjust. *Harvard Business Review*.

Eisenhardt, K. M., & Martin, J. A. (2000). Dynamic capabilities: What are they? *Strategic Management Journal*, *21*(10–11), 1105–1121.

Eisenhardt, K. M., & Sull, D. (2001, January). Strategy as simple rules. *Harvard Business Review*.

Gatignon, H., Tushman, M. L., Smith, W., & Anderson, P. (2002). A structural approach to assessing innovation: Construct development of innovation locus, type, and characteristics. *Management Science*, *48*(9), 1103–1122

Gioia, D. A., Patvardhan, S. D., Hamilton, A. L., & Corley, K. G. (2013). Organizational identity formation and change. *Academy of Management Annals*, *7*(1), 123–193.

Gioia, D. A., Price, K. N., Hamilton, A. L., & Thomas, J. B. (2010). Forging an identity: An insider-outsider study of processes involved in the formation of organizational identity. *Administrative Science Quarterly*, *55*(1), 1–46.

Gramling, K., Orschell, J., & Chernoff, J. (2021, May 11). How e-commerce fits into retail's post-pandemic future. *Harvard Business Review*. https://hbr.org/2021/05/how-e-commerce-fits-into-retails-post-pandemic-future

Harreld, J. B., O'Reilly III, C. A., & Tushman, M. L. (2007). Dynamic capabilities at IBM: Driving strategy into action. *California Management Review*, *49*(4), 21–43.

Helfat, C. (2013, July 2). How Apples and IBM learn to change with the times. *U.S. News.* https://www.usnews.com/opinion/blogs/economic-intelligence/2013/07/02/apple-and-ibm-show-the-power-of-dynamic-capabilities

Jacobides, M. G., & Reeves, M. (2020). Adapt your business to the new reality. *Harvard Business Review.* https://hbr.org/2020/09/adapt-your-business-to-the-new-reality

Lenox, M., & King, A. (2004). Prospects for developing absorptive capacity through internal information provision. *Strategic Management Journal, 25*(4), 331–345.

Liao, J., Welsch, H., & Stoica, M. (2003). Organizational absorptive capacity and responsiveness: An empirical investigation of growth–oriented SMEs. *Entrepreneurship Theory and Practice, 28*(1), 63–86. https://doi.org/10.1111/1540-8520.00032

McKinsey Quarterly. (2008, September 1). *Enduring ideas: The GE-McKinsey nine-box matrix.* https://www.mckinsey.com/business-functions/strategy-and-corporate-finance/our-insights/enduring-ideas-the-ge-and-mckinsey-nine-box-matrix

Morris, J. A., Brotheridge, C. M., & Urbanski, J. C. (2005). Bringing humility to leadership: Antecedents and consequences of leader humility. *Human Relations, 58*(10), 1323–1350.

Ou, A. Y., Waldman, D. A., & Peterson, S. J. (2015). Do humble CEOs matter? An examination of CEO humility and firm outcomes. *Journal of Management, 44*(3), 1147–1173. https://doi.org/10.1177/0149206315604187

Padolny, J. M., & Hansen, M. T. (2020). How Apple is organized for innovation. *Harvard Business Review.* https://hbr.org/2020/11/how-apple-is-organized-for-innovation

Park, K. (2007). Antecedents of convergence and divergence in strategic positioning: The effects of performance and aspiration on the direction of strategic change. *Organization Science, 18*, 386–402. https://doi.org/10.1287/orsc.1060.0240

Porter, M. E. (1979). How competitive forces shape strategy. *Harvard Business Review* (March).

Ravasi, D., & Schultz, M. (2006). Responding to organizational identity threats: Exploring the role of organizational culture. *Academy of Management Journal, 49*(3), 433–458.

Rajaram, K. (2021). *Evidence-Based Teaching for the 21st Century Classroom and Beyond, Innovation-Driven Learning Strategies.* Springer.

Rigby, D., Elk, S., & Berez, S. (2020). The Agile C-Suite – A new approach to leadership for the team at the top, *Harvard Business Review.*

Rigby, E. (2008). Seeds of Woolworths' demise sown long ago. *Financial Times* (November 29).

Rosen, E. (2018, May 14). Japan Airlines to start new international budget airlines. *Forbes.* https://www.forbes.com/sites/ericrosen/2018/05/14/japan-airlines-to-start-new-international-budget-airline/?sh=4e896b0c573a

Satell, G. (2019, August 27). 4 tips for managing organizational change. *Harvard Business Review.* https://hbr.org/2019/08/4-tips-for-managing-organizational-change

Savage, G. T., Nix, T. W., Whitehead, C. J., & Blair, J. D. (1991). Strategies for assessing and managing organizational stakeholders. *Academy of Management Perspectives, 5*(2), 61–75.

Schaninger, B., & Lauricella, T. (2020, April 14). The questions you ask drive the action you see. *McKinsey & Company.* https://www.mckinsey.com/business-functions/people-and-organizational-performance/our-insights/the-organization-blog/the-questions-you-ask-drive-the-action-you-see

Scott, S. G., & Lane, V. R. (2000). A stakeholder approach to organizational identity. *Academy of Management Review, 25*(1), 43–62.

Teece, D. J. (2012). Dynamic capabilities: Routines versus entrepreneurial action. *Journal of Management Studies, 49*(8), 1395–1401.

Teece, D. J. (2020). Fundamental issues in strategy: Time to reassess? *Strategic Management Review, 1*(1), 103–144. https://doi.org/10.1561/111.00000005

Teece, D. J., Pisano, G., & Shuen, A. (1997). Dynamic capabilities and strategic management. *Strategic Management Journal, 18*(7), 509–533.

Tilles, S. (1963, July). How to evaluate corporate strategy. *Harvard Business Review.* https://hbr.org/1963/07/how-to-evaluate-corporate-strategy

Trainer, D. (2019, December 11). Disney's strategy is working. *Forbes.* https://www.forbes.com/sites/greatspeculations/2019/12/11/disneys-strategy-is-working/?sh=740394cd56b0

Trevor, J., & Varcoe, B. (2016, May 16). A simple way to test your company's strategic alignment. *Harvard Business Review.* https://hbr.org/2016/05/a-simple-way-to-test-your-companys-strategic-alignment

Van den Oever, K., & Martin, X. (2019). Fishing in troubled waters? Strategic decision-making and value creation and appropriation from partnerships between public organizations. *Strategic Management Journal, 40*(4), 580–603. https://doi.org/10.1002/smj.2975

Vaara, E., Harju, A., Leppälä, M., & Buffart, M. (2021, June 7). How to successfully scale a flat organization. *Harvard Business Review.* https://hbr.org/2021/06/how-to-successfully-scale-a-flat-organization

Vera, D., & Rodriguez-Lopez, A. (2004). Strategic virtues: Humility as a source of competitive advantage. *Organizational Dynamics, 33*(4), 393–408.

Volini, E., Schwartz, J., Mallon, D., Van Durme, Y., Hauptmann, M., Yan, R., & Poynton, S. (2020, May 15). Knowledge management: Creating context for a connected world. *Deloitte Insights.* https://www2.deloitte.com/us/en/insights/focus/human-capital-trends/2020/knowledge-management-strategy.html

Vorhies, D. W., & Morgan, N. A. (2003). A configuration theory assessment of marketing organization fit with business strategy and its relationship with marketing performance. *Journal of Marketing, 67*(1), 100–115.

Wade, M., Joshi, A., & Teracino, E. A. (2021, September 2). 6 principles to build your company's strategic agility. *Harvard Business Review.* https://hbr.org/2021/09/6-principles-to-build-your-companys-strategic-agility

Wong, A. (2016, August 22). The key to keeping up: Dynamic capabilities. *California Management Review.*

Chapter 5

Corporate Governance and Ethics

> The character of a leader and the deeply rooted culture of an organisation is well reflected on the moral values that are upheld in the most challenging situations.

Kumaran Rajaram, PhD

PART 1 CORPORATE GOVERNANCE AND ETHICS

5.1 Introduction

In the digital era, organizations face various issues concerning the data including privacy, accountability, surveillance, and transparency (Etter, Fieseler, & Whelan, 2019). It is hence critical for organizational leaders and members to adopt the mindset concerning how to ethically conduct business in the digital era. As such, Lobschat and colleagues (2021) proposed a novel construct called corporate digital responsibility (CDR), which is defined as "the set of shared values and norms guiding an organization's operations with respect to the creation and operation of digital technology and data" (p. 876). They argued that CDR would apply to various domains of the management of organizations, including marketing management, consumer behavior and psychology, human–computer interactions, computer ethics, and so

DOI: 10.4324/9781003286288-7

on. They developed a conceptual framework of CDR in which they described how its culture can be fostered by both social and organizational contexts. Moreover, CDR culture has key implications in organizations, individual actors, and society at large, and engagement in CDR practices is expected to generate long-term benefits.

5.2 Digitalization: Corporate Governance

The rapid digitalization also highlights the potential of new technologies that enables more effective corporate governance. Sama, Stefanidis, and Casselman (2021) argued that given the significant shift in the business environments due to digitalization and complexity of new technologies, traditional corporate governance mechanisms might not be effective or become obsolete in the future. Organizations are required to adopt governance mechanisms by incorporating digital consideration. For example, Hilb (2020) discussed how adoption of artificial intelligence (AI) in the practice of corporate governance can contribute to and promote effective decision making and judgment. Organizations can use AI in many different ways, while they do not necessarily automate the decision-making processes but rather combine human intelligence and machine intelligence to achieve the most optimal outcomes (for example, using AI as an assisting tool to better comprehend market and operational data and to inform organization's strategic decision making; using AI to navigate coaching programs in human resources and make compensation decisions). At the same time, Hilb pointed out several ethical considerations entailed in AI-based corporate governance such as, bias in and by AI, monopolization of intelligence, the moral basis of the decisions made by AI, and potential constrains on individuals' and company's free will or autonomous decision making. However, if appropriately utilized, AI will serve as a powerful tool to improve corporate governance practice.

5.3 Application: Case Studies with Insights on Corporate Governance and Ethics

Let us relate and appreciate the imperativeness of corporate governance and ethics with the examples as per illustrated. Starbucks is known for their good ethical standards. In 2018, the 12th consecutive year, Starbucks was named one of the World's Most Ethical Companies by the Ethisphere Institute. This was a milestone and no easy feat, given that only 135 companies in the entire globe were acknowledged. Part of their successful ecosystem with effective ethical strategies can be attributed to former CEO and Chairman, Howard Schultz, who aimed to prove the power of a business model that balances profit with social responsibility (Schwartz, 2011). Starbucks puts in both money and effort towards ethical efforts such as addressing local needs in the communities it serves, fostering sustainable farming communities and ethically sourcing coffee, and packaging and transporting its products while considering the environmental impact. Starbucks proves by its actions to show how being ethical does not necessarily mean compromising on profits. While Starbucks resembles an organization that is strongly and positively connected to ethics, Facebook does otherwise. In 2018, it was revealed that the political data firm Cambridge Analytica had harvested the public profile data of up to 87 million of its users (Frenkel, Rosenberg, & Confessore, 2018). Upon this revelation, Facebook's public relations engaged in a self-defeating argument on what constituted a data breach. It took them five days before founder and CEO Mark Zuckerberg made a public statement, with promises to reform the company's policies on privacy (Wong, 2019). We could conclude from this evidence-based case that the priority on Facebook's actions did portray the users' best interests at heart. Walsh (2019) reported that in this case, Facebook's product is the consumer's data that was sold to the advertisers. Facebook has also been accused of other data scandals, for example with the most recent one being a leak of more than 500 million users' phone numbers and personal information. These incidents show how Facebook administrating a poor ethical code of conduct can potentially create such repercussions that have caused to spiral out of control. Facebook's lack of care and concern towards its users were further amplified when responses (or lack thereof) from representatives came across as disconnected, empathetic, and uncaring. These illustrations reiterate and emphasize the importance of creating a strong ethical culture and practicing moral ethos in corporate governance. Organizations must give due considerations on the varying types of ethical issues such as gender and racial equality, environmental sustainability, privacy and data protection, and more. In the face of an ethical scandal, companies must develop thorough processes and mechanisms that will allow them to effectively deal with the required and ensure the situation is not made even worse.

Another example that highlights the importance of corporate social responsibility and ethical issues is the Volkswagen's scandal that was found in September 2015 (Groysberg, Lin, Serafeim, & Abrahams, 2016). The Environmental Protection Agency (EPA) found that a device in diesel engines – called a "defeat device" – that could improve results for testing of emission was installed in many of their vehicles sold in the United States (Hotten, 2015). Volkswagen intentionally set such controls on its diesel engines, and it misrepresented the emission levels, which affected over 10,000 cars. Because of this scandal, the company lost its reputation and brand image entirely. Volkswagen's stock price immediately plunged. Furthermore, this scandal led to the investigations from governments in North America, Europe, and Asia. The then CEO had to step down, and other executives were also suspended. This example of Volkswagen shows that when companies failed to address their ethical issues, not only will organizations likely suffer from the consequences but also the career of the executives of these companies will be put in jeopardy. Groysberg et al. (2016) reported that executives who previously worked in scandal-tainted organizations, even if they had nothing to do with scandals, would be paid nearly 45 less than their peers. Compliance to ethical standards is thus critical not just for protecting organizations' reputation and their current employees but also the future career of the members working for them.

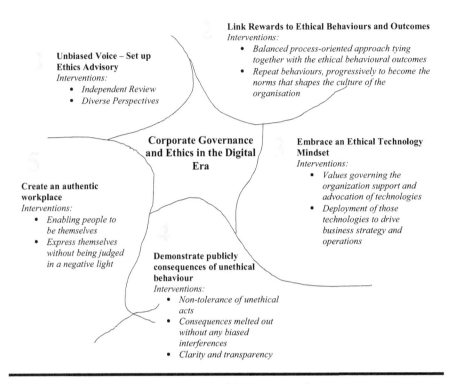

Figure 5.1 Corporate Governance and Ethics Framework

We advocate five vital tested and proven strategies organizations can adopt to effectively deal with the potential ethical issues (from the corporate governance and ethics dimension) that they might get entangled with. This framework is presented in Figure 5.1.

5.4 Strategy 1: Unbiased Voice – Set Up Ethics Advisory Board

Establishing an Ethics Advisory Board (EAB) enables an organization to gain perspectives from diverse, external stakeholders when making ethical decisions, with regard to anything from a new product launch to a pandemic response plan. Liautaud (2021) highlighted eight strategies that can help an organization successfully set up an EAB, which help them avoid pitfalls and construct a strong ethical foundation for their business operations. Firstly, there must be a unified mission for the EAB. Creating silos will only result in disconnected groups that focus on specific problems. Broad and common ethical issues must be duly considered through a unified ethical mission where an EAB would be required to thoroughly investigate them.

The second strategy is to ensure that the EAB comprises of a small group of independent experts, avoiding anyone directly related to the company. If the EAB members are required to pay for the services, its finances must be handled judiciously, to avoid conflict of interest or biased opinions. Thirdly, the EAB's scope of responsibility and authority must be clearly defined, where its role is purely advisory and have no authority in decision making. Fourthly, EAB meeting agendas should be specific and targeted. A vague agenda or generic questions can divert people's attention from its true aspects of the ethical issues at hand. Next, another strategy is for the EAB to duly consider the perspectives of various stakeholders that includes customers, employees, shareholders, and others. They must carefully examine everyone's perspectives collectively and ensure that no one group is being negatively affected by the actions of the organization. Next, ethics reports provided by the EAB should provide nuanced advice rather than prescriptive directives. However, it is ultimately the responsibility of the organization who is accountable to implement the EAB's advice. Organizations must provide honest inputs when engaging with the EAB. Perhaps, the recommended approach is not to direct the conversation towards the desired conclusion instead ask open-ended questions to engage and collate genuine perspectives on the situation. Finally, the time to consult EAB should be made speedily without procrastination, especially when making key decisions. This act assists organizations to identify any potential issues before it is too late. In a nutshell, setting up an EAB can be of tremendous help and value-add to an organization. It provides them with unbiased and new perspectives that could seriously help address the "gaps" on their ethical standards, processes which will affect their reputation.

In terms of promoting unbiased voice, organization should pay attention to board diversity. Board diversity is critical in enhancing effectiveness of monitoring and governance. For example, designing gender-diverse boards improves the boards' ability to monitor financial reporting quality (Dobija, Hryckiewicz, Zaman, & Pulawska, 2021). Having female board members enables more varied perspectives and experiences compared to less gender-diverse boards, and the number of women in boards is positively related to strategic and corporate social responsibility controls. Furthermore, Dobjia et al. reported that the financial reporting quality improves when women are chairing the board. Other studies also demonstrated the value of having female board members in facilitating organizations' compliance with codes of ethics (García-Sánchez, Rodríguez-Domínguez, & Frías-Aceituno, 2015; Rodríguez-Domínguez, Gallego-Alvarez, & García-Sánchez, 2009). Having female board members also reduce the likelihood of fraud (Cumming, Leung, & Rui, 2015). Beji, Yousfi, Loukli, and Omri (2021) reported how different types of board diversity contribute to different dimensions of corporate social responsibility (CSR) performance. Gender diversity is positively associated with human rights and corporate governance dimensions, while age diversity is conducive to better CSR performance on corporate governance, human resources, human rights, and environmental activities. Furthermore, they reported that having foreign directors contribute to environmental performance and community involvement. Also, board size and CEO duality would play a key role in promoting unbiased voice. Research shows that there was a positive relation between board size and corporate social responsibility (CSR) disclosure while CEO duality is negative associated with CSR disclosure (Alabdullah, Ahmed, & Muneerali, 2019). Beji et al. (2021) also found that organizations with larger board size would have better CSR performance. Another approach is to enhance morality and to motivate ethical behaviors of board members. For example, the study done by Lee, Choi, Youn, and Chun (2017) showed how ethical leadership can translate into greater moral voice from employees through increased moral efficacy. This study suggests that the chairperson of the boards and/or CEO can adopt ethical leadership so that board members might be more attentive to ethical issues and engage in more voice behaviors to improve corporate governance.

5.5 Strategy 2: Link Rewards to Ethical Behaviors and Outcomes

Not everyone may be intrinsically motivated to act ethically. This is why we often see executives acting out of greed and unethically when financial incentives are overly linked to solely on outcome performance, instead with a more balanced process-oriented approach with other varying interventions. Hence, organizations are recommended to duly consider linking rewards to ethical outcomes instead, for example, Southwest Airlines, a company that adopted executive scorecard that ties compensation to its core values where each of it is exhibited by an objective measurement (Epley & Kumar, 2019). The scorecard displays how their ethical values line up with business success, reminds employees to pay attention to them explicitly, and suggests to employees the actions they should take to acquire them. Other ways to reward employees for specific ethical actions include giving public recognition in presentations and/or publications. This motivates the employees to repeat such behaviors that help to progressively be ingrained as norms that influences the culture within the organization. Organizations must also create opportunities for employees to act ethically towards one another. For instance, advocate and encourage employees to pay it forward by repaying good deeds. Acts of kindness can be contagious and create a positive ethical culture within the organization itself. Extrinsic rewards influence employees to shape their behaviors and actions to be ethically bounded.

Hannah, Avolio, and May (2011) developed a comprehensive framework that illuminates what leads to one's moral decisions and actions. Moral cognition processes are determined by moral complexity, meta-cognitive ability, and moral identity, which they called moral maturation capacities as a whole. Moral conation processes are based on moral identity, moral ownership, moral efficacy, and moral courage, and the latter three constitute what they called moral conation capacities. Furthermore, they argued that moral maturation capacities and moral conation capacities are both shaped by one's experiences, reflection, and feedback of moral actions. Their proposal points out several important factors that can help organizations facilitate employees' compliance with the code of ethics. For instance, Fudge and Schlacter (1999) emphasized that the development of employees' knowledge and skills are critical in fostering their moral actions, which resonates the moral conation capacities in the Hannah et al.'s (2011) model. Thus, to be driven to act ethically, the aspects of competence and capability of acting ethically should not be overlooked. Furthermore, DeCelles, DeRue, Margolis, and Ceranic (2012) argued that the link between moral motivation can be attenuated when people possess power given that self-interested behaviors would be more likely to be facilitated in the presence of power. Indeed, they found that power and moral identity interacted to influence self-interested behavior through moral awareness, showing that organizations should be especially careful about those in the positions of power. Though not explicated in detail in the earlier model by Hannah et al. (2011), contextual factors such as climate, leadership, and HRM practices also play an important role in shaping one's moral actions. A line of research on ethical leadership, ethical climate, and corporate ethical values within organizations generally support their direct, positive impacts on employees' ethical behaviors (Mayer, Kuenzi, & Greenbaum, 2010; Baker, Hunt, & Andrews, 2006; Bedi, Alpaslan, & Green, 2016; Manroop, Singh, & Ezzedeen, 2014). However, incentives for prompting ethical behaviors should not be implemented haphazardly. Some research suggests unintentional countervailing influence of incentives for ethical behaviors (also see the recent review done by Park, Park, & Barry, 2021). For example, Baucus and Beck-Dudley (2005) argued that mere reliance on rewards and punishments might encourage people to do the right thing just for the sake of avoiding punishments. Other researchers also pointed out that the psychological effects of monetary incentives might vary depending on the contexts (Gneezy, Meier, & Rey-Biel, 2011; Wang & Murnighan, 2017). As such, though carefully designed incentive programs for ethical conducts may be effective, organizations should simultaneously invest in helping their employees deepen the understanding of why and how they need to conduct business more ethically.

5.6 Strategy 3: Embrace an Ethical Technology Mindset

Embracing the "ethical technology" mindset is a strategy to deal with ethics in a digital era. Ethical technology as defined by Bannister, Sniderman, and Buckley (2020) is a set of values governing the organization's approach in its support and advocacy of technologies and ways in which employees at all levels deploy those technologies to drive business strategy and operations. It comprises various aspects such as data privacy, replacing humans with machines, and bias in algorithms. The ethical tech mindset refers to the cultural and social characteristics that both leaders and employees can adopt to support their efforts in working towards ethical decision making. The seven characteristics that are illustrative of the ethical technology mindset are (a) drive towards a shared, inclusive cross-functional responsibility;

(b) be ethically driven from the start; (c) make ethical tech part of a holistic, tech-savvy approach; (d) make the framework relevant, specific and flexible; (e) make sure it goes beyond compliance; (f) equip employees with the resources to respond, and (g) ensure the approach can evolve (Bannister et al., 2020). While organizations continue to espouse new and contemporary technologies, they must duly consider and thoroughly evaluate the ethical associations. Hence, organizations can better anticipate and respond to ethical issues that occur by equipping with an ethical, technologically agile, and inclined mindset.

In addition to organizational efforts of promoting among employees such global mindsets concerning new technology and digitalization, it would be also essential to comprehend the types of recommendations researchers have made thus far with respect to more specific technologies that have recently evolved in business settings. For example, adopting artificial intelligence (AI) and machine learning in corporate decision-making processes has recently gained prominence in both research and practice. In terms of ethical considerations, it is critical to consider that the use of AI could suppress our own autonomy in operating business (Hilb, 2020; Nabbosa & Kaar, 2020). For example, some of the hiring and selection procedures have been replaced by AI-adopted technology but human autonomy needs to be maintained, as "people should not be treated as mere data subjects, but as individuals" (Hagendorff, 2020, p. 110). Similarly, job automation technologies can increase efficiency and productivity at the expense of some employees, who work in the domain of manufacturing and service sectors, being deprived of current and future job opportunities. Organizations thus need to consider various ethical consequences and corporate responsibility in terms of technological unemployment which refers to the job loss stemming from automation in the workplace (Kim & Scheller-Wolf, 2019; Martin, Shilton, & Smith, 2019). Adnan, Nordin, bin Bahruddin, and Ali (2018) discussed the implications of autonomous vehicles that would replace human drivers with AI-based machines to some extent if not completely. Rather than focusing on unemployment issues that could ensue due to automation, they focused on illustrating a number of specific safety and legal issues raised by such type of job automation, including: What if there is a critical situation to be handled that would cause an accident if the driver were in charge, but the system does not react as well as the driver would have, which resulted in more severe consequences? What if the driver activated the system when it is not appropriate? It is thus crucial to consider the extent of liability and due diligence of the driver when adopting autonomous vehicle innovations. Also, Pollard, Karimi, and Ficcaglia (2017) explored some ethical concerns in incorporating technology in healthcare services (i.e., telehealth service delivery model). Telehealth service is cost-effective and especially efficient in providing necessary care and service to those living in rural areas. Pollard and colleagues (2017) listed several ethical challenges such as development of a clinical infrastructure support system (for example, ensuring high quality service, monitoring of implementation of service being delivered) and client protection (for example, informed consent, privacy and confidentiality, data). The last example pertains to counseling. Harris and Birnbaum (2014) argued several ethical and legal challenges present in the adoption of technology in counseling. While online counseling promotes accessibility and asynchronous communication between counselors and clients, it could also cause such issues as absence of non-verbal behavioral cues, misunderstandings and misinterpretation, and online security. Overall, each business model would evidently face unique ethical challenges and concerns with respect to digitalization and adoption of new technologies. Organizations need to be thorough and comprehensive about potential issues that might be caused when incorporating technologies into their businesses and need to develop relevant ethical guidelines for employees to strictly follow.

5.7 Strategy 4: Demonstrate Publicly Consequences of Unethical Behavior

While rewarding ethical behavior is effective, punishing unethical behavior must also be viewed from that positive dimension. Organizations must emphasize and show their stakeholders that unethical behaviors and acts are not tolerated. Firstly, allegations of ethical violations must be meticulously investigated (Chesnut, 2020) to emphasize only factual and accurate allegations are confronted with. When claims are proven to be accurate and fair, reasonable consequences must be carried out without any biased interferences. Leaders and top performers must also be subjected to the same treatment should they act unethically, which shows clarity and transparency in the process. The ecosystem must earn the employees trust and confidence to avoid doubts that potentially make less people reporting violations. Transparency can be achieved with the release of reports that signify the total number of reports generated, types of violations recorded, number of investigations carried out, substantiated, and the types of consequences.

Pfarrer, DeCelles, Smith, and Taylor (2008) developed a model that navigates how organizations can restore the legitimacy after they engage in corporate unethical actions. Their model involves four sequential stages – discovery, explanation, penance, and rehabilitation. The discovery stage concerns public's awareness that organizations committed transgressions. The model proposes that when organizations engage in more actions to discover the facts about transgressions (for example, actively disclosing unethical acts), they can restore their reputation and legitimacy more quickly and more likely. At the explanation phase, organizations that provide more adequate and sincere explanations by acknowledging their wrongdoing and accepting responsibility are expected to regain trust from their stakeholders. The third stage is penance which concerns both official and unofficial punishment towards organizations. At this stage, organizations' willingness to accept punishment as well as the level of punishment would determine how quickly organizations can move to the next stage (i.e., rehabilitation). For example, when stakeholders perceive official punishments not severe enough, they might potentially seek to levy their own unofficial punishments on organizations accused of wrongdoing. Finally, at the rehabilitation stage, organizations need to demonstrate what internal and external changes they have made so as not to repeat the same transgressions. While a macro-level unethical behaviors needs to be immediately corrected and punished to maintain the organizations' integrity and legitimacy, within the context of organizations, research has also emphasized that it is critical for organizations to uphold ethical standards and adopt corrective actions when employees engage in unethical behaviors to reduce future unethical behavior (Kaptein, 2011). One of the early studies done by Hegarty and Sims (1978) that investigated some antecedents of unethical behaviors demonstrated that environmental rewards and punishments would play a vital role in promoting and hindering unethical behaviors. When organizations fail to punish or even reward unethical behaviors, employees would continue to engage in them. In addition, Trevino and Ball (1992) reported that such failures in denouncing unethical behaviors would also affect others' cognition and behaviors. In their experiment, they found that responses to unethical behaviors influenced observers' justice evaluations and emotional reactions, such that the harshest punishment towards unethical behaviors led to the most positive justice evaluations and emotions. Implementation of effective corporate ethics program (i.e., punishment, monitoring, and internal reporting) should reduce employees' unethical acts by increasing their threat appraisal (Jannat, Alam, Ho, Omar, & Lin, 2021). Thus, punishment of unethical behaviors has important social consequences within organizations and forgoing appropriate corrective actions towards unethical deeds would likely beget another unethical behavior from the same employees who engaged in the behavior and/or others.

5.8 Strategy 5: Create an Authentic Workplace

Design and structure a working environment that values authenticity. Research reports that enabling people to be themselves at work gives them a heightened sense of authenticity and empowerment that eventually makes them to behave and act more ethically (Kouchaki, 2019). The efforts taken to align the company values with that of employees' helps prevent ethical lapses. People largely desire to feel trustworthy at work and do not want professional responsibilities to force them to compromise on their personal beliefs and/or values. Moreover, they also want to express themselves without being judged in a negative light while not missing out on opportunities in advancing their careers. A reliable work climate and environment can certainly lessen the risks of unethical behavior and acts.

The role played by leaders is critical with regard to promoting ethical behaviors among employees. Liu, Fuller, Hester, Bennett, and Dickerson (2018) reported that authentic leadership, defined as "a process that draws from both positive psychological capacities and a highly developed organizational context, which results in both greater self-awareness and self-regulated positive behaviors on the part of leaders and associated, fostering positive self-development" (Luthans & Avolio, 2003, p. 243), would lead to subordinates' proactive behaviors while reducing their workplace deviance. They developed a serial mediation model that links authentic leadership and such employees' behaviors, and specifically, authentic leadership increases proactive behavior and reduces workplace deviance through increasing (a) supervisory identification, (b) psychological safety, and then (c) job engagement. Authenticity in leaders also influences subordinates' moral identity and actions and creates a more ethical climate within work teams (Zhu, Avolio, Riggio, & Sosik, 2011). Research done by Cianci, Hannah, Roberts, and Tsakumis (2014) also suggests that employees may be less likely to engage in unethical decision making even in the presence of temptation or incentive to do so, when they are exposed to authentic leadership. However, if leaders fail to act authentically but engage in unethical behaviors themselves, employees experienced reduced moral courage and identification with organizational values (Hannah, Avolio, & Walumbwa, 2011; Hannah et al., 2013). It is thus critical to design a workplace and organization in the way that employees are always guided by authentic leaders. Also, Steckler and Clark (2019) argued potential importance of authenticity in corporate governance. Specifically, they discussed how authenticity would play out within corporate governance at the individual and board levels. For example, they emphasized that it is critical for individual board members to be clear about personal moral values, transparent and confident in moral convictions, capable of recognizing, evaluating ethical issues, and taking appropriate actions to uphold ethical standards and harmonize individual values and objectives with responsibilities and interests of firm. With regard to the board-level interaction, four key points are advocated: namely, board members need to express and advocate for moral beliefs during decision-making processes, to be committed to encouraging other board members to also uphold ethical standards and behaviors, to appreciate multiple perspectives, and deeply contemplate and reflect on any decisions made through board member interactions (Steckler and Clark, 2019). Finally, in order to increase authenticity in corporate governance, it is critical to (a) select the directors with "true to self" criteria (for example, possessing strong moral values and principles), (b) consistently engage in cultivation of moral values and train and educate board members about how they can express personal values and become more aware of ethical versus unethical conducts, and (c) foster enactment of important ethical values by constantly engaging in discussion and reflection among board members. It is thus critical for practitioners to recognize authenticity as a personal quality that should be considered when it comes to running an effective board in the organization.

References

Adnan, N., Md Nordin, S., bin Bahruddin, M. A., & Ali, M. (2018). How trust can drive forward the user acceptance to the technology? In-vehicle technology for autonomous vehicle. *Transportation Research Part A: Policy and Practice, 118,* 819–836.

Alabdullah, T. T. Y., Ahmed, E. R., & Muneerali, M. (2019). Effect of board size and duality on corporate social responsibility: What has improved in corporate governance in Asia? *Journal of Accounting Science*, *3*(2), 121–135.

Baker, T. L., Hunt, T. G., & Andrews, M. C. (2006). Promoting ethical behavior and organizational citizenship behaviors: The influence of corporate ethical values. *Journal of Business Research*, *59*(7), 849–857.

Bannister, C., Sniderman, B., & Buckley, N. (2020, January). *Ethical tech: Making ethics a priority in today's digital organization*. Deloitte.

Baucus, M. S., & Beck-Dudley, C. L. (2005). Designing ethical organizations: Avoiding the long-term negative effects of rewards and punishments. *Journal of Business Ethics*, *56*(4), 355–370. https://doi.org/10.1007/s10551-004-1033-8

Bedi, A., Alpaslan, C. M., & Green, S. (2016). A meta-analytic review of ethical leadership outcomes and moderators. *Journal of Business Ethics*, *139*(3), 517–536. https://doi.org/10.1007/s10551-015-2625-1

Beji, R., Yousfi, O., Loukil, N., & Omri, A. (2021). Board diversity and corporate social responsibility: Empirical evidence from France. *Journal of Business Ethics*, *173*(1), 133–155. https://doi.org/10.1007/s10551-020-04522-4

Chesnut, R. (2020, July 30). How to build a company that (actually) values integrity. *Harvard Business Review*.

Cianci, A. M., Hannah, S. T., Roberts, R. P., & Tsakumis, G. T. (2014). The effects of authentic leadership on followers' ethical decision-making in the face of temptation: An experimental study. *The Leadership Quarterly*, *25*(3), 581–594.

Cumming, D., Leung, T. Y., & Rui, O. (2015). Gender diversity and securities fraud. *Academy of Management Journal*, *58*(5), 1572–1593. https://doi.org/10.5465/amj.2013.0750

DeCelles, K. A., DeRue, D. S., Margolis, J. D., & Ceranic, T. L. (2012). Does power corrupt or enable? When and why power facilitates self-interested behavior. *Journal of Applied Psychology*, *97*(3), 681–689. https://doi.org/10.1037/a0026811

Dobija, D., Hryckiewicz, A., Zaman, M., & Puławska, K. (2021). Critical mass and voice: Board gender diversity and financial reporting quality. *European Management Journal*. https://doi.org/10.1016/j.emj.2021.02.005

Epley, N., & Kumar, A. (2019). How to design an ethical organization. *Harvard Business Review*.

Etter, M., Fieseler, C., & Whelan, G. (2019). Sharing economy, sharing responsibility? Corporate social responsibility in the digital age. *Journal of Business Ethics*, *159*(4), 935–942. https://doi.org/10.1007/s10551-019-04212-w

Frenkel, S., Rosenberg, M., & Confessore, N. (2018, April 10). Facebook data collected by quiz app included private messages. *The New York Times*.

Fudge, R. S., & Schlacter, J. L. (1999). Motivating employees to act ethically: An expectancy theory approach. *Journal of Business Ethics*, *18*(3), 295–304. https://doi.org/10.1023/A:1005801022353

García-Sánchez, I.-M., Rodríguez-Domínguez, L., & Frías-Aceituno, J.-V. (2015). Board of directors and ethics codes in different corporate governance systems. *Journal of Business Ethics*, *131*(3), 681–698. https://doi.org/10.1007/s10551-014-2300-y

Gneezy, U., Meier, S., & Rey-Biel, P. (2011). When and why incentives (don't) work to modify behavior. *Journal of Economic Perspectives*, *25*(4), 191–210. https://doi.org/10.1257/jep.25.4.191

Groysberg, B., Lin, E., Serafeim, G., & Abrahams, R. (2016, September). The scandal effect. *Harvard Business Review*.

Hagendorff, T. (2020). The ethics of AI ethics: An evaluation of guidelines. *Minds and Machines*, *30*(1), 99–120. https://doi.org/10.1007/s11023-020-09517-8

Hannah, S. T., Avolio, B. J., & May, D. R. (2011). Moral maturation and moral conation: A capacity approach to explaining moral thought and action. *Academy of Management Review, 36*(4), 663–685. https://doi.org/10.5465/amr.2010.0128

Hannah, S. T., Avoli, B. J., & Walumbwa, F. O. (2011). Relationships between authentic leadership, moral courage, and ethical and pro-social behaviors. *Business Ethics Quarterly, 21*(4), 555–578. https://doi.org/10.5840/beq201121436

Hannah, S., Schaubroeck, J., Peng, A., Lord, R., Trevino, L., Kozlowski, S., ... Doty, J. (2013). Joint influences of individual and work unit abusive supervision on ethical intentions and behaviors: A moderated mediation model. *The Journal of applied Psychology, 98.* https://doi.org/10.1037/a0032809

Harris, B., & Birnbaum, R. (2014). Ethical and legal implications on the use of technology in counselling. *Clinical Social Work Journal, 43.* https://doi.org/10.1007/s10615-014-0515-0

Hegarty, W. H., & Sims, H. P. (1978). Some determinants of unethical decision behavior: An experiment. *Journal of Applied Psychology, 63*(4), 451.

Hilb, M. (2020). Toward artificial governance? The role of artificial intelligence in shaping the future of corporate governance. *Journal of Management and Governance, 24*(4), 851–870. https://doi.org/10.1007/s10997-020-09519-9

Hotten, R. (2015, December 10). *Volkswagen: The scandal explained.* BBC News.

Jannat, T., Alam, S. S., Ho, Y.-H., Omar, N. A., & Lin, C.-Y. (2021). Can corporate ethics programs reduce unethical behavior? Threat appraisal or coping appraisal. *Journal of Business Ethics.* https://doi.org/10.1007/s10551-020-04726-8

Kaptein, M. (2011). Understanding unethical behavior by unraveling ethical culture. *Human Relations, 64*(6), 843–869.

Kim, T. W., & Scheller-Wolf, A. (2019). Technological unemployment, meaning in life, purpose of business, and the future of stakeholders. *Journal of Business Ethics, 160*(2), 319–337. https://doi.org/10.1007/s10551-019-04205-9

Kouchaki, M. (2019, June 19). Why authentic workplaces are more ethical. *Harvard Business Review.*

Lee, D., Choi, Y., Youn, S., & Chun, J. U. (2017). Ethical leadership and employee moral voice: The mediating role of moral efficacy and the moderating role of leader–follower value congruence. *Journal of Business Ethics, 141*(1), 47–57. https://doi.org/10.1007/s10551-015-2689-y

Liautaud, S. (2021, January 21). How to set up an ethics advisory board. *Harvard Business Review.*

Liu, Y., Fuller, B., Hester, K., Bennett, R. J., & Dickerson, M. S. (2018). Linking authentic leadership to subordinate behaviors. *Leadership & Organization Development Journal, 39*(2), 218–233.

Lobschat, L., Mueller, B., Eggers, F., Brandimarte, L., Diefenbach, S., Kroschke, M., & Wirtz, J. (2021). Corporate digital responsibility. *Journal of Business Research, 122,* 875–888.

Luthans, F., & Avolio, B. J. (2003). Authentic leadership development. In Cameron, K. S., Dutton, J. E., and Quinn, R. E. (Eds.), *Positive organizational scholarship* (pp. 241–258). Berrett-Koehler.

Manroop, L., Singh, P., & Ezzedeen, S. (2014). Human resource systems and ethical climates: A resource-based perspective. *Human Resource Management, 53*(5), 795–816. https://doi.org/10.1002/hrm.21593

Martin, K., Shilton, K., & Smith, J. (2019). Business and the ethical implications of technology: Introduction to the symposium. *Journal of Business Ethics, 160*(2), 307–317.

Mayer, D. M., Kuenzi, M., & Greenbaum, R. L. (2010). Examining the link between ethical leadership and employee misconduct: The mediating role of ethical climate. *Journal of Business Ethics*, *95*(1), 7–16.

Nabbosa, V., & Kaar, C. (2020). *Societal and ethical issues of digitalization*. Paper presented at the proceedings of the 2020 international conference on Big Data in Management, Manchester, United Kingdom.

Pfarrer, M. D., Decelles, K. A., Smith, K. G., & Taylor, M. S. (2008). After the fall: Reintegrating the corrupt organization. *Academy of Management Review*, *33*(3), 730–749.

Pollard, J. S., Karimi, K. A., & Ficcaglia, M. B. (2017). Ethical considerations in the design and implementation of a telehealth service delivery model. *Behavior Analysis: Research and Practice*, *17*(4), 298–311.

Rodríguez-Domínguez, L., Gallego-Alvarez, I., & García-Sánchez, I. M. (2009). Corporate governance and codes of ethics. *Journal of Business Ethics*, *90*(2), 187–202. https://doi.org/10.1007/s10551-009-0035-y

Sama, L. M., Stefanidis, A., & Casselman, R. M. (2021). *Rethinking governance for the digital era: The role of stewardship*. Business Horizons.

Schwartz, T. (2011, April 4). Why I appreciate Starbucks. *Harvard Business Review*.

Steckler, E., & Clark, C. (2019). Authenticity and corporate governance. *Journal of Business Ethics*, *155*, 951–963.

Trevino, L. K., & Ball, G. A. (1992). The social implications of punishing unethical behavior: Observers' cognitive and affective reactions. *Journal of Management*, *18*(4), 751–768.

Walsh, M. (2019, November 7). Does your AI have users' best interests at heart? *Harvard Business Review*.

Wang, L., & Murnighan, J. K. (2017). How much does honesty cost? Small bonuses can motivate ethical behavior. *Management Science*, *63*(9), 2903–2914. https://doi.org/10.1287/mnsc.2016.2480

Wong, J. C. (2019, March 18). The Cambridge Analytica scandal changed the world – but it didn't change Facebook. *The Guardian*.

Zhu, W., Avolio, B. J., Riggio, R. E., & Sosik, J. J. (2011). The effect of authentic transformational leadership on follower and group ethics. *The Leadership Quarterly*, *22*(5), 801–817.

PART 2 ETHICAL LEADERSHIP IN AN UNPRECEDENTED AND EVOLVING WORLD

5.9 Ethical Leadership: Is There Magic and Unspoken Nuances to Be Moral?

The internet of things has made it much easier for ethical scandals to be more publicized than ever. Social media, in particular, has transformed the business and communication landscape (Kaul et al., 2015). A single tweet from an angry consumer or a lengthy exposé written by a critic can go 'viral' and spread like wildfire, tainting the image of the brand. Leaders today play a key role in managing their company's reputation. They are often what personifies their company to stakeholders and their personality will influence where the organization is headed (Davies & Chun, 2009). In actuality, research does suggest that leaders should, and do, influence organizational ethics (Treviño & Brown, 2005). Hence, it is no surprise that organizational leadership is under constant scrutiny. Any backlash from ethical scandals can seriously damage the company's reputation and leaders' credibility. A recent example of ethical scandal would be Tesla's $1.5 billion bitcoin purchase as the mining of the cryptocurrency causes greenhouse gas emissions that impact the world's climate. This action of Tesla is viewed as hypocritical given that its mission is to speed up the world's transition to sustainable energy (Calma, 2021). This purchase decision implicates Telsa's CEO Elon Musk who was already been implicated and accused of other ethical scandals in the past. This induces us to advocate on the significance of ethical leadership, explicitly to re-examine the nuances that limit leaders' ability to recognize and address the unethical practices.

Ethical leadership is defined as the appropriate conduct through personal actions and interpersonal relationships, and the promotion of such conduct to followers through two-way communication, reinforcement, and decision-making (Brown & Treviño, 2006). As summarized by Brown and Mitchell (2010), the first formal investigations that concentrated on defining ethical leadership from a descriptive point of view and were carried out by Treviño and colleagues. Their studies suggest that ethical leaders can be best described along two related dimensions: moral person and moral manager. The dimension of the 'moral person' refers to the qualities of the ethical leader as a person, while the 'moral manager' dimension refers to how a leader uses leadership tools to promote ethical behavior at work. For a person to be seen as an ethical leader by their employees, they must be both a strong moral person and moral manager. This is because leader who is only a strong moral manager may be perceived as a hypocrite by colleagues. On the other hand, an individual who is only a strong moral person may be seen as an ethically 'neutral' leader.

Leaders serve as a vital source of ethical guidance for employees and are in many ways responsible for their moral development. This is supported by a study conducted by Moore et al. (2018), who found that leader behavior corresponds to how employees construe decisions with ethical import. They also found that ethical leadership has a direct causal impact on employee moral disengagement. Ethical leadership is vital as it influences both its corporate climate and organizational culture. Research shows that ethical leadership is positively related to (a) considered behavioral aspects, interactional fairness, honesty, and traits of transformational leadership (b) affective trust in the leader while negatively related to abusive supervision (Brown, Treviño, & Harrison, 2005). Ethical leadership improves followers' moral actions by generating their moral emotions (Zhang, Zhou, & Mao, 2018). Employees are less likely to engage in unethical behaviors when a leader models ethical behavior and uses appropriate rewards, punishments to ensure that their subordinates are acting ethically (Mayer, Aquino, Greenbaum, & Kuenzi, 2012). It also has strong links to follower outcomes such as employee job satisfaction, organizational commitment, willingness to report problems to supervisor, willingness to put in additional effort at work, voice behavior, and perceptions of organizational culture and ethical climate (Brown & Mitchell, 2010).

Unethical leadership, on the other hand, which is defined as "a process of intentional or unintentional, passive or active, and recurrent influencing that harms others, being it individuals, organization and/or society as a whole" (Lašáková & Remišová, 2015). This results in employees experiencing decreased trust in the leader, less commitment to the organization, and an increased likelihood to leave the organization altogether. It also damages relationships, negatively impacts employee performance, and decreases organizational effectiveness (Fehr, Fulmer, & Keng-Highberger, 2019). Other consequences of unethical leadership include employee anxieties, feelings of helplessness, and work alienation. Altogether, unethical leadership harms both individual employees and organizations. The framework on effects of unethical leadership is presented in Figure 5.2, leveraging from the advocates made by Lašáková and Remišová (2015) and Fehr et al. (2019) as well as improvised add-ons to make it a holistic practice-oriented guide.

5.10 Why Do Leaders Engage in Unethical Practices?

Despite organizations adopting and adhering to the relevant ethical standards, many leaders still fall into the trap of acting unethically. Unethical behaviors include committing fraud, stealing from the company, mistreating employees, and other similar actions (Fehr et al., 2019). Unethical actions may be purposeful or accidental, though in either case, the repercussions can be massive. Take for instance the case of Enron, a U.S. energy company that collapsed after it was uncovered that its executives carried out one of the biggest accounting frauds in history. According to Johnson (2003), the company's bankruptcy was ultimately caused by the ethical shortcomings of its executives. This included abuse of power, excess privilege, deceit, inconsistent treatment of internal and external constituencies, misplaced and broken loyalties, and irresponsible behavior. In total, 21 people were convicted in the scandal. There are

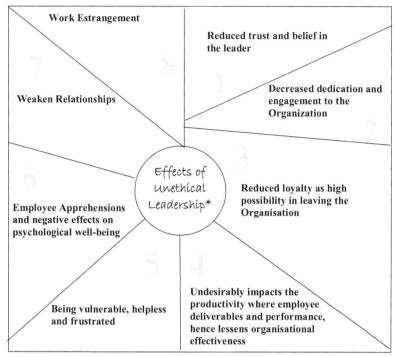

Unethical Leadership can be defined as the *means of deliberate or inadvertent, adhoc, inactive or active, and persistent interventions that serve as influences that have negative impact on organizations and/or employees (individuals) and/or society as a whole.*

Figure 5.2 Framework on Effects of Unethical Leadership

many possible reasons as to why leaders might act unethically, where broadly, these include shareholder pressure for growth, senior leadership trying to achieve their goals, imminent financial losses, greed, ignorance, and more (Hegarty & Moccia, 2018). At the most basic level, the focus and emphasis placed on tangible organizational outcomes. Unfortunately, there is often a disparity between corporate profitability and social responsibility. Leaders may frequently find themselves considering a trade-off between profit and ethics. For instance, a company may find that inappropriately disposing waste could significantly cut down company costs. At the same time, leaders at the organization know that doing so could have a devastating impact on the environment (Minkes, Small, & Chatterjee, 1999). Hence, when considering outcomes, a leader might make a decision that skews more in favor toward measurable outcomes, especially if it influences the firm's finances. The authors also describe the issue of corporate competition which also affects ethical leadership. Leaders often influence the degree to which an organization is prepared to act ethically or unethically given increased competition.

The social expectations placed on these leaders are a major contributor to their ethical failures (Hoyt, Prince, & Poatsy, 2013). Research points out that the expectations of goal achievement led leaders to over-value group goals making them more confident in the moral permissibility of the means used to achieve these goals. It also implies that the pressure leaders feel can significantly blur their lines of morality and cause them to either purposely or inadvertently act in an unethical manner to meet the expectations bestowed on them. Furthermore, research also reports that leaders who perceived their goals to be "worthier" than others were more likely to feel justified in using unethical means to achieve them. The constant pressure leaders face can limit the willpower needed to act according to ethical norms and standards, leading to unethical behavior (Joosten, van Dijke, van Hiel, & De Cremer, 2013). Besides exemplifying ethical behavior, leaders are held responsible for ethically bounded decisions to be made and dealing with tasks on moral grounds despite them being potentially overwhelmed. When leaders are required to make multiple decisions and take on varying functions in demanding environments, they are less likely to maintain the mental energy or cognitive resources needed to deal with other processes such as ethical decision-making. This lack of mental energy can result in negative consequences such as racial and gender discrimination, theft, and more. A study conducted by Robertson and Rymon (2001) exemplified this. When examining the behaviors of purchasing agents toward sellers, the authors found that perceived pressure to perform along with ethical ambiguity is correlated to the agents' unethical behavior.

Another possible reason for unethical practices could boil down to the leader's personality. Research study by Boddy (2016) reported that ethical scandals and failures have been characterized by the presence of CEOs who scored highly on a measure of corporate psychopathy. Psychopaths are people who lack a conscience and are unable to feel guilt, love, concern, or empathize with others. This inability is linked to neurobiological factors associated with irregular brain connectivity or chemistry. Corporate psychopaths are often more motivated in climbing to the top of the ladder, capable of conning others, and are often able to talk themselves out of trouble. Examples of potential corporate psychopaths include individuals such as Robert Maxwell and Bernard Madoff. In these cases, unethical practices are seemingly unavoidable because the leaders are innately prone to unethical behaviors. Narcissism is another potential trait that may cause a leader to act unethically. Research evidence indicates that positive correlation between narcissism and behaviors are linked to unethical leadership such as one-way communication, control of power, insensitivity to others, and more (Blair, Helland, & Walton, 2017). Narcissism in leaders may also manifest itself as an excessive pre-occupation with the self. This sense of individualism can make it more difficult for leaders to engage in ethical practices as they become more obsessed with their own image as a leader rather than with their ethical responsibility to others (Knights & O'Leary, 2005).

The behavior of followers can also influence leaders to engage in unethical practices. When followers perform organizational citizenship behaviors, leaders are more likely to give themselves leeway to act unethically (Ahmad, Klotz, & Bolino, 2020). Narcissistic leaders or leaders who identify with their followers are more likely to give themselves moral credit because of their followers' good deeds. It is not merely just the leader-follower relationship, rather it is a two-way street when it comes to one influencing the other in regard to ethical behavior. Unethical followers can create unethical leaders; hence, this does not mean that followers should act unethically for leaders to act ethically. Instead, both leader and follower should be encouraged to display ethical behavior in the workplace. For instance, a study by Mostafa, Farley, and Zaharie (2020) found that while ethical leadership does benefit employee attitudes by reducing disengagement, this relationship was moderated by co-worker social undermining. Co-worker social undermining, according to the authors, is "a form of workplace mistreatment that reduces a person's ability to create and maintain good relationships, success, and a positive reputation at work". Essentially, the authors discovered that the effectiveness of ethical leadership can be diminished when social rules are broken by a source other than the supervisor. Similarly, Moore et al. (2018) found evidence that the centrality of an employee's moral identity plays a significant role in the relationship between ethical leadership and employee unethical decisions and behavior. While leadership is crucial, other factors beyond the character of the leader can be a key factor in determining the overall ethical, or lack thereof, behavior of an organization.

A more materialistic inclined reason could be attributed to the potential financial incentives which are made available to leaders should they act in an unethical manner. Organizations' leaders might be tempted by greed and act in a way which aims to benefit themselves over the organization. For example, financial misreporting might occur when there are financial incentive schemes in place to reward unethical behavior (Chen, 2010). Misreporting financial performance is influenced by the CEO's personal assessment of the potential benefits versus the potential penalties. They may be even more incentivized should they own stock options in the organization or if their bonus is linked to the performance of the company. In actuality, the degree to which a leader is materialistic may also be influenced by his or her personality. A study by Hong, Koh, and Paunonen (2012) found that low scores on Agreeableness in the Big Five model of personality were the most prolific predictor of both materialism and unethical behavior.

It is imperative to emphasize that unethical behaviors are unacceptable as they can harm an organization's stakeholders and seriously compromise its reputation. For instance, employees can be negatively impacted by unethical leadership which causes them feelings of anxiety, helplessness, and frustration (Lašáková & Remišová, 2015). Hence, it is vital that organizations not only implement ethical standards and rules but also ensure that they are followed and exemplified by leaders.

5.11 Ubiquitous Ethical Oversight

While ethical leaders can inspire followers to behave ethically as well, being in a position of leadership poses unique challenges to one's ability to act ethically. As we saw, social expectations and constant pressure to achieve group goals (e.g., company KPIs) can compete with ethical motivations. Furthermore, studies suggest that as an individual rises through the ranks in an organization, they become less likely to dissent from the actions of the organization, regardless of whether those actions are ethical or not (Kennedy & Anderson 2017). Lower-ranking individuals, by contrast, are more likely to dissent against unethical group practices. The reason is evidently that holding higher rank tends to increase one's identification or "sense of oneness" with the organization. This makes it difficult for high-ranking leaders to think critically about an organization's activities and perceive the organization as behaving unethically. Thus, the rank associated with leadership positions can leave leaders ethically compromised. A similar phenomenon is observed in employees as well in the form of moral disengagement. As stated by Fehr et al. (2019), not all employees react adversely to unethical leadership behaviors. In fact, employee reactions often vary greatly. The authors argue that moral disengagement propensity (MDP), which is "an individual difference that captures the tendency of an individual to morally disengage", is what enables employees to maintain their trust and support for a leader even after they have seen them act unethically. The term 'moral disengagement' refers to "an interrelated set of cognitive justification mechanisms that allow individuals to act unethically while circumventing the self-sanctions that normally inhibit such behaviour" (p. 74). When employees convince themselves that ethical standards do not apply to them in the work environment, they are subduing their ability to feel guilty about partaking in unethical behavior. Overall, the authors found that employees with high MDPs engage in cognitive processes which allow them to respond less negatively to the unethical behaviors of their leaders.

On the other hand, additional studies revealed that when individuals who strongly identify with a group *do* perceive the group's activities as ethically problematic, they are more likely to dissent (Packer, 2009). This suggests that if leaders could preserve a keen ethical sensibility, in spite of their high rank, they could be particularly effective champions of ethical standards. After all, research has shown that working for an ethical leader is linked to lower turnover intentions and higher levels of job satisfaction and organizational commitment (Mostafa et al., 2020). Additionally, a leader's level of moral reasoning has been found to influence the moral reasoning used by group members in their decision-making. Altogether, leaders should remain a key source of ethical guidance given the authority and power they have over their employees (Treviño & Brown, 2005).

How then might leaders uphold their sense of right and wrong while also maintaining a healthy critical distance from the organizational status quo? One strategy is to invite lower-ranking employees to voice criticisms of the organization's practices. Due to being less identified with the organization, lower ranking may have invaluable insight into the ethical status of the organizational norms. Another strategy is to let lower-level employees sit on ethics review boards and provide assessments of upper-management decisions. Ethics review boards may even be granted the power to intervene in organizational decisions, much like unions and boards of trustees do. The mission of ethics review boards would strictly be to give voice to the interests of all stakeholders affected by the organization's activities. As indicated by Lam, Loi,

Chan, and Liu (2016), ethical leaders have high moral standards and will clearly relay to employees their standards and expectations of appropriate and inappropriate workplace conduct. Hence, these leaders are more likely to be open to and encourage employees' voice as a way to improve workplace conditions. Their study also found that ethical leaders can influence employees through the motivational state of cognitive engagement. This explains why, under ethical leadership, it is more probable for employees to express their opinions and less likely to exit the company.

For either of these strategies to be effective, the organization's culture should support dissent from lower-ranking employees. Employees ought to be invited by leaders to speak up when they believe something going on in their firm is not right. People need assurance that they won't be penalized or ostracized for expressing critical views about decisions taken by superiors. Channels for whistleblowing should be established, and the anonymity of whistle-blowers must be guaranteed. Only with such measures, among others, will rank-and-file employees feel that it is safe to vocalize a critical and potentially unpopular opinion. It is also important to note that leader-follower congruence acts as a boundary condition for the effect of ethical leadership on moral efficacy. Essentially, ethical leadership becomes more salient and effective when employees hold on to values that are consistent with that of their leader's. Therefore, organizations must also pay attention to the value congruence between leaders and followers. To do so, a leader may wish to frequently do a check on the extent to which his or her followers understand and accept their values or ideals (Lee, Choi, Youn, & Chun, 2017).

Moreover, ethics review boards should be established at the appropriate levels, given the structure of the organization. If the organization has a "flat" structure, with relatively few ranked levels of authority and relatively many departments at the same level, ethics review boards would wield greater influence with more "horizontal" placements in different units at the same level. If the organization has a "tall" structure, with relatively more ranked levels of authority but few departments at any one level, ethics review boards could be formed at each level in the hierarchy. Making ethical oversight ubiquitous in this fashion will not only ensure accountability throughout the organization, it will also empower employees of all ranks to address ethical challenges that are in close proximity to their normal work domains and expertise. Even at the highest level of oversight, however, it is important to include the voices of lower-level members, since their lower rank may render them less susceptible to biases stemming from over-identification with the organization's goals. On a similar note, leaders can also choose to establish an Ethics Advisory Board (EAB). This is a newer concept that organizations may wish to pursue that can provide them with vital perspectives from diverse, external stakeholders on ethical decisions relating to any organizational activity such as a new product launch or a pandemic response plan. An EAB differs from an ethics review board in the sense that an EAB should not include any company stakeholders such as employees, shareholders, customers, advisors, close family members, or anyone who falls in a similar category. Instead, the EAB should be made up of a small, diverse group of independent experts such as academic ethicists, policymakers, lawyers, technologists, or any other relevant expert. While internal representatives may be present during EAB meetings, they should not have any voting privileges (Liautaud, 2021). Doing this ensures that ethical decisions made are not only informed but also free from bias.

Leaders may also choose to approach ethics on a more personal level. As stated by Knights (2016), the fundamental of developing ethical leaders is to increase values to a higher level of consciousness and to raise awareness of how their behavior impacts their own performance and that of their employees. Essentially, a leader must be able to introspect and understand where their values lie and how they can incorporate them into building an ethical organization. Additionally, at the individual scale, a leader may also choose to grow their moral identity. A study by Mayer et al. (2012, p. 164) found that moral identity can "act as a source of motivation for leaders to behave in a manner consistent with a self-schema organized around a set of traits (e.g., honest, caring, compassionate, hard-working) associated with a moral prototype". Leaders who score highly on measures of moral identity are also expected to display behaviors that are congruent to their moral identity, including exhibiting ethical leadership. This is because doing otherwise would lead to a sense of discomfort and self-condemnation. The authors also suggest that the tendency for people to express their moral identity outside of work may also predict whether they do so within the organization. Hence, it is important that leaders ensure that they remain committed to their own moral goals.

5.12 Concluding Thoughts

While ethical leaders are necessary to keeping organizations from crossing ethical lines, we have made the case that lower-ranking individuals can provide a unique and important source of ethical oversight as well. Indeed, we caution against the assumption that being an ethical leader requires having high rank. More than anything, ethical leadership calls for thinking independently, being an advocate, and inspiring others to do and best their best. From this perspective, even an entry-level worker can take up the mantle of ethical leader, provided that there are institutional mechanisms that enable them to do so.

References

Ahmad, M. G., Klotz, A. C., & Bolino, M. C. (2020). Can good followers create unethical leaders? How follower citizenship leads to leader moral licensing and unethical behavior. *Journal of Applied Psychology*, 1–17. https://doi.org/10.1037/apl0000839

Blair, C. A., Helland, K., & Walton, B. (2017). Leaders behaving badly: the relationship between narcissism and unethical leadership. *Leadership & Organization Development Journal*, *38*(2), 333–346. https://doi.org/10.1108/lodj-09-2015-0209

Boddy, C. R. (2016). Unethical 20th century business leaders. *International Journal of Public Leadership*, *12*(2), 76–93. https://doi.org/10.1108/ijpl-12-2015-0032

Brown, M. E., & Mitchell, M. S. (2010). Ethical and unethical leadership: Exploring new avenues for future research. *Business Ethics Quarterly*, *20*(4), 583–616. https://doi.org/10.5840/beq201020439

Brown, M. E., & Treviño, L. K. (2006). Ethical leadership: A review and future directions. The Leadership Quarterly, 17(6), 595–616. https://doi.org/10.1016/j.leaqua.2006.10.004

Brown, M. E., Treviño, L. K., & Harrison, D. A. (2005). Ethical leadership: A social learning perspective for construct development and testing. *Organizational Behavior and Human Decision Processes*, *97*(2), 117–134. https://doi.org/10.1016/j.obhdp.2005.03.002

Calma, J. (2021, February 9). *Tesla's $1.5 billion bitcoin purchase clashes with its environmental aspirations.* https://www.theverge.com/2021/2/9/22275243/teslas-bitcoin-purchase-clashes-climate-change-mission

Chen, S. (2010). Bolstering unethical leaders: The role of the media, financial analysts and shareholders. *Journal of Public Affairs*, *10*(3), 200–215. https://doi.org/10.1002/pa.356

Davies, G., & Chun, R. (2009). The leader's role in managing reputation. *Reputation Capital*, 311–323. https://doi.org/10.1007/978-3-642-01630-1_21

Fehr, R., Fulmer, A., & Keng-Highberger, F. T. (2019). How do employees react to leaders' unethical behavior? The role of moral disengagement. *Personnel Psychology*, *73*(1), 73–93. https://doi.org/10.1111/peps.12366

Hegarty, N., & Moccia, S. (2018). Components of ethical leadership and their importance in sustaining organizations over the long term. *Journal of Values-Based Leadership*, *11*(1), 1–10. https://doi.org/10.22543/0733.111.1199

Hong, R. Y., Koh, S., & Paunonen, S. V. (2012). Supernumerary personality traits beyond the Big Five: Predicting materialism and unethical behavior. *Personality and Individual Differences*, *53*(5), 710–715. https://doi.org/10.1016/j.paid.2012.05.030

Hoyt, C. L., Price, T. L., & Poatsy, L. (2013). The social role theory of unethical leadership. *The Leadership Quarterly*, *24*(5), 712–723. https://doi.org/10.1016/j.leaqua.2013.07.001

Johnson, C. (2003). Enron's ethical collapse: Lessons for leadership educators. *Journal of Leadership Education*, 2(1), 45–56. https://doi.org/10.12806/v2/i1/c2

Joosten, A., van Dijke, M., van Hiel, A., & De Cremer, D. (2013). Being "in Control" may make you lose control: The role of self-regulation in unethical leadership behavior. *Journal of Business Ethics*, 1–14. https://doi.org/10.1007/s10551-013-1686-2

Kaul, A., Chaudhri, V., Cherian, D., Freberg, K., Mishra, S., Kumar, R., Pridmore, J., Lee, S. Y., Rana, N., Majmudar, U., & Carroll, C. E. (2015). Social media: The new mantra for managing reputation. *Vikalpa: The Journal for Decision Makers*, *40*(4), 455–491. https://doi.org/10.1177/0256090915618029

Kennedy, J. A., & Anderson, C. (2017). Hierarchical rank and principled dissent: How holding higher rank suppresses objection to unethical practices. *Organizational Behavior and Human Decision Processes*, *139*, 30–49. https://doi.org/10.1016/j.obhdp.2017.01.002

Knights, D., & O'Leary, M. (2005). Reflecting on corporate scandals: the failure of ethical leadership. *Business Ethics: A European Review*, *14*(4), 359–366. https://doi.org/10.1111/j.1467-8608.2005.00417.x

Knights, J. (2016). *How to develop ethical leaders.* Routledge. https://www.routledge.com/rsc/downloads/Transpersonal_Leadership_WP1.pdf

Lam, L. W., Loi, R., Chan, K. W., & Liu, Y. (2016). Voice more and stay longer: How ethical leaders influence employee voice and exit intentions. *Business Ethics Quarterly*, *26*(3), 277–300. https://doi.org/10.1017/beq.2016.30

Lašáková, A., & Remišová, A. (2015). Unethical leadership: Current theoretical trends and conceptualization. *Procedia Economics and Finance*, *34*, 319–328. https://doi.org/10.1016/s2212-5671(15)01636-6

Lee, D., Choi, Y., Youn, S., & Chun, J. U. (2017). Ethical leadership and employee moral voice: The mediating role of moral efficacy and the moderating role of leader–follower value congruence. *Journal of Business Ethics, 141*(1), 47–57. https://doi.org/10.1007/s10551-015-2689-y

Liautaud, S. (2021, January 21). How to set up an ethics advisory board. *Harvard Business Review*. https://hbr.org/2021/01/how-to-set-up-an-ethics-advisory-board

Mayer, D. M., Aquino, K., Greenbaum, R. L., & Kuenzi, M. (2012). Who displays ethical leadership, and why does it matter? An examination of antecedents and consequences of ethical leadership. *Academy of Management Journal, 55*(1), 151–171. https://doi.org/10.5465/amj.2008.0276

Minkes, A. L., Small, M. W., & Chatterjee, S. R. (1999). Leadership and business ethics: Does it matter? Implications for management. *Journal of Business Ethics, 20*(4), 327–335. https://doi.org/10.1023/a:1005741524800

Moore, C., Mayer, D., Chiang, F. F. T., Crossley, C. C., Karlesky, M. J., & Birtch, T. A. (2018). Leaders matter morally: The role of ethical leadership in shaping employee moral cognition and misconduct. *SSRN Electronic Journal*, 1–70. https://doi.org/10.2139/ssrn.3289593

Mostafa, A. M. S., Farley, S., & Zaharie, M. (2020). Examining the boundaries of ethical leadership: The harmful effect of co-worker social undermining on disengagement and employee attitudes. *Journal of Business Ethics*, 1–14. https://doi.org/10.1007/s10551-020-04586-2

Packer, D. J. (2009). Avoiding groupthink: Whereas weakly identified members remain silent, strongly identified members dissent about collective problems. *Psychological Science, 20*(5), 546–548. https://doi.org/10.1111/j.1467-9280.2009.02333.x

Robertson, D. C., & Rymon, T. (2001). Purchasing agents' deceptive behavior: A randomized response technique study. *Business Ethics Quarterly, 11*(3), 455–479. https://doi.org/10.2307/3857849

Treviño, L. K., & Brown, M. E. (2005). The role of leaders in influencing unethical behavior in the workplace. *Managing Organizational Deviance*, 69–96. https://doi.org/10.4135/9781452231105.n3

Zhang, Y., Zhou, F., & Mao, J. (2018). Ethical leadership and follower moral actions: Investigating an emotional linkage. *Frontiers in Psychology, 9*, 1–11. https://doi.org/10.3389/fpsyg.2018.01881

Chapter 6

Agile to Digitalization and Technological Change

Technology is in every aspect, and it is no longer an option but a must to have it incorporated in the future of education so that the workplace and its leaders are well equipped and trained with the skills to cope in a world dependent on rapidly evolving technology.

Kumaran Rajaram, PhD

6.1 Introduction

In today's digital era, technological innovations are constantly developed at an increasingly rapid pace. New technologies largely include for example blockchain, virtual reality, augmented reality, artificial intelligence, and machine learning. This evolution has led to the creation of new digital ecosystems where non-traditional competitors are offering new forms of customer value which threaten to eliminate outmoded industry barriers (Wade, Tarling, Assir, & Neubauer, 2017). For example, in the cases of AirBnB and Uber, both companies adopted the usage of digital platforms and unique business models to disrupt the hospitality and transport industries, respectively. Hence, as such the incumbent organizations found it even more difficult to maintain their market share and differentiate themselves. The pace of technological change has further increased since the coronavirus pandemic. Companies that have planned their digital strategies to be executed progressively in one-to-three-year phases are now put under time pressure where they are literally

DOI: 10.4324/9781003286288-8

forced to scale them within weeks or even days (McKinsey & Company, 2020). In a European survey by McKinsey & Company (2020), 70% of executives said that the pandemic will potentially fasten the pace of their digital transformation. The current rapid speed in which digitalization is occurring is suggestive of the future direction in which businesses are headed towards. Going digital will be crucial for organizations to sustain and compete in the new global market. Companies must reassess and commence their digital initiatives as soon as they can. Being agile in the digital climate is of utmost importance.

6.2 Organization's Agility: Digitalization and Technological Disruption

An agile organization is one that can respond speedily and resourcefully and is able to adapt to the rapidly changing environments (Mathiassen & Pries-Heje, 2006). While speed and efficacy are of essence, organizations must also ensure that their digital transformation efforts are performed in an appropriate manner so as to safeguard the interests of their stakeholders. Technological interventions have both their pros and cons. For instance, many employees have long been concerned over the thought of robots taking over their jobs. Labor economists largely agree that the digital revolution has resulted in a greater wealth divide (Cascio & Montealegre, 2016). On top of that, technology can be easily exploited by companies for their own selfish and unethical agenda that benefits them exponentially. For example, Huawei, the world's largest telecommunications equipment provider and second-largest smartphone manufacturer, faced much scrutiny and was banned in the United States over spying allegations. These concerns were valid given that in August of 2019, the Wall Street Journal found that Huawei had worked with governments from at least two African countries to spy on political opponents (Slate, 2020). Organizations must understand the nuances of digitalization in terms of the strong benefits it offers as well as the threats it potentially poses if not handled well while remaining agile at the same time.

Keeping up with technological innovations and development is critical for organizations. For example, organizations can capitalize on AI in three important ways (Davenport & Ronanki, 2018). First, most typically, organizations adopt AI to facilitate process automation. Organizations can render easy mundane tasks such as updating customer information and records and extracting necessary information from legal and contractual documents. The second type is concerned with gaining cognitive insight based on machine learning and using algorithms to facilitate detection of patterns from a significant amount of data as well as interpretation of the meaning behind it. This intervention is particularly useful when organizations want to predict what certain types of customers would be most likely to purchase, detect credit fraud, and automate personalized advertisement on customers' devices. Machine learning is highly data-intensive, and its accuracy in prediction improves as the organizations have a greater amount of data that they could feed into a given model; in other words, the model developed by AI will improve over time. This type of application is particularly valuable since such automation in detecting and extracting patterns is way beyond human ability. Finally, AI can also handle the tasks that require cognitive engagement, and the examples include chatbots for customer inquiries, internal sites that answer employee questions, and health treatment recommendation systems. Such application of AI could facilitate the interaction with customers and enables 24/7 customer service without adding new staff to the organizations, helping reduce personnel cost. However, digital innovation and transformation cannot happen in one day. Digital transformation requires having right talent in four domains of organizations (Davenport & Redman, 2020). The first domain is technology, as all technological innovations are primarily driven by the capability of organizations' Information Technology (IT) departments. Also, leaders in IT departments must be able to communicate with organizations what values they could produce and how such value can address business needs. The second area is data. Digital transformation often requires understanding and interpretation of massive, unstructured data. Unless having competent individuals, who can make sense of and effectively communicate the meaning, organizations' efforts in digital transformation unlikely bear fruit. The third domain is concerned with process orientation. Organizational leaders must be able to understand how their technological transformations come into play within entire system and structure of the organizations. Organizations can improve efficiency through adopting AI, but such digitalization could also happen in silos and may not be truly transformative, unless organizations align it with their overall strategy. Fourth, organizational change capability is critical to make digital transformation happen. Davenport and Redman particularly stressed that it is important to have leaders with excellent people skills so that organizational initiatives of digital transformation are properly communicated to employees. On a related note, Fountaine, McCarthy, and Saleh (2019) argued that adopting AI requires an alignment with organizational culture and employees' digital mindset; otherwise, implementing AI could backfire. Organizations need to foster agile, experimental, and adaptable cultures since the adoption of AI may not yield success immediately but might require a number of trials and errors. Van Alstyne and Parker (2021) highlighted how organizations should invest in digital technologies. They argued that digital transformation creates the highest value when firms orchestrate the development of products by others instead of creating them solely internally – such firm is called *inverted firm* (Parker, Van Alstyne, & Jiang, 2017). Inverted firms, through engaging with their external partners, are able to capture the greater value than that they could produce by themselves. For example, platform firms like GAFA and Microsoft, leading organizations in internet and technologies, do not author the posts or web pages or write the majority of apps in their platforms by themselves; in other words, these firms do not create value on their own but focuses on the value that they help orchestrate. As it is critical to consider not simply about value creation but also value capture, organizations need to consider how they can capture value based on their digital investments as well. Digitalization is not just for achieving efficiency; rather, organizations can invest in technology in a way that attracts others to join their ecosystems and to share their resources and innovations to achieve an even greater success.

6.3 Application via Case Studies: Organizations That Epitomizes Dexterity in Digitalization and Technological Disruptions

Levi Strauss is one of the companies that resembled and exemplified agility in terms of digitalization of their business. With the pandemic drastically changing how consumers shopped, adapting to the shift became vital for many retailers across the globe including Levi's. The pandemic had thrown them into overdrive, but CEO Harmit Singh responded positively by stating that they were ready for the challenge. In accordance to McKinsey & Company (2020), Levi Strauss had invested in digital technologies including artificial intelligence (AI) and predictive analytics way before the pandemic happened. This enabled them to act swiftly and with certainty when many consumers switched to e-commerce. Further to that, Levi Strauss also accepted online orders through both fulfillment centers and its physical stores in order to meet demand. CEO Harmit Singh claimed that it would have taken them weeks or months to work out this move if it is prior to the pandemic. However, Levi Strauss managed to achieve this shift within days. They launched curbside pickup at around 80% of their US stores and made use of their already established mobile application to connect with consumers in a creative manner. Overall, Levi Strauss has demonstrated the importance of both foresight and agility in digitization today.

Toys 'R' Us, on the flipped side, is an organization that infamously failed to have an agile digital strategy. The organization which was once a market leader in the toy industry filed for bankruptcy in 2017. While their demise can be attributed to several reasons, one of the major contributing factors could be their failure to adapt to changes in the competitive environment and was slow to embrace e-commerce. Even former CEO David Brandon acknowledged that the company was late to the e-commerce game (Albanese, 2017). Their 10-year partnership with Amazon worsens the situation, where they paid the e-commerce company $50 million a year, on top of a percentage of sales to be Amazon's exclusive seller of toys and baby products. While the partnership was initially a success, the agreement meant that Toys 'R' Us had no autonomous online presence. Furthermore, when Amazon realized its success, it started expanding its toy and baby categories with other merchants including Toys 'R' Us competitors. Although the company managed to sue Amazon successfully, it had lost a lot of time to develop a substantial online presence and e-commerce strategy (Knowledge@Wharton, 2018). The failure of Toys 'R' Us highlights the imperativeness of a clear digital strategy and the agility to change.

Singapore Airlines is another representative example of an agile organization with the emphasis on a digital strategy (Singapore Airlines, n.d.). In 2019, Singapore

Airlines announced its launch of a digital innovation lab called KrisLab, as part of the Singapore International Airline (SIA) Group's investment program. KrisLab aims to develop innovative ideas and also collaborate with external partners as well as start-ups to facilitate digitalization and technology across the company's business in various ways. KrisLab particularly focuses on innovations concerning virtual reality, blockchain, AI, and data analytics. Staff are encouraged to submit their ideas and solutions for business problems, and once the ideas are approved, they will be further developed into a prototype. This initiative allows Singapore Airlines to adapt to a variety of business and customer needs quickly and maintain its agility in terms of innovations and technology. KrisLab also collaborates with such research institutions as A*STAR and National University of Singapore to conduct research in deep-tech areas. Such collaboration enhances business operation of SIA in such spheres as revenue management, smart seats, virtual training, and predictive maintenance for aircraft. Last but not least, upon the opening of KrisLab, SIA also launched Learning and Innovation For Everyone (LIFE), a three-day learning festival for SIA employees, to cultivate digital mindsets among employees as part of company-wide initiatives to foster digital transformation and to promote an innovative culture within the organization. During the LIFE festival, staff can attend workshops and talks by business leaders and pioneers of digitalization in the industry as well as an interactive showcase where they can experience new digital technologies.

From the above illustrations, we can conclude that agility in the digital era is crucial for an organization's sustainability, productivity, survivability, and growth. The following recommended strategies advocated in Figure 6.1 serve as a strategic operational guide that organizations must embrace for agility towards digitalization and technological change. Figure 6.1 presents a visual summarized digitalization and technological change framework.

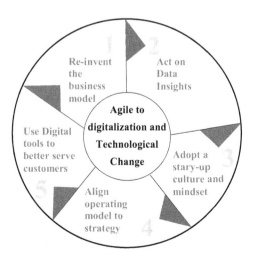

Figure 6.1 Digitalization and Technological Change Framework

6.4 Strategy 1: Reinvent the Business Model

Organizations should focus on developing its business and operating models to give themselves the best opportunity of success in both the short and long term (Blackburn, LaBerge, O'Toole, & Schneider, 2020). In contrary, those organizations that only make minor changes to their business model without addressing the specific root issues have a much higher probability of not been able to meet their goals. We could reason this to the fact where small adjustments generally lead to returns that are below the cost of capital and are often too insignificant when compared to the external pace of disruption. Hence, adopting tools such as Artificial Intelligence (AI) to redefine businesses to be scaled will enable companies to attain greater success. For instance, a business may use algorithms in their supply chain to better comprehend purchase-pattern changes and decide on production numbers accordingly. This approach could be adopted and executed for other business processes as well. When a decision is made to do so, it is vital that it is done on a scale where there will be significant impact, otherwise organizations may find themselves spending too much money and effort for too little of a reward.

According to McKinsey, leading companies in digitalization tend to invest in a variety of strategic dimensions including marketing and distribution, products and services, processes, ecosystems, and supply chains; stated otherwise, these companies adjust their corporate strategies significantly upon digitalization (Bughin, LaBerge, & Mellbye, 2017). The magnitude and scope of investment in digitalization is well beyond the companies that cannot yield significant improvement in economic performance by promoting digitalization. Winners in digitalization invest more boldly than other companies. However, there are not many companies that engage in so-called "digital reinvention" or restructuring companies' portfolios and investing in an aggressive digital strategy by such means as creating new platform business models (Bughin & Catlin, 2017). This attests to the possibility that organizational leaders may have a false assumption that simply investing in technology and digitalization and adopting new tools such as AI can make digital transformation happen. However, as Leinwand and Mani (2021) put, digitalizing isn't the same as digital transformation. It is critical for companies to rethink and reimagine how they create value and what roles digitalization will play. Also, companies need to work together and explore possibilities of collaboration with other companies in the same ecosystem to create even greater values. As such, digitalization should not occur in silo but requires organizations to reconsider their business models and overarching strategies. However, some scholars pointed out that companies may not always have to reinvent business models to capture the full value of digitalization (Furr & Shipilov, 2019). A radical disruption and dramatic change of companies' business may not be always necessary to have successful digitalization, and transformation can also happen in an incremental manner. It is vital to ensure that digitalization does not occur in isolation with other key corporate strategies, but it does not mean that companies need to engage in digitalization of *all aspects* of their business *simultaneously*. It is indeed possible that engaging in digital transformation across all the units and employees at the same time can make the process disruptive – rather companies could also consider taking an incremental step and trial-and-error approach to ensure the successful implementation of digitalization. Equally importantly, companies need to understand how their digitalization can best address and serve customers' needs. For example, Aeroflot, the Russian airline, which used to be one of the worst airline companies in the world, was able to transform itself and became one of the best in the industry by implementing digital technologies into their core activities including operations, reporting, passenger booking, and so on. They also re-purposed the digital architecture so that they can run both of their main airline and a low-cost carrier. Although digitalization did not alter the company's business model dramatically, it helped them become a more efficient and user-friendly airline company. Companies can still reap greater revenues from digitalization that does not involve large-scale transformation of business models than those who make disruptive changes, as long as they can better make use of new technology to meet the customer demands. Organizational leaders need to be aware of that digitalization is not merely about technology but is also about the customers.

6.5 Strategy 2: Act on Data Insights

When organizations make decisions in relation to their business model, they must do so based on data insights that focus on being objective rather than general observation or perceived, opinionated insights or intuition. While advances in data are often focused on AI, machine learning, deep learning, and more, they are not the main differentiator to future-proof an organization (Frankiewicz & Chamorro-Premuzic, 2020). Instead, the ability to harness valuable data, being able to translate it into insights, and to act on those insights is a much bigger competitive advantage. The emphasis should be on the acting of the insights found, largely because many business leaders falsely assume that investing in data technology, tools, or scientists will automatically solve their problems and help them become more technologically advanced. The key strategic advantage for many successful data-driven companies is primarily because they act according to the analysis of the data. In today's ever-changing competitive landscape, data is more imperative than ever. Having the collated data analyzed, organizations can deduce the changes more accurately and make them respond in an efficient and effective way. As such, it is rather essential to not only understand the value of data but also need to act upon what data shows. Although business leaders are sometimes required to make decisions based on their intuitions or gut feelings, especially in situations without any available data or precedents, such instinctive decision making unnecessarily increases a risk when they have some data at hand (Glazer, 2020). It is important for organizations to possess the capability of deriving important insights from data and acting on them, so that they can avoid potential failures in their decision making. Towards these ends, fostering data-driven and digital mindsets among employees is essential (Subrahmanyan & Jalona, 2020). Establishing a data-driven culture in organizations is one of the most efficient ways to promote decision making based on data analytics. Without data-driven and digital mindsets among employees, it may cause some backlash or resistance from them when organizations try to implement solutions based on the insights derived from data. Employees' potential psychological barrier to the reliance on data may need to be removed. Organizations can try a few things to foster a data-driven culture (Davenport & Mittal, 2020). For instance, CEOs can convey the value of data to employees by making important organizational decisions based on data. Also, organizations can conduct educational programs internally whereby employees can learn more about important skills relevant to data analytics. Organizational efforts in promoting a data-driven culture and mindset should help employees fully appreciate the value of data, which eventually encourages them to act on the data insights.

Furthermore, Troyanos (2020) suggested that the following considerations are necessary during data analytics process for organizations to effectively act on data insights: (a) prioritizing high-value key business questions (KBQs) over pipe dreams; (b) building cross-functional teams capable of translating insight into action; and (c) using process formalization as a stand-in for someone who can translate analytics. First and foremost, organizations need to consider forward-looking questions concerning what organizations will do based on the insights obtained from data; then, they need to sort out the priority of those questions. Organizations are required to identify what questions they want to answer using their data. Second, organizations need to translate the insights from data into actions. To this end, it is necessary to assemble cross-functional teams during the data analytics process, since implementing solutions based on data often requires collaboration across employees. When organizations fail to involve other teams and to properly communicate the insights from data analytics to them, there could be some internal resistance that prevents organizations from acting on data insights. Finally, there should be identified individuals based on their expertise who can communicate data insights to the teams being involved. Finding such individuals is crucial to facilitate collaboration among the teams. These three considerations discussed should help organizations act upon the data insights effectively.

6.6 Strategy 3: Adopt a Start-Up Culture and Mindset

Culture and mindset are two significant factors when we advocate digitization in an organization. For an organization to be agile in times of change, it must have a culture that facilitates and embraces digital transformation. For instance, a type of culture that characterizes growth mindset and agility is that of a Silicon Valley start-up. Silicon Valley start-ups are known for their agile decision-making, rapid prototyping, and flat structure (Tabrizi, Lam, Girard, & Irvin, 2019). As the process of digital transformation is inherently uncertain, traditional hierarchies will highly hinder speedy progress, hence a flat organizational structure is significant. This can be attributed to the changes that are required to be implemented and adjusted, decisions to be made quickly, and the belief that groups from all parts of the organization need to play a role. Experimentation of any digitization initiatives takes up a lot of time, hence more delays will occur if every decision must go through multiple layers of management, which is counterproductive and not efficient. Moreover, due to the delayed lag time, the digital initiative may even end up becoming irrelevant or outdated or losing out in terms of first mover advantage by the time it is authorized to be put into actual action. Consequently, organizations may potentially find themselves lagging behind their competitors and losing their position in the market. While organizations do not have to necessarily revamp their entire organizational structure to be agile in the digital era, it is imperative that they facilitate a strong, deep-rooted culture and a growth, agile mindset that enables employees to act in an efficient and decisive manner.

Researchers have advocated several strategies to promote an organizational culture that fosters exploratory and innovative firm behaviors. For instance, Kidder and Geraci (2018) recommended that organizational leaders should make decisions like venture capitals for rapid and effective innovations. Specifically, they argued that organizations should adopt a lean start-up approach that involves a number of iterations throughout product development processes and set up a growth board by having senior executives regularly meet and discuss company's new growth initiatives to decide whether they pursue or let go of them. Given the speed of digitalization and technological development in a modern society, organizations are also required to act swiftly and convene their senior executives as frequently and constantly as possible, instead of having them discuss new ideas in a sporadic manner. Furthermore, when senior leaders of the organization appreciate the value of an agile decision-making process and experimentation, a start-up culture and mindset is more likely to be shared among employees. Also, such an innovative and explorative culture could also derive from organization's HR team. In particular, Gothelf (2014) emphasized the importance of HR teams to build agility in organizations. To promote a start-up culture and mindset, it is crucial for organizations to attract and hire the individuals and talents who have an entrepreneurial mindset and attitude. Also, in terms of performance evaluation and appraisal, organizations should incentivize employees for the behaviors that conduce to organizational agility. As such, how organizations structure HR teams should play a key role in promoting a culture and mindset that leads to digitalization and innovation.

McConnell (2022) recently proposed a "gig mindset" that refers to the mindset whereby employees think and act like freelancers by taking ownership of their personal development and trying to challenge the status quo. Organizations that can foster such individuals should be able to readily adapt to rapid technological changes. Organizations can assess the following aspects to ensure that they cultivate a gig mindset learning culture: flow of information and ideas, teams and experimenting, and horizon scanning. Equally important is to retain gig mind setters, and to do so, managers need to understand the difference between deviance and positive deviance. Gig mind setters, given their tendency to challenge the status quo, can be seen as deviants at work, leading to negative perceptions from managers and subsequently increasing the turnover of the gig mind setters. Managers thus need to understand that deviating behaviors can actually bring benefits in this fast-changing world, so that organizations will not lose valuable talents that can contribute to digital and technological innovations. To this end, organizations should foster so-called *start-up's soul* – something intangible like an energy but "inspires enthusiasm and fosters a sense of deep connection and mutual purpose" (Gulati, 2019). It would become increasingly more difficult to maintain such start-up culture and mindset as the company's business grows over time. Therefore, it is critical for organizations to have a business intent that provides a lofty reason for organization's purpose, cultivates close customer connections, and promotes employee voice and choice to foster their autonomy and creativity. Investing in these dimensions of a start-up's soul should strengthen an entrepreneurial culture and mindset among employees.

6.7 Strategy 4: Align Operating Model to Strategy

Organizations should align their operating model to their strategy for their digital transformation to succeed (Deloitte, 2020). Successful transformations realign the organization to a singular vision while failed ones do not. Hence, leadership teams should relook at and appropriately revise their organization's operating model, where a well-designed one should assist the organization in balancing growth with risk concurrently overcoming organizational barriers. The first step is for the organization to identify the holistic set of capabilities that are needed to meet their strategic ambitions. Then, leaders must source the capabilities, which is the most challenging step as organizations are often resistant to changing their existing ways of working. Subsequently, work must be allocated to the most efficient parts of the organization.

Organizations should expect their operating model to constantly evolve as the business environment changes. To increase an organization's chances in developing an ecosystem to guide a successful digital transformation, it includes, (a) defining clear roles and responsibilities; (b) creating complementary incentives and goals, and (c) establishing cross-functional debriefs. It is quite essential for organizations to reshape various domains of their business to yield successful outcomes from engaging in digitalization. For example, Angevine, Keomany, Thomsen, and Zemmel (2021) argued that changes need to occur in three business processes for digitalization to make real changes. Those three thrusts entail, namely (a) product, service offer, and order fulfillment, (b) commercial strategy and execution, and (c) customer service and transactions. Concerning the first point, companies might have to revamp their delivery systems as well as supply chains to increase transparency during order tracking, so that they can provide the same level of transparency as similar to offline ordering. For the second point, companies might have to consider creating the new distributor and revising sales incentives so that they can shift to online commerce. Regarding the third point, companies need to be able to set up a process for a smooth customer experience. Making changes to these domains is not easy and requires a substantial amount of resources; therefore, organizations need to constantly re-appraise and re-allocate a portfolio of their investment to the areas where they want to achieve the most optimal digitalization outcomes. In other words, digital transformation is no longer something that merely supports limited aspects of business strategy, but rather it should be given first consideration (Harvard Business Review, 2017). Indeed, Fischer, Imgrund, Janiesch, and Winkelmann (2020) also emphasized the importance of strategic alignment and governance between business process management and digital transformation to ensure organizational agility and successful digitalization.

Also, to actualize a better alignment between organizations' business strategies and digitalization initiatives, there must be alignment in the transformation efforts with business results in some measurable ways (Forbes, 2021a). Organizations need to constantly appraise and evaluate how their digitalization efforts contribute to their global business strategy and need to identify where they fall short. Managers must be up to date about whether the companies' digital initiatives do make positive impacts on organizations' main business, largely because a mismatch between them could not only impede digital transformation but also incur a significant amount of financial loss (Harvard Business Review, 2020). Another potentially practical strategy to promote an alignment between organizational strategy and digitalization is to establish a Digital Factory recommended by McKinsey (Khanna, Konstantynova, Lamarre, & Sohoni, 2020). The Digital Factory consists of "dedicated, cross-functional teams that work together on change-the-business programs". One of the key advantages of the Digital Factory that promotes digital transformation is that it facilitates collaboration across various teams within the organization. The Digital Factory could thus not only help coordinate the resources and expertise across teams but also establish common organizational goals. In other words, organizations that adopt the Digital Factory approach should be able to achieve digital transformation in a way that does not deviate from the organization's strategic focus.

6.8 Strategy 5: Use Digital Tools to Better Serve Customers

A common misconception about digital transformations is that they have to be disruptive (Furr & Shipilov, 2019). In contrary, it generally means leveraging on digital tools to meet consumer needs more effectively. Organizations should focus more on serving customers' needs using digital tools rather than investing in radical changes as their value proposition. Whether an organization is disrupted or not largely depends on the value they provide to customers. An incumbent will still prosper when they use digital tools to better meet consumers' needs compared to a disruptive new entrant.

Indeed, the firms that are successful in digitalization do not simply invest in technology but carefully assess their customer needs and revamp processes to enhance customer experiences (Perry, McGrath, & Singh, 2020). E-commerce and online payments are important examples that showcase how organizations respond to new customer needs that were introduced by the COVID-19 pandemic. Due to the outbreak of the pandemic, customers were mandated to stay inside and to avoid physical interactions, which increased the demands for online purchases and non-physical transactions. However, companies need to make many choices and carefully review multiple alternatives. This process enables them to decide the varying kinds of e-commerce and online payment systems they use and how these are adopted so that customers will not find new processes too complicated, complex, and difficult to follow. Companies also need to ensure that their online systems are fast and free of technical difficulties as it can potentially reduce customer satisfaction and loyalty (Forbes, 2021b). Moreover, it is equally important to enhance customer's post-purchase experiences. To this end, companies invest in technologies that enable them to closely monitor and address customer's issues remotely and promptly (Perry et al., 2020). Artificial Intelligence (AI) tools can be adopted to track and analyze customers' inquiries and helps improve their experiences. Also, beyond facilitating online purchase and cashless transaction mode, healthcare industries use medical technologies to promote patients' healthy lifestyle by collecting real-time health-related data with Apple Watch or Fitbit (Terwiesch & Siggelkow, 2021). Also, they use big data to provide customized care programs and interventions for patients (Chilukuri & Van Kiken, 2017).

Having a customer-centric culture and mindset enables the organization to effectively tailor its technological initiative to customer needs. Solis (2021) described several key changes to increase customer centricity within organizations. First, organizations need to start from assessing the current experiences of customers. It is crucial to know whether customers are satisfied with organizations' digital initiatives and online platforms and identify areas of organizations' business where customers would like to see digital changes. Next, organizations need to develop an understanding about what the best customer experiences would entail. In other words, they need to set a specific vision about how organizations can create values for customers through digitalization. Third, organizations are required to identify touchpoints, processes, and training being required for delivering the customer service based on the vision that they developed in the previous step. Fourth, organizations need to set up the system whereby they connect the customer data and records to key touchpoints and transactions so that they can better understand customer experiences. In the context of digitalization, organizations are encouraged to keep a close eye on how customers feel about their online platforms for purchasing their products and services (for example, usability of the platforms, experience of any technical glitches). Fifth, organizations should develop a comprehensive scheme for digital transformation beforehand by defining necessary resources, developing a detailed timeline and roadmap, and devising a plan to evaluate their digital initiatives. Lastly, Solis (2021) also emphasized that internal collaboration across different teams of organizations is essential to make transformation for customers successful. In other words, organizations need to develop a consensus about a shared view of their customers among employees.

References

Albanese, J. (2017, November 9). *The death of a toy retailer: How a lack of digital transformation helped destroy Toys 'R' Us.* Inc.Com.

Angevine, C., Keomany, J., Thomsen, J., & Zemmel, R. (2021, May 27). Implementing a digital transformation at industrial companies. *Harvard Business Review.*

Blackburn, S., LaBerge, L., O'Toole, C., & Schneider, J. (2020, April 22). *Digital strategy in a time of crisis.* McKinsey & Company.

Bughin, J., & Catlin, T. (2017). What successful digital transformations have in common. *Harvard Business Review.*

Bughin, J., LaBerge, L., & Mellbye, A. (2017, February 9). The case for digital reinvention. *McKinsey Quarterly.*

Cascio, W. F., & Montealegre, R. (2016). How technology is changing work and organizations. *Annual Review of Organizational Psychology and Organizational Behavior, 3*(1), 349–375.

Chilukuri, S., & Van Kuiken, S. (2017, April 25). Four keys to successful digital transformations in healthcare. *McKinsey Digital.*

Davenport, T. H., & Mittal, N. (2020). How CEOs can lead a data-driven culture. *Harvard Business Review.*

Davenport, T. H., & Redman, T. C. (2020). Digital transformation comes down to talent in 4 key areas. *Harvard Business Review.*

Davenport, T. H., & Ronanki, R. (2018). Artificial intelligence for the real world. *Harvard Business Review.*

Deloitte. (2020). If you want your digital transformation to succeed, align your operating model to your strategy. *Harvard Business Review.*

Fischer, M., Imgrund, F., Janiesch, C., & Winkelmann, A. (2020). Strategy archetypes for digital transformation: Defining meta objectives using business process management. *Information & Management, 57,* 103262.

Forbes (2021a, June 22). *More than words: Defining digital transformation in a meaningful way for organizations.* https://www.forbes.com/sites/forbestechcouncil/2021/06/22/more-than-words-defining-digital-transformation-in-a-meaningful-way-for-organizations/?sh=6d4f7bac58e3

Forbes (2021b, October 1). *Creating a digital customer experience that drives loyalty and revenue.* https://www.forbes.com/sites/forbestechcouncil/2021/10/01/creating-a-digital-customer-experience-that-drives-loyalty-and-revenue/?sh=f9fee925768f

Fountaine, T., McCarthy, B., & Saleh, T. (2019). Building the AI-powered organization: Technology isn't the biggest challenge. Culture is. *Harvard Business Review.*

Frankiewicz, B., & Chamorro-Premuzic, T. (2020, May 6). Digital transformation is about talent, not technology. *Harvard Business Review.*

Furr, N., & Shipilov, A. (2019). Digital doesn't have to be disruptive: The best results can come from adaptation rather than reinvention. *Harvard Business Review.*

Glazer, R. (2020, February 21). Are you using your data, or just collecting it? *Harvard Business Review.*

Gothelf, J. (2014, November 14). Bring agile to the whole organization. *Harvard Business Review.*

Gulati, R. (2019). The soul of a start-up: Companies can sustain their entrepreneurial energy even as they grow. *Harvard Business Review.*

Harvard Business Review. (2017, July 19). *Embracing digital change requires a clear strategic focus.*

Harvard Business Review. (2020, September 1). *Is your IT department aligned with your business outcomes?*

Khanna, S., Konstantynova, N., Lamarre, E., & Sohoni, V. (2020, May 14). Welcome to the Digital Factory: The answer to how to scale your digital transformation. *Harvard Business Review.*

Kidder, D., & Geraci, J. (2018, May 7). To innovate like a startup, make decisions like VCs do. *Harvard Business Review.*

Knowledge@Wharton. (2018, March 14). *The demise of toys R us: What went wrong.*

Leinwand, P., & Mani M. M. (2021). Digitalizing isn't the same as digital transformation. *Harvard Business Review.*

Mathiassen, L., & Pries-Heje, J. (2006). Business agility and diffusion of information technology. *European Journal of Information Systems, 15*(2), 116–119.

McConnell, J. (2022, January 26). How workers with a "Gig Mindset" can help your company thrive. *Harvard Business Review.*

McKinsey & Company. (2020). *Covid-19: Implications for business in 2020.* https://www.mckinsey.com/capabilities/risk-and-resilience/our-insights/covid-19-implications-for-business-2020

Parker, G., Van Alstyne, M., & Jiang, X. (2017). Platform ecosystems: How developers invert the firm. *MIS Quarterly, 41*(1), 255–266.

Perry, D., McGrath, G., & Singh, H. (2020, September 22). Industrial firms need to give their customers a digital experience. *Harvard Business Review.*

Singapore Airlines. (n.d.). *Singapore Airlines opens digital innovation lab in drive to be world's leading digital airline.* Retrieved on January 30, 2022, from https://www.singaporeair.com/en_UK/es/media-centre/press-release/article/?q=en_UK/2019/January-March/ne0119-190129

Slate. (2020, January 15). The evil list. *Slate Magazine.* https://slate.com/technology/2020/01/evil-list-tech-companies-dangerous-amazon-facebook-google-palantir.html

Solis, B. (2021, July 22). A blueprint for becoming a customer-centered company. *Harvard Business Review.*

Subrahmanyan, S. N., & Jalona, S. (2020, February 28). Building a data-driven culture from the ground up. *Harvard Business Review.*

Tabrizi, B., Lam, E., Girard, K., & Irvin, V. (2019, March 13). Digital transformation is not about technology. *Harvard Business Review.*

Terwiesch, C., & Siggelkow, N. (2021, December 2). Digital transformation: Designing a seamless digital experience for customers. *Harvard Business Review.*

Troyanos, K. (2020, February 24). Use data to answer your key business questions. *Harvard Business Review.*

Van Alstyne, M. W., & Parker, G. G. (2021). Digital transformation changes how companies create value. *Harvard Business Review.*

Wade, M. R., Tarling, A., Assir, R., & Neubauer, R. (2017, May). *Agile leadership in an age of digital disruption.* International Institute for Management Development.

NAVIGATING THROUGH SUCCESSFULLY IN CRISIS MANAGEMENT

3

Chapter 7

Leadership Competencies for Crisis Management

Effective leadership in crisis management epitomizes the fortitude of an individual who leads. The actions and behavior of a leader in crisis in a true realistic test of resilience and competence, both on the technical skills, socially-culturally and emotionally. The ability to know the answers to the unprecedented 'hows' and 'whats' to the rapid evolving changes is imperative. A leader in crisis gives hope and confidence for people to stay calm and self-assured. The traits of compassion, empathy, humility, grit, foresight and eye for details are primary competencies that requires a leader in crisis to embrace.

Kumaran Rajaram, PhD

7.1 Introduction

In today's volatile and unpredictable environment, organizational instability is becoming a common issue that arises more frequently. Hence, being able to lead an organization through a crisis is vital and will certainly continue to be an essential aspect as crises are at times inevitable despite much planning is done as a foreseeable strategy. Crisis management refers to the process in which indicators of crisis are assessed for the risk of a potential crisis and the required measures

DOI: 10.4324/9781003286288-10

taken in order to experience minimum loss during crisis (Fener & Cevik, 2015). Someone who leads others through turbulent times can be described as a crisis leader, which is defined by DuBrin (2013) as an individual who leads a team during an abrupt and largely unanticipated, negative, and emotionally draining circumstance. There are some essential traits, characteristics, and behaviors that are recurrently associated with effective leadership in crisis situations. The word "effective" or "effectiveness", in this context, refers to factors such as productivity, survival, and preserving morale.

7.2 Leadership: Crisis Management

Research evidence shows that the characteristics of a crisis leader require one to be charismatic and inspiring, to think strategically, and to have the ability and desire to empathize by relating and expressing sadness and compassion (James, Wooten, & Dushek, 2011). First, a leader who is charismatic helps employees in coping with feelings of distress triggered by the crisis. When employees perceive their leader to be charismatic, they tend to experience lesser job stress and avoid the overwhelming feel of being in a crisis mode. Charisma from a behavioral action-oriented aspects could help leading a company out of crisis. Charisma inspires employees through stabilizing emotions while instilling grit to continue working towards getting out of the crisis, with the hope of making them more resilient. Second, the ability to think strategically and see the holistic picture serves as a contributing factor to success for a leader to effectively manage a crisis. Cognitive skills are vital when employees are bogged down by the challenges, for them to think critically and search quick ways to resolve them. Last, but not least, it is crucial that leaders are able to deal with their own effectively as well as that of his or her employees during a crisis as it could be a prolonged and fluctuating emotionally challenging event. A leader must relate, empathize with the varying situational aspects, expressing and relating to desolation about the crisis, and show compassion towards affected employees. This exemplifies the care and concern extended for their employees. Research study shows that leaders who took the responsibility during the crisis occurring received more favorable evaluations than those who did not.

Waldman, Ramirez, House, and Pranam (2001) revealed that charismatic leadership had a strong impact on organizational performance under uncertainty than under certainty. Petrieglieri (2020) also made similar points relevant to compassion and emotional comfort for the employees who are affected by a given crisis. He emphasized leaders' capability of *holding* during the time of crises and argued that there are two important defining factors – containing and interpreting. Containing involves soothing distress, while interpreting refers to "the ability to help others make sense of a confusing predicament" (Petriglieri, 2020, p. 3). Holding can be done at the interpersonal and institutional levels, and leaders' holding behaviors help reassure and empower colleagues and followers while minimizing their emotional distress.

Crisis leadership is by no means critical for effectively handling unprecedented events and thereby improving firm performance under ambiguous circumstances (James et al., 2011). Wooten and James (2008) revealed a set of leadership competencies that are significant throughout crisis management. A crisis has five phases: (a) signal detection (sense-making; perspective taking); (b) preparation and prevention (issue selling; organizational agility; creativity); (c) damage control and containment (decision making; communicating; risk taking); (d) business recovery (promoting organizational resilience); and (e) reflection and learning. Each phase requires different competencies, as detailed in Figure 7.1. For example, during signal detection, leaders are supposed to be aware of and to understand early signals about a potential crisis. In other words, it is critical for leaders to engage in sense-making or organizing and interpreting individual discrete events that may not be overtly connected but potentially result in a crisis. Also, one of the competencies highlighted in the second stage (i.e., preparation and prevention) is issue selling, a skill in bringing important issues that leaders discovered under the radar of top management. When leaders' issue-selling behaviors are not effective, organizations would likely fail to prepare for and respond to a crisis. James and colleagues (2011), in their review on crisis management, argued that the way in which leaders frame crises is of considerable importance. When leaders interpret given crises as threats, their cognition and behaviors likely become conservative. However, when they view them as opportunities, organizations can leverage them and translate them into positive changes or innovations.

Leaders should adopt a more directive leadership with extensive yet comprehensive communication to be reached out to the varying stakeholders. They should take decisive action to correct the situation as the more dire a crisis is, the less time they will have to solve it. Once a well thought-through execution plan is decided, a leader must communicate it to all employees in the organization and reassure them that actions and measures are taken to address the specific issues. Those who take visible action are more likely to be viewed as competent leaders. Aside this, there must be adequate, honest, and effective engagement with the varying stakeholders of the organization, where the leader must know the who, what, when, and how of communication. Besides this, Table 7.1 illustrates the core behaviors to be embraced by leaders that contribute to improving the effectiveness of handling a crisis.

To have the contents illustrated in a holistic and comprehensive visual framework, Figure 7.1 is presented.

Table 7.1 Leaders Mindsets and Behaviors and Action Plans for Crisis Management

Mindsets and Behaviors of Leaders	Action Plan
Think ahead – Initiative and Proactiveness	**Devise a Contingency Crisis Management Plan** ◼ **Strategic Actions:** such as integrating crisis management (CM) into strategic planning and official policies ◼ **Technical and Structural actions:** such as creating a CM team and dedication a budget to CM ◼ **Evaluation and diagnostic actions:** such as conducting audits of threats and liabilities, establishing tracking systems for early warning signals ◼ **Communication actions:** such as providing training for dealing with media, local communities, police and government officials ◼ **Psychological and cultural actions:** such as showing a strong top management commitment to CM, providing training, psychological support services regarding the human and emotional impact of crisis (Bateman & Konopaske, 2021)
Engage the Stakeholders	◼ Care for your team by empathizing with the team's circumstances and challenges ◼ Uplift their spirits, clearly, succinctly, and thoroughly communicate new goals and information
Coach and mentor to equip your team's enhanced crisis leadership skills and knowledge	◼ Invest in coaching and mentoring to boost leaders' effectiveness ◼ Review the roles and responsibilities of your team for post-crisis world and whether our key executives are leveled and positioned for success ◼ Identify talent and nurture the team to propel through the current crisis and in the longed-for tomorrow as the new normal emerge
Speedy and informed decision making over precision	◼ Process available information, quickly determine the priorities, and decide with conviction ◼ Focus on business continuity through prioritizing with trade-offs ◼ Advocate to go with an easy to understand, simple and scalable framework
Avoid procrastination of the problem	◼ Acknowledge the issues raised by employees ◼ Prioritize and take actions to resolve it, even if it requires time to be solved fully. The action in wanting to solve the issue itself is effective (Rajaram, K. 2021)

Mindsets and Behaviors of Leaders	Action Plan
Review the workflow, processes, and re-establish the work routine	■ Examine if changes or tweaks or improvisations are required in the existing workflow and processes. If yes, have that sorted out with the relevant stakeholders through engagement and receiving relevant feedback. This allows the organization to stay relevant and agile ■ Map out the work routine that best functions to achieve efficiency and effectiveness assigned to company's goals and business deliverables
Create a culture of accountability through empowerment	■ Establish new metrics to monitor performance that is carefully aligned to the varying roles and responsibilities of employees ■ Align team focus with adequate interventions on individual responsibility ■ Advocate values such as empowerment, autonomy, and trust that become the rooted ethos in shaping the culture
Recognition for exhibiting the appropriate behavioral traits and accomplishments tied to performance	■ Shift the behaviors through recognizinçg the essential behaviors, for example, embracing of digitalization ■ Tie rewards to the outcomes with key aspects in the process being fulfilled versus the number of hours spent. This helps to focus on productivity yet instilling a work-life balance, especially when the boundary could be mostly blurred in a crisis phase
Signal detection	■ Sense-making: Making sense for individual discrete events as well as a series of events that may seem unrelated ■ Perspective taking: ensuring the well-being of those who are affected by given crises and demonstrate compassion and empathy towards them (Wooten & James, 2008)
Framing of a crisis	■ Issues can be interpreted as threats or opportunities, and how they are framed influences leaders' subsequent cognition and behaviors (e.g., strategic decisions, how, and what to communicate to relevant stakeholders) (James, Wooten, & Dushek, 2011)

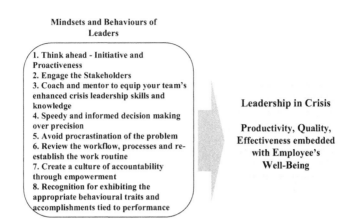

Figure 7.1 Leaders Mindsets and Behaviors for Crisis Management

7.3 Case Studies: Leadership in Crisis Management

Crises take many varying forms, where some disrupt businesses globally while others impact certain industries more than the other and individual organizations. For instance, a sudden sharp downturn in business, natural disasters, workplace accidents, a massive product recall, workplace abuse, or even a sex scandal involving a senior executive would all be labeled a crisis (DuBrin, 2013). A recent example would be the COVID-19 pandemic which saw countries closing their borders, major disruptions in work and school environments, changes in consumer behaviors, and many other spill-over effects. The economic uncertainty and financial impact brought about by this crisis has impacted many organizations across the globe, where some companies are seeing slower growth and lower revenues. Small businesses were particularly affected with 43% of them in the United States reporting to have temporarily closed (Bartik et al., 2020). The large scale of the outbreak along with its unpredictability made it challenging for business leaders and their teams to respond as expected. Nonetheless, some companies managed to swiftly respond to the crisis, where some businesses in Singapore as reported by Gilchrist (2020) on the strategies adopted in which they tackled the challenge. For instance, the manufacturer 3M applied lessons learnt from the SARs outbreak in 2003 and ran its manufacturing lines 24/7 to double the global production of N95 respirators. They worked with local authorities in Singapore to keep the business moving and to rehouse staff who frequently commuted daily from Malaysia as border closures threatened to impact output.

Effectiveness in leadership during a crisis allows a company to recover from any setbacks that may have arisen. The Tylenol crisis faced by Johnson and Johnson (J&J) is a prime example that we could use to illustrate crisis management. In 1982, several people died after being poisoned by cyanide-laced Tylenol capsules, a painkiller medication. Prior to the incident, J&J had 35% of the $1.2 billion painkiller market share, and after the deaths, their market share dropped to a mere

7%. Although recovery may have seemed rather impossible, under the leadership of former CEO James Burke, J&J swiftly responded. Under his leadership, the company used $100 million to recall 31 million Tylenol bottles and re-launched the product in just two months with tamper-proof packaging. Burke had not only saved the company's reputation but the imperatively Tylenol's brand as well. By the end of 1983, slightly more than a year after the incident, the brand's market share had returned to 35% (Knowledge@Wharton, 2012). Burke had displayed exemplary leadership on crisis management. He had reacted swiftly to the crisis and assured customers by adding the tamper-proof seals to their products. In fact, J&J produced the first industry-leading tamper-evident packaging and revolutionized the way over-the-counter medicines were packaged.

While J&J's CEO exemplified good crisis management, United Airlines' leadership failed to meet the same level of success when they faced their own set of crises in 2017. The first issue arose when the company barred two teenage girls from boarding their plane because a gate agent had deemed their leggings to be inappropriate. This sparked outrage on social media with many labeling the act sexist and intrusive. Nonetheless, the company defended itself and remained supportive of the gate agent's decision (Stack, 2017). Shortly after that, a video surfaced online showing a customer being beaten and dragged off a flight. This was because the company was substituting four crew members in exchange to passengers who were already seated. While three passengers accepted travel vouchers, no one else volunteered to give up their seat. Security personnel then forcefully removed a passenger, David Dao, from the flight. His injuries included a concussion, a broken nose, and two lost teeth. Instead of apologizing, CEO Oscar Munoz initially attempted to downplay the situation and shifted the blame to Dao and suggested that it was his behavior that caused the altercation. He did, however, apologize to the other passengers on the flight and not Dao. This response was spread all over social media, making things even worse for the company. A poll revealed that the percentage of consumers who thought United Airlines had a "bad" or "very bad" reputation had drastically increased from 7% in 2016 to 42% after the incident (Benoit, 2018). While there is no one "right" way or fixated template to deal with crises, it is of paramount importance that organization's leader can play a significant role in influencing the post-crisis outcome. While the Tylenol example highlights that an organization can always recover from a crisis with the presence of a good leader, the United Airlines example shows how a leader can, in contrary, make thing worse. A leader must act appropriately and in the best interests of the company when faced with a crisis.

The final example is the previous CEO of Marriott International, Arne Sorenson, who demonstrated great leadership in response to the COVID-19 pandemic. He forfeited his salary for the year, and the executives of the company also cut their salary by 50% to mitigate financial burdens imposed upon their employees (Gibbons, 2020). He also made a decision of donating the rooms of Marriott's hotels across a number of cities including New York, Chicago, Los Angeles, and Detroit to healthcare workers who then fought against COVID-19 in the front line and needed a room so as not to expose themselves with their family members (Hansen, 2020). Furthermore, Sorenson

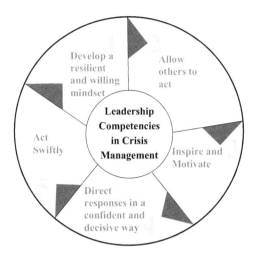

Figure 7.2 Leadership Competencies in Crisis Management Framework

sent a video message to the employees, customers, and shareholders, where he conveyed the negative impacts of COVID-19 that the Marriott International had to cope with in a sincere and authentic manner (Gallo, 2020). Despite that Marriott was one of the companies that was most severely impacted by the pandemic, then company CEO remained steadfast in committing himself to their employees and communities that are in a need of dire help. Although the company had to furlough many of their employees, it is still positively perceived by general public (Johnson, 2020).

Although every crisis varies and the organization's circumstances are different, there are key recommendations and strategic approaches that an organization's leader must undertake in order to overcome the challenges that they could potentially face. Figure 7.2 presents five core strategies from a leadership competencies dimension to deal with crisis management.

7.4 Strategy 1: Develop a Resilient and Winning Mindset

Leaders do not necessarily require a redefined response plan to successfully tackle a crisis (D'Auria and De Smet, 2020). Instead what they need is the (a) correct outlook and the right mindset (to see, appreciate the opportunities that lie within the challenges or setbacks), (b) behaviors (attitude in approaching tough situations; responding calmly and firmly; embracing team and collective acts), and (c) mindsets (growth mindset: learning and growing; open mindset – focusing on facts and thinking optimally; promotion mindset: attaining goals and outward mindset – lifting others (Ryan & Rajaram, 2021) that will prevent them from being defensive, complacent, or overreacting, rather that put them in a good state to look ahead. The first action is for the leader to acknowledge and recognize that the company is facing a crisis. This is easier to be said than done due to the normalcy bias that causes leaders to underestimate the possibility of a crisis occurring and the impact it may potentially cause. This may be especially challenging when the crisis does not occur suddenly but instead grows out of an accustomed circumstance. Hence, it is vital that a leader speedily foresee and identify a crisis as soon as possible. Once the crisis is recognized, only then can they begin to craft a response.

Research suggests that leaders' mindset is crucial in shaping followers' affective states and resilience under a crisis (Sommer, Howell, & Hadley, 2016); specifically, transformational leaders can elevate the optimism and confidence among the followers, as they are likely to adopt an outward mindset that inspires their followers with such qualities as charisma and intellectual stimulation. James and Wooten (2005) also stressed the value of leaders' mindsets amid a crisis. For example, they argued that leaders with an expansive mindset – which may be part of an open mindset discussed above – who take a big-picture approach should be able to identify opportunities embedded in a crisis and thereby leverage the crisis to their firms' advantages. This is because leaders with an expansive mindset can look at given crises from multiple angels and perspectives. A qualitative study about entrepreneurial business leaders also revealed three theoretical dimensions of leader mindset (Subramaniam & Shanker, 2020), which could inform the crisis leadership, given that both crisis leaders and entrepreneurs need to effectively manage uncertainty. These dimensions include people-oriented mindset, purpose-oriented mindset, and learning-oriented mindset. People-oriented mindset and learning-oriented mindset largely correspond to outward mindset and growth mindset, respectively. Crisis leaders must be equipped with a purpose-oriented mindset, as the emergence of crises could potentially limit leaders' attention and focus, resulting in short-sighted solutions, while forgoing long-term perspectives and goals. As pointed out by organizational researchers, it is critical for leaders to be patient when dealing with uncertain circumstances (Ashford, Sytch, & Greer, 2020). Evidence also emphasizes the value and significance of resilient leadership. Renjen (2020) provided a guide for leaders to build resilient organizations in response to the COVID-19 pandemic. Specifically, he listed five items: (a) design from the heart … and the head; (b) put the mission first; (c) aim for speed over elegance (i.e., taking necessary actions as immediately as possible); (d) own the narrative (i.e., communicating information with relevant stakeholders in a prompt, thorough manner); and (e) embrace the long view. These five leadership qualities are critical for organizations to not just respond to and recover from a given crisis such as COVID-19 but also to thrive. CEOs who have clear, long-term visions and purposes should be able to inspire their followers and persevere through a crisis.

7.5 Strategy 2: Allow Others to Act

Another strategy is to organize a network of teams to promote rapid problem solving and execution under high stress (D'Auria and De Smet, 2020), through the act of empowerment, heightening the trust level by enabling others to make decisions at various levels appropriately. Such accountability bestowed on team leaders improves their self-responsibility and reiterates the high level of trust to be placed on them. As a leader, you are unlikely to solve a crisis on your own or with just a small group of executives. Hence, it is vital to mobilize other employees to carry out responses outside of the usual operations and to adjust routine business activities. A network of teams comprises of a highly adaptable assembly of groups with a common purpose. In most cases, the network of teams includes an integrated nerve center covering four domains: workforce protection, supply-chain stabilization, customer engagement, and financial stress testing. No matter what the functional scope of the teams is, a leader should consistently encourage collaboration and transparency by distributing authority and sharing of information. A leader must also promote psychological safety so that ideas, questions, and concerns can be openly discussed without fear of repercussions.

Leaders' efforts in promoting empowerment and collaboration among employees as well as teams are critical in weathering crises. Brafford and Ryan (2020), revolving around the self-determination theory, argued that leaders can instill motivation in teams by focusing on the three kinds of basic human needs, namely relatedness, competence, and autonomy. For relatedness, leaders can invest some resources to building positive bonds with their followers to make it known that they are valued at work. To enhance a sense of employees' competence, leaders can provide constant feedback about their achievements and discuss their progress. Also, the need for autonomy would be satisfied when leaders do not micromanage employees but rather encourage self-initiation and proactivity. In doing so, employees become more intrinsically motivated and work more effectively during time of a crisis. Chima and Gutman (2020) proposed a new leadership style called Sapient Leadership, which helps to foster empowerment among employees and teams. This leadership style is focused on leader humility, authenticity, and openness and enhances employees' perceptions of trust and psychological safety. Sapient Leadership is argued to be effective in promoting continuous learning and growth of organizations during a crisis that is characterized by three-dimensional changes that are perpetual, pervasive, and exponential. Developing this new construct of leadership style, Chima and Gutman also emphasized the importance of leaders' role in promoting employee empowerment. Empirical research has also shown that team empowerment is predicted by the extent of organizational decentralization, and the positive association is weakened as the level of formalization increases (Hempel, Zhang, & Han, 2012). Though the research is not conducted specifically under the context of a crisis, the findings suggest that teams can be less empowered when leaders are too controlling and directive.

At the same time, it is important to build a network and connection between teams that are empowered to function in an adaptive and flexible manner during the time of a crisis. Specifically, McKinsey (Alexander, De Smet, Kleinman, & Mugayar-Baldocchi, 2020) proposed four steps for building a network of teams: (a) launching teams fast and building as you go; (b) getting out of the way but staying connected; (c) championing radical transparency and authenticity; and

(d) turbocharging self-organization. Empowered networks of teams would facilitate processing and exchanging information, devising new strategies, and implementing them, all of which are imperative aspects of crisis management.

7.6 Strategy 3: Inspire and Motivate

Several core elements of transformational leadership can be used to successfully tackle a crisis, one of which is inspirational motivation (Pillai, 2013). While enabling others to act is a preliminary step to taking ownership in dealing with a crisis, a leader who can inspire followers to act will be more effective. A crisis filled with overwhelming emotions and emerging changes can cause employees not able to see the end-goals, making them feel depressed and helpless. Thus, a transformational leader who can inspire confidence during dire times makes a huge positive impact in elevating the spirit and reassuring the direction set ahead. A leader can further motivate their employees by communicating their confidence in their employees' abilities to achieve goals. These leaders also help to suggest alternatives to the status quo and provide unique solutions to the problems faced.

Empirical evidence has also demonstrated that transformational leadership is effective, especially under the circumstances of organizational crises and adversities. Zhang, Jia, and Gu (2012) collected the data from medical workers from hospitals following the earthquake that struck China in 2008. Specifically, they reported that transformational leaders were effective in managing the crisis because they were capable of promoting the congruence between the leaders' and followers' values through inspirational motivation and vision. Furthermore, transformational leaders who are capable of controlling their own emotions and have developed high-quality relationships with their followers are more effective in facilitating the value congruence as well as leader effectiveness. Transformational leaders are also seen as "change agents" who could initiate important changes for organizations (Lee, 2014), which is critical during the time of crises when organizations might need to implement novel strategies and initiatives. Indeed, when employees need to undergo significant changes in their work conditions, transformational leaders provide social resources with their employees and enhance their quality of work life by increasing the employees' commitment to the changes (Kim, Im, & Shin, 2021). Taken together, the roles that transformational leaders would play in inspiring and motivating the followers are critical in helping them stay resilient against crises.

Given the practical value and utility of transformational leadership in helping navigate followers through organizational crises, it is vital to give due consideration to the types of behaviors transformational leaders adopt and how organizations can foster transformational leaders. For example, leaders can focus on developing and communicating powerful narratives about the future to employees (Anthony & Schwartz, 2017). In order to reinforce the visions that organizations have, leaders need to repeatedly share what the purposes of making changes are and how the changes would aid the organizations to cope with a given crisis that they are currently facing through their words and messages. Furthermore, such messages should be tailored to individual divisions and work groups (for example, call center employees and line workers might be inspired in different ways). Also, Lancefield and Rangen (2021) provided a useful piece of advice about the behavior of transformational leaders, using Xavier Rolet, who made transformation in London Stock Exchange, as an example. They emphasized the importance of *working the edges of the organization*. Specifically, organizational leaders must not stay in the "center" but try to listen to and gain inputs from the "edges" – customers, partners, and employees – to understand their issues and challenges that need to be addressed. For example, Lancefield and Rangen suggested that leaders could initiate company-wide community to pick up the voice from the front-line employees and customers. Such leaders' efforts should not only motivate and inspire employees to provide their own opinions but also help organizations respond to a given crisis more flexibly and effectively by incorporating diverse viewpoints and opinions.

7.7 Strategy 4: Direct Responses in a Confident and Decisive Way

Leaders must provide clear and precise direction for employees to work towards resolving a crisis from their respective roles and responsibilities. Weak and non-decisive instructions from a leader will potentially have employees doubt the business strategies and processes, where the process of devising solutions will become convoluted. The ability to remain calm and deal with a crisis in a systematic yet decisive manner requires a competent leader with essential skills and confidence (Yukl & Gardner, 2019). A leader must articulate and provide employees clear directions and guidance on crisis response while convincing employees of the effectiveness of their decisions. A leader must be open and forward looking without being defensive and judgmental in hearing out the perspectives and feedback of the subordinates that enables to resonate well with the ground and respond appropriately.

During times of crisis, it is crucial for leaders to provide clear visions and engage in transparent decision-making processes by incorporating followers' inputs. Authentic leaders are capable of analyzing relevant data and information objectively and share information and their own emotions in an open but appropriate manner (Avolio, Walumbwa, & Weber, 2009). Such characteristics of authentic leaders help promote the followers' positive emotions and trust in leaders, while reducing negative emotions, during the time when an organization is going through changes (Agote, Aramburu, & Lines, 2016). Holtom, Edmondson, and Niu (2020) emphasized the importance of leaders' efforts in communication with followers under the COVID-19 pandemic because the way leaders convey information matters to employees' commitment and motivation. Also, taking Jacinda Ardern, New Zealand Prime Minister, as an example who navigated the country through the challenging times during the COVID-19 pandemic, Kerrissey and Edmondson (2020) indicated that the directions and messages need to be communicated in a clear, honest, and compassionate way. Instead of downplaying the threat of the pandemic, Ardern communicated the country's situation in a transparent manner to the people and provided explicit guidelines about what to do during the critical time. Such communication style would likely enhance followers' trust in the leaders and inspire their spontaneous actions to resolve the crisis.

Knight (2020) also provided several suggestions when it comes to communication with followers. For example, it is important to reflect upon and think from employees' perspectives instead of leaders' own viewpoints. When failing to fully take into account what employees are concerned and anxious about during a crisis, leaders' messages can be seen less effective and might be received less positively. Also, leaders must be open and transparent and need to acknowledge honestly what they do not know. If leaders try to sugarcoat a current reality or hide some negative information from employees, the employees' trust in the leaders would likely decline (Edmondson, 2020). Hiding bad news does more harm than good, and instead, leaders must speak up early and quickly start engaging in problem solving. With respect to this point, Sundheim (2020) provided an example about how leaders could act upfront in front of employees. The CEO of Gravity Payments, Dan Price, was facing a significant reduction in revenue due to the pandemic and he was left no choice but to fire the employees to avoid bankruptcy. However, he decided to have meetings with a group of employees, and the company ended up reducing employees' salaries instead of laying them off. Also, the company leaders privately consulted with staff members to gain their input on how much reduction they could accept instead of applying a certain proportion of reduction in pay to everyone. Taken together, organizational leaders, when facing crises, need to act as authentically as possible and transparently communicating current situations with their key stakeholders (Desyatnikov, 2020).

7.8 Strategy 5: Act Swiftly

When a crisis occurs, leaders must act speedily to reassure the organization's stakeholders. Speed and time become a leader's adversary during a crisis (Garcia, 2006). Often times, leaders are late to understand that business-as-usual practices must be suspended. Crisis management professionals often speak of the Golden Hour of crisis response which relates to the observation that incremental delays in responding to a crisis lead to greater than incremental impact on the outcome. Therefore, it is not only essential that a leader delivers a well thought through and articulated response but also that the response is to be delivered in a speedily manner.

If leaders fail to act promptly when a crisis occurs, their organizations will likely experience a serious downfall and setback in firm performance and effectiveness. Thus, during times of crisis, leaders often need to prioritize speed over precision when making decisions and taking actions accordingly (Nichols, Hayden, &

Trendler, 2020). During a crisis, leaders must determine priorities and make trade-offs for effective decision-making processes. When organizational leaders try to seek perfect solutions to a given situation, organizations would likely have to slow down their decision-making processes (Hougaard & Carter, 2020). Also, severe punishments imposed upon mistakes and missteps can restrict employees' proactivity in response to a crisis, so it is necessary for leaders to embrace followers' actions even if they did not yield the best outcomes (Nichols et al., 2020). Additionally, Schakel and Wolbers (2021) argued that sensitive situational awareness would be a critical factor for leaders for decision making and fast responses. Such situational awareness can be learned from an accumulation of past experiences but also can be fostered through mental simulation of a crisis event. Other key factors include accurately assessing the situation, gathering relevant information and input, formulating concrete action plans, and monitoring the outcomes of employees' actions (Bhiman-prommachak, 2020). In order to promote speedy organizational actions, leaders' sense-making practices of scrutinizing and unpacking situations are essential, as a crisis often involves high degrees of ambiguity and uncertainty (Faraj & Xiao, 2006; Fortunato, Gigliotti, & Ruben, 2018). Furthermore, coordination among employees needs to be fostered to improve the speed of organizational responses, since when employees' actions are aligned and directed to common goals, organizations would be able to respond to the crisis in a prompt manner (Schakel & Wolbers, 2021).

There are specific recommendations for improving the speed of organizational responses to a crisis. For example, Forster and Heinzel (2021) reported that countries where their politicians possessed a technocratic mentality (operationalized as having a PhD) were able to react to the COVID-19 in a prompt manner in the beginning of the pandemic. Also, Hougaard and Carter (2020) described three challenges that could potentially hinder organizational responses and how to overcome them. First, leaders must fight against distractions and sustain their mental agility in shifting between focus and awareness, since leaders must need to be able to direct their attention to specific issues while still maintaining a big-picture thinking. Second, leaders are required to overcome their ego. When leaders are fixated on their own styles and methods that worked effectively in the past, they would likely fail to act in an agile manner. Hougaard and Carter proposed that being selfless is one way to combat our challenge of ego – in other words, it is important to inspire leaders to serve the mission of their organizations without being too concerned about their own reputation and fame. Lastly, empathy can be a hindrance for leaders to take swift actions, especially when the actions involve difficult decisions that could hurt employees' feelings (for example, layoff, salary deduction). Instead of empathy, leaders should engage in compassion as it is not just about understanding but involves an intent and conduct of help. Adopting a compassionate mindset instead of empathetic one would be a vital strategy for leaders to provide comfort to their employees during a crisis while not compromising the speed of their actions.

In a nutshell, this chapter discusses and explains how crises must be dealt with in an effective and efficient manner to protect the longevity of an organization and have its business deliverables sustained. Slow response times or a lack of measures in place could significantly reduce a company's survivability. A leader must be agile in responding to deal with crisis effectively, better still to turn the situation to your favor just like Johnson and Johnson did with Tylenol. While acknowledging the importance of agility, it is essential to keep yourself grounded, understand the nuances explicitly, and think thoroughly before responding. While a quick response is good, it may not always be right, with the mantra of never to tackle a crisis ill-equipped. Leaders should always learn from the past successes but more so on failures, for example, the unsuccessful business strategies, operational processes, and what went wrong in leading people during a crisis. While crises are never 100% alike, certain common and familiar patterns may emerge. By reflecting on past events, a leader learns and enhances the ability to create, articulate, and provide a much more superior response. This is portrayed by leaders at 3M, who have learnt from the SARs outbreak and by leveraging on those experiences have successfully managed their business in current conditions. Dealing and overcoming a crisis is often a collaborative effort, although a good crisis leader gets others to act and ensures the welfare, mental well-being, and health of their employees. They communicate clearly and assertively, and work effectively with employees to reach a common goal. They protect the interest of the organization, rather than merely themselves.

References

Agote, L., Aramburu, N., & Lines, R. (2016). Authentic leadership perception, trust in the leader, and followers' emotions in organizational change processes. *The Journal of Applied Behavioral Science*, *52*(1), 35–63. https://doi.org/10.1177/0021886315617531

Alexander, A., De Smet, A., Kleinman, S., & Mugayar-Baldocchi, M. (2020, April 8). To weather a crisis, build a network of teams. *McKinsey & Company*.

Anthony, S. D., & Schwartz, E. I. (2017, May 8). What the best transformational leaders do. *Harvard Business Review*.

Ashford, S. J., Sytch, M., & Greer, L. L. (2020, August 20). 5 ways a crisis can help you cultivate a growth mindset. *Harvard Business Review*.

Avolio, B. J., Walumbwa, F. O., & Weber, T. J. (2009). Leadership: Current theories, research, and future directions. *Annual Review of Psychology*, *60*, 421–449.

Bateman, T.S & Konopaske, R. (2021). Management, Leading and Collaborating in a Competitive World, Global Edition, 14/E.

Bartik, A. W., Bertrand, M., Cullen, Z., Glaeser, E. L., Luca, M., & Stanton, C. (2020). The impact of COVID-19 on small business outcomes and expectations. *Proceedings of the National Academy of Sciences*, *117*(30), 17656–17666.

Benoit, W. (2018). Crisis and image repair at United Airlines: Fly the unfriendly skies. *Journal of International Crisis and Risk Communication Research*, *1*(1), 11–26.

Bhimanprommachak, V. (2020, July 20). Leading your team through a crisis. *Harvard Business Publishing*. https://www.harvardbusiness.org/leading-your-team-through-a-crisis/

Brafford, A. M., & Ryan, R. M. (2020, September 25). 3 ways to motivate your team through an extended crisis. *Harvard Business Review*.

Chima, A., & Gutman, R. (2020, October 29). What it takes to lead through an era of exponential change. *Harvard Business Review.*

D'Auria, G., & De Smet, A. (2020, March 16). Leadership in a crisis: Responding to the coronavirus outbreak and future challenges. *McKinsey & Company.*

Desyatnikov, R. (2020, July 17). Management in crisis: The best leadership style to adopt in times of crisis. *Forbes.* https://www.forbes.com/sites/forbestechcouncil/2020/07/17/management-in-crisis-the-best-leadership-style-to-adopt-in-times-of-crisis/?sh=4e7132f7cb4a

DuBrin, A. J. (2013). *Handbook of research on crisis leadership in organizations.* Edward Elgar Publishing.

Edmondson, A. C. (2020, March 6). Don't hide bad news in times of crisis. *Harvard Business Review.*

Faraj, S., & Xiao, Y. (2006). Coordination in fast-response organizations. *Management Science, 52*(8), 1155–1169. https://doi.org/10.1287/mnsc.1060.0526

Fener, T., & Cevik, T. (2015). Leadership in crisis management: Separation of leadership and executive concepts. *Procedia Economics and Finance, 26,* 695–701.

Forster, T., & Heinzel, M. (2021). Reacting, fast and slow: How world leaders shaped government responses to the COVID-19 pandemic. *Journal of European Public Policy, 28*(8), 1299–1320.

Fortunato, J. A., Gigliotti, R. A., & Ruben, B. D. (2018). Analysing the dynamics of crisis leadership in higher education: A study of racial incidents at the University of Missouri. *Journal of Contingencies and Crisis Management, 26*(4), 510–518.

Gallo, C. (2020, March 21). Marriott's CEO demonstrates truly authentic leadership in a remarkably emotional video. *Forbes.* https://www.forbes.com/sites/carminegallo/2020/03/21/marriotts-ceo-demonstrates-truly-authentic-leadership-in-a-remarkably-emotional-video/?sh=5ce33de41654

Garcia, H. F. (2006). Effective leadership response to crisis. *Strategy & Leadership, 34*(1), 4–10.

Gibbons, S. (2020, April 30). 3 things you can learn from Marriott about taking care of employees. *Forbes.* https://www.forbes.com/sites/serenitygibbons/2020/04/30/3-things-you-can-learn-from-marriott-about-taking-care-of-employees/?sh=4d130f-972bca

Gilchrist, K. (2020, August 23). *How big businesses in Singapore are managing the challenges of coronavirus.* CNBC.

Hansen, D. (2020, April 9). Marriott to provide rooms to medical workers battling the coronavirus crisis. *Washington Business Journal.* https://www.bizjournals.com/washington/news/2020/04/09/marriott-to-provide-rooms-to-medical-workers.html

Hempel, P. S., Zhang, Z.-X., & Han, Y. (2012). Team empowerment and the organizational context: Decentralization and the contrasting effects of formalization. *Journal of Management, 38*(2), 475–501.

Holtom, B., Edmondson, A. C., & Niu, D. (2020, July 9). 5 tips for communicating with employees during a crisis. *Harvard Business Review.*

Hougaard, R., & Carter, J. (2020, April 16). Perfectionism will slow you down in a crisis. *Harvard Business Review.*

James, E. H., & Wooten, L. P. (2005). Leadership as (Un)usual: How to display competence in times of crisis. *Organizational Dynamics, 34*(2), 141–152.

James, E. H., Wooten, L. P., & Dushek, K. (2011). Crisis management: Informing a new leadership research agenda. *Academy of Management Annals, 5*(1), 455–493. https://doi.org/10.5465/19416520.2011.589594

Johnson, S. K. (2020, May 14). How CEOs can lead selflessly through a crisis. *Harvard Business Review*.

Kerrissey, M. J., & Edmondson, A. C. (2020, April 13). What good leadership looks like during this pandemic. *Harvard Business Review*.

Kim, H., Im, J., & Shin, Y. H. (2021). The impact of transformational leadership and commitment to change on restaurant employees' quality of work life during a crisis. *Journal of Hospitality and Tourism Management, 48*, 322–330. https://doi.org/10.1016/j.jhtm.2021.07.010

Knight, R. (2020, April 20). How to talk to your team when the future is uncertain. *Harvard Business Review*.

Knowledge@Wharton. (2012, October 2). *Tylenol and the legacy of J&J's James Burke.*

Lancefield, D., & Rangen, C. (2021, May 5). 4 actions transformational leaders take. *Harvard Business Review*.

Lee, M. (2014). Transformational leadership: Is it time for a recall? *International Journal of Management and Applied Research, 1*(1), 18–29.

Nichols, C., Hayden, S. C., & Trendler, C. (2020, April 2). 4 behaviors that help leaders manage a crisis. *Harvard Business Review*.

Petriglieri, G. (2020). The psychology behind effective crisis leadership. *Harvard Business Review*.

Pillai, R. (2013). Transformational leadership for crisis management. In A. J. DuBrian (Ed.) *Handbook of Research on Crisis Leadership in Organizations* (pp. 47–66). Edward Elgar Publishing.

Rajaram, K. (2021, June). *Leadership in crisis management.* Expert Panelist and Invited Keynote Speaker, Webinar, Asia Pacific Think Tank Summit.

Renjen, P. (2020, March 16). The heart of resilient leadership: Responding to COVID-19: A guide for senior executives. *Deloitte Insights*.

Ryan, G., & Rajaram, K. (2021, May 12). *Elevate leaders' operating systems to navigate disruptive conditions.* Association of Talent Development.

Sommer, S. A., Howell, J. M., & Hadley, C. N. (2016). Keeping positive and building strength: The role of affect and team leadership in developing resilience during an organizational crisis. *Group & Organization Management, 41*(2), 172–202.

Subramaniam, R., & Shankar, R. K. (2020). Three mindsets of entrepreneurial leaders. *The Journal of Entrepreneurship, 29*(1), 7–37. https://doi.org/10.1177/0971355719893498

Schakel, J. K., & Wolbers, J. (2021). To the edge and beyond: How fast-response organizations adapt in rapidly changing crisis situations. *Human Relations, 74*(3), 405–436. https://doi.org/10.1177/0018726719893450

Stack, L. (2017, March 26). After barring girls for leggings, United Airlines defends decision. *The New York Times*.

Sundheim, D. (2020, April 23). When crisis strikes, lead with humanity. *Harvard Business Review*.

Waldman, D. A., Ramirez, G. G., House, R. J., & Puranam, P. (2001). Does leadership matter? CEO leadership attributes and profitability under conditions of perceived environmental uncertainty. *Academy of Management Journal, 44*(1), 134–143.

Wooten, L. P., & James, E. H. (2008). Linking crisis management and leadership competencies: The role of human resource development. *Advances in Developing Human Resources, 10*(3), 352–379.

Yukl, G. A., & Gardner, W. L. (2019). *Leadership in organizations* (9th ed.). Pearson.

Zhang, Z., Jia, M., & Gu, L. (2012). Transformational leadership in crisis situations: Evidence from the People's Republic of China. *International Journal of Human Resource Management, 23*(19), 4085–4109. https://doi.org/10.1080/09585192.2011.639027.

Chapter 8

Sustainability and Agility in Navigating an Unprecedented Phase

> Companies should be able to sense the pulse of its customers' and stakeholders' changing needs and the external rapidly evolving changes to response and act speedily. The fortitude of a company could be seen in its ability to unlearn and relearn quickly to adapt and re-align its business processes, strategies, and models to operate in the most challenging terrains.

Kumaran Rajaram, PhD

8.1 Introduction

Today's corporate environments are continuously evolving due to rapid advancements in technology, new innovations, more competitors emerging, changes in consumer dynamics, and unpredicted events or occurrences. As such, organizations are facing much greater challenges to survive and thrive in this ever-complex climate and environment. Boston Consulting Group (2019) reported that companies' life spans are shrinking, where only 44% of industry leaders today have held their positions for at least five years. This is a decrease from 77% 50 years ago. Furthermore,

DOI: 10.4324/9781003286288-11

one out of three public companies will no longer exist in their current form over the next five years.

Organizations are ever more likely to face crises. While some crises may cause minor roadblocks, others might cause disruption on an unprecedented level. For instance, the 2008 global financial crisis and the COVID-19 pandemic impacted the entire world's economy resulting in recessions and job losses in many nations globally. Even companies that have a strong standing can lose their footing. Companies such as Lehman Brothers, Enron, and Arthur Anderson were supposedly performing companies until their abrupt collapse shocked many. For organizations to survive such episodes, sustainability and agility when facing change are two crucial interlinking factors that come into play.

8.2 Organizations: Traversing and Sustaining in an Unprecedented Phase

The demise of many organizations can be attributed to reluctance in engaging in organizational change and learning (Khan, 2015). Organizational longevity, or the continued existence of an organization even after the founding members leave, is one aspect that can categorize the sustainability of an organization. For an organization to sustain itself, it must be stable, continuous, and long-lived. For organizations to survive an unpredictable dynamic business climate, it is crucial that they invest in attaining business success in the area of managerial processes such as innovation and technology process systems, project management, communication systems, management of change, and resource management (Galadanchi & Bakar, 2018).

To sustain itself, an organization must be agile in responding to changes in the environment. Agility in the 21st century is no longer a choice but a necessity (Harraf, Wanasika, Tate, & Talbott, 2015). Constant evolving changes in the environment require speedy responsiveness and adaptability. The size and market can blind and hinder an organization's ability to detect and speedily respond to changes which could have improved its competitiveness. Agility, as a measure of responsiveness, can be grouped into two parts: flexibility and adaptability. Anticipated responses to an external stimulus are indicative of an organization's overall flexibility while the responses they make in relation to environmental stimuli are a measure of their adaptability. However, there is a tradeoff between agility and efficiency, where many organizations face a challenge of balancing an approach that favors scale efficiency, stability, and long-term focus, with another that focuses on agility, speed, and rapid response (Prats, Siota, Gillespie, & Singleton, 2018).

One important antecedent of agility is organizational learning culture. Cetindamar, Katic, Burdon, and Gunsel (2021) viewed agility as part of dynamic capability that enables organizations to re-configure and re-structure their resources to thrive in changing environments. They further argued that organizations with a strong learning culture should be able to identify and handle potential issues and to effectively learn from the experience. Employees embedded in the organization with a learning culture should be able to acquire new information and integrate it with existing knowledge base, which helps their organization better adapt to external changes. Furthermore, they found that organization's big data capability strengthened the positive effect of organizational learning culture on organizational agility. In other words, building a learning culture in the organization should be particularly important during a crisis when organizations are expected to act and make changes swiftly.

De Smet, Gagnon, and Mygatt (2021) have proposed nine key pointers for organization to become future-ready and remain sustainable in the face of a crisis. They include the following: (a) take a stance on purpose; (b) sharpen your value agenda; (c) use culture as your 'secret sauce'; (d) radically flatten structure; (e) turbocharge decision making; (f) treat talent as scarcer than capital; (g) adopt an ecosystem view; (h) build data-rich tech platforms; and (i) accelerate learning as an organization. Cetindamar et al. (2021), De Smet et al. also stressed the importance of learning as a key driver for an organization to be better prepared for potential crises. Obviously, employees cannot adopt a new mindset in a single day and fostering a learning culture after a large-scale crisis occurs is too late to effectively handle the situation. Thus, organizations should consider learning as one of the most crucial imperatives where organizations need to continuously invest. Also, researchers have argued that organizational sustainability can derive from resilience, which refers to "a firm's capability to survive, adapt and grow in a dynamic and uncertain environment" (Rai, Rai, & Singh, 2021). Resilient organizations should be able to monitor their external environments for any changes and to adapt to them in an agile manner. They tend to be prepared for potential crises, adaptable in turbulent business environments, collaborative and fostering learning and sharing information within the organization, trustworthy, and responsible (Renjen, 2021). According to Rai and colleagues (2021), there are three important aspects with regard to resilience, namely, *crisis anticipation* that entails organization's capability to foresee any potential risks in the future, *organizational robustness* that is concerned with organization's capability of hedging, minimizing, and handling the risks, and *organization's recoverability* or the capability of reconfiguring a portfolio of organizational resources so that organizations can restore their previous states or even bounce back following the occurrence of the crisis. On top of resilience, Bella, Barboza, Quelhas, Meiriño, and França (2021) highlighted the value of spirituality – "the recognition that employees have an inner life that nourishes and is nurtured by meaningful work that takes place in the context of the community" (Ashmos & Duchon, 2000) – for organization and its employees to remain sustainable even amid the unprecedented time of a crisis. According to the authors, spirituality has intrapersonal, interpersonal, and institutional aspects, and each corresponds to inner life, purpose at work, and sense of community, respectively. Even if top management champions the value of agility in the organization during the crisis, the organization would be likely to fail to resonate with their employees who do not identify with the organization. As such, it is crucial to foster shared values and a sense of commitment among employees so that the organization could reduce its risk of being vulnerable when a crisis occurs.

8.3 Case Studies: Organizational Agility and Sustainability in Crisis

Alibaba is a good example that exemplifies of how agility contributes to organizational sustainability, especially during turbulent times. In 2003, Alibaba was still a relatively small enterprise and had only turned its first annual profit the year prior. That same year, the SARS pandemic severely impacted China's economy including Alibaba's business. Manufacturers were affected by factory closures while retail sales dropped significantly. To make things worse for Alibaba, in May 2003, an employee contracted SARS and the company was forced to quarantine all its staff in their homes. It had seemed like the pandemic had struck the company at the worst possible time as the company had been preparing to launch Taobao, an online marketplace. However, the company managed to turn the situation around. Jack Ma, one of the founders and former Chief Executive at Alibaba, sent his workers back home to prevent the spread of the disease within the company (Huddleston Jr., 2020). Workers took their computers back home to ensure that their e-commerce platform would remain operating, and the company's hotline was redirected to staff's home phone lines during the quarantine. At the same time, a team of executives and developers stayed in Ma's apartment to finish building the Taobao website. As a result, the site was released on time. Furthermore, during this period, businesses and consumers were becoming more inclined to buy and sell online due to fears of contracting the disease. This benefitted Alibaba, making it one of the leading online marketplaces in the country.

A more recent example of a company typifying agility would be AirAsia. With the COVID-19 pandemic forcing borders to close and national lockdowns around the globe, organizations operating in the airline industry have suffered immensely as travel becomes restricted for most consumers. Tony Fernandes, founder of AirAsia Group, needed to respond quickly to ensure that the business remains afloat in such a volatile situation. As such, AirAsia launched a food delivery service, competing with companies such as Grab, FoodPanda, and Deliveroo. He also quickly embraced mental health services and other support systems for AirAsia staff (Pesek, 2021). Another initiative implemented by AirAsia is to digitally transform its supply chain (AirAsia, 2020). The company, through its partnership with AC2 Group, installed Blue Yonder's (an American software company) warehouse management solution to achieve enhanced supply chain capabilities and operational agility. The implementation of a digital supply chain enables greater efficiency by not only improving the customer experiences of booking but also helping the company tailor their products to passenger preferences on specific flights. As can be seen from this partnership, AirAsia places great importance on digitalization to thrive in the COVID-19 pandemic. Indeed, AirAsia also committed themselves to digital transformation and becoming more data-driven (Kaur, 2021) so that it can sustain its agility and take a holistic approach towards such an unprecedented crisis. AirAsia launched the airline's official online ticketing platform called airasia.com. They also developed an application that gives an experience of whole services being offered by AirAsia called "super app" which allows customers to not only book flights and hotels but also order food and groceries. As such, AirAsia's efforts in transforming themselves to be a digital airline epitomizes the case concerning how organizations can remain unwavering amid large-scale crises.

John Deere, a farm equipment company with their headquarter in the United States (US), has also demonstrated its agility in the midst of the global challenges of the COVID-19 pandemic. Having adopted the Agile operation model (Tobenkin, 2021), they were able to adapt to the crisis quickly (Jayaram, 2020). For example, they supported over 21,000 employees to transit to remote work within just two weeks. Furthermore, they could quickly respond to customers' needs for alternatives to payment options and process over 45 times the number of customer payment modifications in the United States and Canada in 2020 compared to a typical year. Their investment in technology and digitalization to achieve organizational agility helped them support their customers during the pandemic as well, and the company was able to achieve dramatic growth in net sales and revenue despite the global crisis (Tobenkin, 2021). Their focus on digitalization and technology has also provided them a unique competitive edge in the industry, as epitomized by their novel integration of AI and computer vision into their machinery, so that they could provide service bundles for precision agriculture; this technological innovation allows farmers to monitor operations while allowing real-time adjustment of machinery, and other organizations follow in John Deere's footstep (Gurumurthy, Nanda, & Schatsky, 2021). Having invested in technological competence has enabled the company to successfully survive the detrimental impacts of the COVID-19 pandemic.

From the above illustrations, we can conclude that agility in the digital era is crucial for an organization's sustainability, productivity, survivability, and growth. The following recommended strategies, presented in Figure 8.1 advocates that organizations must embrace for agility towards digitalization and technological change.

8.4 Strategy 1: Re-evaluate Human Resources

Organizations need to strategize to plan and execute successfully by being agile to navigate through unprecedented times. One strategy is to ensure the human resources function is responsive to evolving changes in the culture and work style of the organization. ING Group is an example that resembles the notion of building agility through HR (Gothelf, 2017). ING understood well that an agile Human Resource enables the right people to be put in place to practice and refine new processes. To do this, they made every employee at its headquarters, which comprised

SUSTAINABILITY AND AGILITY IN NAVIGATING AN
UNPRECEDENTED
PHASE FRAMEWORK

Figure 8.1 Digitalization and Technological Change Framework

of nearly 3,500 people, to be re-interviewed for their jobs. This resulted in 40% of their employees being shifted to new positions or parted ways with the company. While many employees had highly relevant skill sets, not all had the mindset that the organization needed for success. Their human resource team had to play a key role in understanding the appropriate mindsets required and match the employees who had those types of mindsets, where they have to decide of who could be potentially trained, and who had to be let go. To work through unstable and unpredictable times, organizations must have their leaders at various levels and employees trained and equipped with the skills to overcome the obstacles. Gothelf (2017) elaborates two activities which Human Resources can conduct to help an organization become more agile. Firstly, they should engage the varying clusters of teams based on their roles and job functions. During these ground visits, human resource team should facilitate open and honest talk to comprehend the likes and dislikes of their jobs, the traits they desire their colleagues to have, and other job performance related aspects. These engagements enable them to have a good sense of the ground and the array of qualities and essentials the organization requires to support agile working. Aside from this, another strategy is to conduct human resource retrospectives which is a biweekly meeting with a team involved in a particular project or initiative to review how things have evolved since the last retrospective. These involvements and engagements help highlight and evaluate the impact of progressive changes over a short period of time.

Organizational agility is fundamentally achieved by the people working in the organization, and therefore, organizations need to focus on their resources and investments into human resources management to foster employees who can think and act in an agile and transformational manner. Without an in-depth involvement of human resources, efforts in building organizational agility will not bear fruits. Human resources will be significant in several ways (Goldberg & Kramer, 2020). For instance, organizations might implement an agile transformation by setting up a team being dedicated to developing a plan and strategy to promote and scale agile practices to new business units. However, failing to include human resources will make it difficult for the team to engage in the agile transformation, since the transformation often involves changes in reporting lines and other personnel-related decisions. Engaging human resources is thus critical to smooth and effective workforce planning that is necessary for promoting the initiatives concerning agile transformation. Deloitte (n.d.-a) coined a term *Exponential HR* whereby human resources depart from traditional way of thinking and pointed out the importance of reimagining the work of human resources. In particular, they emphasized that human resources need to be adaptable, agile, architecting, and augmented. Achieving these characteristics would demand human resources to fundamentally restructure and rethink their current roles and practices. Building a data-driven mindset within human resources is one of such initiatives that would enhance agility and adaptability. Also, when Deloitte designed a new way of performance management, they prioritized speed over perfection. Specifically, they adopted a trial-and-error approach whereby they develop and experiment prototypes and improve them through gathering lots of feedback (Mazor, 2020). To enhance organizational agility, it is valuable to start from human resources and transform HR team to become also agile and capable of making quick actions.

Gothelf (2014) also described how the human resource team can contribute to building organizational agility. Traditionally, the human resource team hires individuals to fill a gap in a discipline-specific silo and to simply meet quotas. However, such approach does not build organizational agility. Instead, the human resource team needs to consider hiring non-conformists with an entrepreneurial mindset or the candidates who are creative, collaborative, and inquisitive. To this end, the hiring process and procedure might have to be fundamentally redesigned and restructured (for example, recruiting practices, interview processes, and so on). Gothelf (2014) further argued that financial compensation may not necessarily serve as a strong motivator to such individuals with an entrepreneurial mindset. It is thus important for the human resource team to re-consider their incentive packages to hire and retain these individuals who are likely to play a key role in promoting organizational agility.

8.5 Strategy 2: Develop an Agile Culture

One of the most vital elements for an organization to be agile is achieved through its people. By creating an environment within the organization that promotes well-defined values, behaviors, and practices that enable agility, the employees of the organization are more likely to be more adaptive, flexible, innovative, and resilient in times of uncertainty and change. A business must ensure there is congruence in their arti-facts, espoused values, and underlying assumptions to shape a culture that exemplifies agility (Agile Business Consortium, 2017). An agile culture is contextual as behaviors and appropriateness of certain practices may be influenced by different cultural norms across the globe. Hence, in the process of shaping an organization's culture to be agile, the suitability and appropriateness of the culture must be examined first.

Aghina et al. (2018) maintained that an agile culture is centered around people in the organization. In an agile organizational culture, people are empowered and encouraged to create values in a collaborative manner. Leadership plays a key role in fostering such a culture, and therefore, organizations need to invest in fostering leaders who can inspire employees to act in an agile manner and build entrepreneur-ship and relevant skills which are conducive to organizational agility. Aghina et al. (2018) further argued that people in agile organizational culture are more likely to take ownership of the goals and performance in their teams and organization and proactively identify and leverage novel opportunities to develop new services and initiatives – leaders' roles are to continue to empower employees to act this way and sustain such entrepreneurial mindset and drive among employees. To foster an agile culture, leaders should make consistent efforts in making the culture more personal to each employee (Jurisic, Lurie, Risch, & Salo, 2020). Specifically, leaders can ask their employees to define what agile culture and mindset are to them and what spe-cific actions they could take in line with their definitions. This way, employees do not only develop a deeper understanding of the meaning of the agile organizational culture but also come up with an action plan to work in an agile way.

Deloitte is known for its *experiment-hungry* culture, which fosters organizational agility (O'Farrell, 2017). Organizations can foster such a culture by specifying and defining a set of behaviors for employees so that they can continuously engage in the behaviors in their daily work routines and projects. Specifically, O'Farrell (2017) proposed three pointers to promote an experiment-hungry culture: (a) encouraging employees to adopt a 'test & learn' approach; (b) encouraging risk-taking attitudes and behaviors and not severely punishing those who made mistakes out of the inten-tion of being agile and developing innovations; and (c) granting a high level of autonomy while ensuring high alignment among employees. These strategies help organizations empower their employees to take swift actions, which in turn translate into an agile organizational culture.

8.6 Strategy 3: Marketing Strategies and Outreach to Be Relevant

Consumers today have much shorter attention spans especially due to the over-whelming amount of information made available to them due to the Internet and other media forms. By releasing outdated advertisements or targeting the wrong demographic clusters, an organization could see less sales of their products and services which will ultimately result in lowered competitiveness and lost market share. Hence, the sustainability of an organization relies on, to an extent, the agility of its marketing function. Companies that take long to create, redesign, and approve marketing campaigns might have their deliverables irrelevance by the time it is launched (Edelman, Heller, & Spittaels, 2016). Digital technology enables marketing teams to meet their consumers' needs in a more innovative and effective manner. As a result, organizations need to be much more agile and responsive to take leverage and advantage of the opportunities presented by digital technologies. This means using data and analytics to continuously look out for potential leads or solutions to problems real time. An organization must also test and evaluate results of the campaigns speedily. To do so, the organization must have a clear idea of what they want to accomplish with their marketing strategies as well as have the essential data and infrastructure in place. An agile marketing team enables an organization to maintain connectivity and relevance with consumers who are increasingly exposed to wide range of marketing campaigns.

Based on an in-depth qualitative study with semi-structured interviews, Hagen, Zucchella, and Ghauri (2019) also argued that the role being played by marketing is crucial in increasing two dimensions of firms' strategic agility: flexibility and selective responsiveness. Specifically, marketing can contribute to agility in four different ways. First, through sustaining communication and interactions with key customers and partners for refinement of current products and development of new ones, marketing can improve *selective customer/partner intimacy and intensity for market sensing*. Second, through constantly addressing customer feedback to improve current products and having key customers and partners involved in the process of co-creation, marketing can engage *selective experimentation and testing for innovation and business development*. Marketing can also enhance strategic agility through *coordination and harmonization of multiple stakeholders and resources* or choosing right partners who are appropriate and relevant to the business and mobilizing the resources lacking in or complementary to the firms. Finally, *creative management and extension of resources* are critical pathways for firms to become agile. Examples concerning this theme includes identifying new ways to organize and leverage firms' resources or promoting flat hierarchy within the firms. Similar themes emerged in Moi and Cabiddu (2021). Their model called the four-stage maturity framework for the development of an agile marketing capability is grounded in four dimensions: customer-oriented responsiveness, high flexibility, human collaboration, and quick and continuous improvement. Thus, marketing needs to be highly flexible and learning oriented in order to add values to firms' strategic agility. Deloitte provided an example concerning how marketing departments can work on enhancing organizational agility (O'Brien, Main, Kounkel, & Stephan, 2019). The method is *adopting newsroom-style operation* which involves bringing different teams come together to enhance cross-functionality and proximity. Taco Bell restructured their teams that used to operate separately and had them work together, enhancing operational efficiency (for example, reduced lead time, quicker decision making). Also, marketing departments can be more agile by adopting new technology. Artificial Intelligence (AI) is one such example. The adoption of AI can be about either task automation or machine learning, and it can be either isolated from or integrated into other platforms, consisting of four ways of implementing AI in marketing business (Davenport, Guha, & Grewal, 2021): stand-alone task automation application (for example, basic consumer service chatbots), stand-alone machine-learning application (for example, Olay skin advisor – an online platform for skin analytics), integrated task automation application (for example, inbound customer call routing), and integrated machine-learning application (for example, predictive sales-lead scoring in customer relationship management). Adoption of AI in marketing cannot be stressed enough as it can not only help companies build their relationships with their customers but also facilitate the process of customer segmentation (Deloitte, n.d.-b).

8.7 Strategy 4: Create Innovation Units

Innovation can be promoted through the development of the organization's research and development. In a study, 70% of the organizations rated the importance of innovation units in achieving greater organizational agility as "high" or "very high" (Prats et al., 2018). Innovation units are designed to break out from today's business models and explore new, competing ways of working. At instances where companies are facing greater levels of change, innovation units are more likely to play a critical role. Innovation units can take many forms, depending on the specific needs of individual organizations. In fact, there is no one or best way to structure and operate an innovation unit. There are four steps that an organization adopts to manage its innovation units (Stetter, 2019). They are: (a) identify the kind of innovation needed, (b) find the best source(s) of new ideas, (c) determine how much of the innovation needs to be owned, and (d) create a process. Through these steps, companies will be able to effectively navigate turbulent times through innovation and within their specific contexts. The agility by organizations to response to unprecedented and increasingly turbulent times is imperative to sustain their business operations. More organizations are struggling to stay afloat and require suitable measures in place to deal with unprecedented situations. To do so, a company should examine its different business functions and adjust them accordingly to make them more agile and operate with a growth innovative mindset. Further to that, an organization should not only focus on its processes but more importantly its people as well. The people within an organization, including its leaders, play a crucial role in the sustainability of the business.

Winby and Worley (2014) identified four key routines that are conducive to agility as well as organizational innovations. These include strategizing, perceiving, testing, and implementing. Agile organizations should be constantly engaging in developing and testing their hypotheses to improve their current products and learning from their experiments (i.e., testing and implementing). In order to do so, strategizing is a key part in improving agility, and top management teams need to be committed to fostering an innovative culture within the organization (i.e., strategizing). Perceiving is another important routine for an agile organization. No matter how much investments organizations make in innovations, unless the organizations have an accurate grasp of customers' needs or external environments, their innovations could be likely futile. It is critical for organizations and their members to come up with the innovations that are aligned with what is required by external environments. Innovation thus plays a key role in fostering organizational agility. This point is reiterated by Harraf et al. (2015). They posited that organizations need to be active in terms of opportunity seeking and alertness. Organizational members need to be proactive in looking for novel opportunities and absorbing new knowledge and information so that organizations can develop new innovations. Furthermore, they highlighted various aspects of organizations (e.g., empowerment, tolerance for ambiguity, vision, strategic direction, change management, communication) as enablers of organizational agility.

Furthermore, organizations need to promote a right mindset among employees so that organizational agility and innovations can be sustained. In particular, learning plays a key role, and organizations are encouraged to foster the individuals who are "continually able to jettison skills, perspectives, and ideas that are no longer relevant, and learn new ones that are" (Flaum & Winkler, 2015). According to Flaum and Winkler (2015), those who can enable learning agility often engage in following behaviors: innovating (challenging the status quo and long-held assumptions), performing (overcoming ambiguity and unfamiliar challenges), reflecting (looking for feedback and acting on it), and risking (stretching themselves and trying to learn outside their comfort zones). Vandewalle (2012) also highlighted the importance of feedback seeking behavior, experimentation, and reflection to make learning more agile. In contrast, those who fail to enable learning agility tend to be more defending. Such individuals are called the "learning-agility derailer" and should likely impede organizational learning and innovations (Flaum & Winkler, 2015). In order to promote innovations, as repeatedly emphasized, having right people who can make learning agile is critical. Also, organizations can provide trainings to new hires about the behaviors concerning agile learning (innovating, performing, reflecting, and risking) and try to tie the behaviors to an employee performance appraisal program, so that the learning and innovative mindset is firmly developed in employees' mindsets.

8.8 Strategy 5: Deploy Migration Strategies

Migration strategies are required in building a resilient business (Reeves & Whitaker, 2020). An example of a migration strategy is to shift the organization's portfolio mix across products, channels, geographies, or business models to maximize opportunities and minimize adversity. Most companies tend to spread their resources rather equally across different businesses and units. However, in extreme and unprecedented circumstances (for example, COVID-19 pandemic), organizations need more decisive reallocation. This requires both the business intelligence and mental agility to identify new risks and opportunities before they become known in the industry. Hence, for an organization to sustain itself, it needs to know how to change business models and sufficiently re-allocate resources when required.

Strategic agility can be achieved through various means of resource allocation. For example, organizations can engage in diversification via merger and acquisitions to attain resources that they do not have access to and build capabilities of remaining agile and resilient during unprecedented times. Merger and acquisitions can be classified into various types, such as those concerning product acquisitions, technology and talent acquisitions, platform acquisition, and bolt-on acquisition (a product extension or a market extension into an adjacent product-market category) (Brueller, Carmeli, & Drori, 2014). Platform acquisition is typically very large-scale, and organizations engage in this type of acquisition in order to gain an established market position. Bolt-on acquisition tends to be geared towards obtaining new products and technologies. Having diversified organizations' business portfolios is crucial for them to sustain competitive advantages and responsiveness, while reducing risks and uncertainty when the organizations face novel challenges and situations. Diversification is not only about company's business portfolio but also about other domains of business operation. For instance, Lin, Fan, Shi, and Fu (2021) conducted a study to examine how diversification in supply chain can help organizations thrive during the COVID-19 pandemic. Based on the data from 1,424 Chinese manufacturing firms, they found that firms with a larger supply and a diversified customer base were better able to cope with the COVID-19 crisis. As such, organizations need to pay deliberate attention to how and in what areas they could possibly engage in diversification.

In *McKinsey Quarterly*, Sull (2009) stressed the importance of portfolio agility as well. Specifically, Sull argued that organizations will lose portfolio agility when executives control the organizations for a too long time, because they might be susceptible to risk and loss aversion, leading to be less willing to re-consider and re-structure their current business portfolio. To break such tendency of the executives or even managers, Gulati and Wiedman (2020) proposed two strategies. The first proposal concerns *the strategic frame for resource allocation decisions*. Specifically, the leaders need to focus on the future instead of the previous successes and achievements that they have made. This shift in the leaders' focus should help their decisions on resource allocation more attuned to organizations' strategic goals. The second approach is *reforming the budgeting process*. This concerns organizations explicitly setting a rule about the projects that they will fund or not and about how the organizations evaluate the current and future projects. As such, overcoming risk aversion in resource allocation decisions requires cognitive changes and bias reduction techniques in decision-making processes of organizational leaders (Atsmon, 2016). Sull (2009) also explained that organizations need to re-allocate their people to ensure portfolio agility. For example, organizations can have their employees rotate different functions and roles. By doing so, organizations become able to redeploy their personnel more easily during the time of a crisis.

References

Aghina, W., Ahlback, K., De Smet, A., Lackey, G., Lurie, M., Murarka, M., & Handscomb, C. (2018, January 22). The five trademarks of agile organizations. *McKinsey & Company.* https://www.mckinsey.com/business-functions/people-and-organizational-performance/our-insights/the-five-trademarks-of-agile-organizations

Agile Business Consortium. (2017). *Towards an agile culture.* https://www.agilebusiness.org/page/Resource_paper_TowardsanAgileCulture

AirAsia. (2020, December 30). *Preparing for a travel comeback, AirAsia boosts supply chain capabilities and agility with AC2 Group.* https://newsroom.airasia.com/news/airasia-boosts-supply-chain-capabilities-and-agility-with-ac2-group

Ashmos, D. P., & Duchon, D. (2000). Spirituality at work: A conceptuality and measure. *Journal of Management Inquiry, 9,* 134–145. https://doi.org/10.1177/105649260092008

Atsmon, Y. (2016, August 30). How nimble resource allocation can double your company's value. *McKinsey & Company.* https://www.mckinsey.com/business-functions/strategy-and-corporate-finance/our-insights/how-nimble-resource-allocation-can-double-your-companys-value

Bella, R. L. F., Barboza, D. V., Quelhas, O. L. G., Meiriño, M. J., & França, S. L. B. (2021). Resilience meets sustainable and spiritual background into an initial review for the new normal after the COVID-19 pandemic. *Frontiers in Sustainability, 2.* https://doi.org/10.3389/frsus.2021.638570

Boston Consulting Group. (2019). *How to thrive in the 2020s.* BCG. https://www.bcg.com/featured-insights/how-to/thrive-in-the-2020s

Brueller, N. N., Carmeli, A., & Drori, I. (2014). How do different types of mergers and acquisitions facilitate strategic agility? *California Management Review, 56*(3), 39–57.

Cetindamar, D., Katic, M., Burdon, S., & Gunsel, A. (2021). The interplay among organisational learning culture, agility, growth, and big data capabilities. *Sustainability, 13*(23), 13024.

Davenport, T. H., Guha, A., & Grewal, D. (2021). How to design an AI marketing strategy. *Harvard Business Review.*

Deloitte (n.d.-a). *Exponential HR: Break away from traditional operating models to achieve work outcomes.* https://www2.deloitte.com/global/en/pages/human-capital/articles/gx-exponential-hr.html

Deloitte. (n.d.-b). *How to leverage AI in marketing: Three-ways to improve consumer experience.* https://www2.deloitte.com/si/en/pages/strategy-operations/articles/AI-in-marketing.html

De Smet, A., Gagnon, C., & Mygatt, E. (2021, January 11). Organizing for the future: Nine keys to becoming a future-ready company. *McKinsey & Company.* https://www.mckinsey.com/business-functions/people-and-organizational-performance/our-insights/organizing-for-the-future-nine-keys-to-becoming-a-future-ready-company

Edelman, D., Heller, J., & Spittaels, S. (2016, November 9). Agile marketing: A step-by-step guide. *McKinsey & Company.*

Flaum, J. P., & Winkler, B. (2015, June 8). Improve your ability to learn. *Harvard Business Review.*

Galadanchi, H., & Bakar, L. J. (2018). A study of factors that support longevity of business enterprises. *IOSR Journal of Business and Management, 20*(1), 53–59.

Goldberg, Z., & Kramer, L. (2020, January 23). Agile transformation and the critical role of HR in creating positive, lasting change. *IBM Smarter Business Review.* https://www.ibm.com/blogs/services/2020/01/23/agile-transformation-and-the-critical-role-of-hr-in-creating-positive-lasting-change/#:~:text=Travel%20and%20transportation-, Agile%20trans-formation%20and%20the%20critical%20role, in%20creating%20positive%2C%20lasting%20change&text=Modern%20enterprises%20recognize%20that%20strategic, with%20customers%20and%20manage%20employees

Gothelf, J. (2014, November 14). Bring agile to the whole organization. *Harvard Business Review.*

Gothelf, J. (2017, June 19). How HR can become agile (and why it needs to). *Harvard Business Review.*

Gulati, R., & Wiedman, M. (2020, September 2). What really prevents companies from thriving in a recession. *Harvard Business Review.*

Gurumurthy, R., Nanda, R., & Schatsky, D. (2021, April 22). Putting digital at the heart of strategy. *Deloitte.* https://www2.deloitte.com/xe/en/insights/topics/digital-transformation/digital-acceleration-in-a-changing-world.html

Hagen, B., Zucchella, A., & Ghauri, P. N. (2019). From fragile to agile: Marketing as a key driver of entrepreneurial internationalization. *International Marketing Review, 36*(2), 260–288.

Harraf, A., Wanasika, I., Tate, K., & Talbott, K. (2015). Organizational Agility. *Journal of Applied Business Research (JABR), 31*(2), 675–686.

Huddleston Jr., T. (2020, March 26). *The SARS epidemic threatened Alibaba's survival in 2003—Here's how it made it through to become a $470 billion company.* CNBC.

Jayaram, G. (2020, August 12). John Deere Global IT uses agility to help our stakeholders overcome COVID-19 challenges. *LinkedIn.* https://www.linkedin.com/pulse/john-deere-global-uses-agility-help-our-stakeholders-overcome-ganesh

Jurisic, N., Lurie, M., Risch, P., & Salo, O. (2020, November 16). Real-world lessons to jumpstart an agile culture shift. *McKinsey & Company.* https://www.mckinsey.com/business-functions/people-and-organizational-performance/our-insights/the-organization-blog/real-world-lessons-to-jumpstart-an-agile-culture-shift

Kaur, D. (2021, February 26). How AirAsia pivoted its airline business to survive a pandemic. *Techwire Asia.* https://techwireasia.com/2021/02/heres-how-airasia-pivoted-its-airline-business-to-survive-the-pandemic/

Khan, M. M. S. (2015). The longevity of large enterprises: A study of the factors that sustain enterprises over an extended period of time. *The Journal of Developing Areas, 49*(5), 41–52.

Lin, Y., Fan, D., Shi, X., & Fu, M. (2021). The effects of supply chain diversification during the COVID-19 crisis: Evidence from Chinese manufacturers. *Transportation Research Part E, 155,* 102493.

Mazor, A. (2020, November 16). Exponential HR: Six practices HR can do right now to enable breakout performance results. *LinkedIn.* https://www.linkedin.com/pulse/exponential-hr-six-practices-can-do-right-now-enable-breakout-mazor

Moi, L., & Cabiddu, F. (2021). An agile marketing capability maturity framework. *Tourism Management, 86,* 104347.

O'Brien, D., Main, A., Kounkel, S., & Stepham A. R. (2019). Diffusing agility across the organization: How leading brands are building capabilities to market for moments.

Deloitte Insights. https://www2.deloitte.com/us/en/insights/topics/marketing-and-sales-operations/global-marketing-trends/2020/agile-marketing.html

O'Farrell, K. (2017, June 8). Enabling agility through an experiment hungry culture. *Deloitte.* https://www2.deloitte.com/au/en/blog/adaptability-blog/2019/enabling-agility-through-experiment-hungry-culture.html

Pesek, W. (2021, March 9). How AirAsia's Tony Fernandes smashed a COVID-19 home run. *Nikkei Asia.*

Prats, J., Siota, J., Gillespie, D., & Singleton, N. (2018). *Organizational agility.* https://www.oliverwyman.com/content/dam/oliver-wyman/v2/publications/2018/april/Organizational_Agility.pdf

Reeves, M., & Whitaker, K. (2020, July 2). *A guide to building a more resilient business.* Harvard Business Review.

Rai, S. S., Rai, S., & Singh, N. K. (2021). Organizational resilience and social-economic sustainability: COVID-19 perspective. *Environment, Development and Sustainability*, 1–18. https://doi.org/10.1007/s10668-020-01154-6

Renjen, P. (2021, January 25). Building the resilient organization: 2021 Deloitte Global resilience report. *Deloitte.* https://www2.deloitte.com/us/en/insights/topics/strategy/characteristics-resilient-organizations.html?id=us:2pm:3ad:firmfy21:awa:greendot:em:covid:cn:bldgresorg:1x1:hbr:030121:1081886615

Stetter, J. (2019, March 29). *Four ways to get your innovation unit to work.* MIT Sloan Management Review. https://sloanreview.mit.edu/article/four-ways-to-get-your-innovation-unit-to-work/

Sull, D. (2009, December 1). Competing through organizational agility. *McKinsey & Company.* https://www.mckinsey.com/business-functions/people-and-organizational-performance/our-insights/competing-through-organizational-agility

Tobenkin, D. (2021, August 7). The Agile journey: Companies need to commit to agility from the top down. *SHRM.* https://www.shrm.org/hr-today/news/all-things-work/pages/the-agile-journey.aspx

Vandewalle, D. (2012). A growth and fixed mindset exposition of the value of conceptual clarity. *Industrial and Organizational Psychology*, *5*(3), 301–305.

Winby, S., & Worley, C. G. (2014). Management processes for agility, speed, and innovation. *Organizational Dynamics*, *43*, 225–234.

Chapter 9

Re-strategize and Prepare for Future Business

Organizations must adopt the growth mindset where they need to transform and heighten up their capabilities, leverage on their R&D capabilities to meet the changing needs of stakeholders and re-align their business processes and strategies to prepare for the future.

Kumaran Rajaram, PhD

9.1 Introduction

Change is part and parcel of life, where it is crucial that we embrace it. Hence, it is vital that organizations prepare and take a second look by reviewing their strategy as they look forward. While it is merely impossible to predict the future of business with all certainty, there are certain trends and drivers that are indicative of the direction the business is currently headed towards. For instance, the COVID-19 pandemic in 2021 was unpredictable but reactions from businesses and consumers were rather analogous to that of during the SARS pandemic in 2003. The most recent pandemic is indicative of factors that are likely to influence businesses in the near future. Kevin Sneader, a global managing partner of an entity, shared eight forces he believed will reshape the post-pandemic business landscape. This includes acceleration of digitization and innovation, increased government action and engagement, recommitment to and reinvention of healthcare, greater balance between social and economic goals, push for a green economic recovery, redefinition of work and the

DOI: 10.4324/9781003286288-12

role of cities, shifting geopolitics and international flows, and movement towards greater resilience and efficiency (McKinsey & Company, 2020). Other changes may generally stem from social, ethical, and environmental changes (Hahn, Kolk, & Winn, 2010). By examining such patterns closely and carefully, businesses become more prepared to deal with whatever comes in the future, more inclined towards the unprecedented and unexpected.

Re-strategizing comes hand in hand upon analyzing the potential impacts of the future of business. Taking the "business as usual" route when it comes to strategy formulation is not adequate for an organization to sustain itself in the long run. In fact, being adaptable becomes a competitive advantage that enables it to create advantages for an organization. Nonetheless, choosing to ignore changes will only harm or cause negative ripple effects for the company. Thus, an organization should be constantly re-evaluating, improvising, and/or changing their strategy, primarily because traditional approaches to strategy assume businesses to be acting in a relatively stable and predictable world (Reeves & Deimler, 2011). However, the 21st century is far from that and instead, it is characterized by an era of instability and uncertainty. Therefore, anticipation and adaptability are two highly relevant characteristics for businesses to have now and in the future.

9.2 Re-strategizing Organization's Business Plans

Re-strategizing organization's business plans and operation plays a vital role in helping the organization become future-ready. It is too late if organizations start considering about re-strategizing after a crisis occurred. In order to be able to best deal with any unpredictable changes and challenges, business leaders need to adopt a future-oriented mindset. For example, Pauga (2020) described five important considerations for business leaders in a constantly changing business world, which are (a) not being complacent, (b) visualizing weakness, (c) thinking about worse-case scenario, (d) having a lofty vision and building it, and (e) securing control over what you can control. Re-strategizing always starts from executives of an organization, and therefore, leaders must not be satisfied with the status quo and need to constantly keep in mind the possibility that one day their business could experience a downturn because of an unexpected crisis just like what we experienced during the COVID-19 pandemic. Organizations that invested digital capabilities and technology could take advantage of the COVID-19 situation, whereas those that did not appreciate their value likely failed to bounce back from the crisis. Mygatt, Steele, and Voloshchuk (2020) provided other sets of recommendations for business leaders to become future-ready. First, the leaders must focus on the purpose, value agenda, and culture of the organization to inspire their stakeholders including employees, customers, and their business partners. Second, the organization needs to adopt a nimble attitude by flattening the structure, turbocharging decision making, and valuing talent that the organization possesses. Finally, organizational leaders must set up a comprehensive plan about how their organization achieves growth by taking an ecosystem view, building a data-rich technology platform, and fostering learning at the organizational level. The organizations with the leaders with future-oriented mindsets who can constantly reflect on and make amends to their business strategies can adapt to external changes that may be unprecedented and unforeseeable.

In order to be future-ready and effectively modify or alter strategic foci when crises occur, organizational leaders must learn about how to deal with uncertainty as well. Sometimes, devising a very detailed, concrete plan can make organizations too rigid and inflexible about external changes. Webb (2019) offered a useful proposal regarding this point. Specifically, she argued for the value of adopting a futurist's framework for strategic planning. Leaders should not think of *time* in a manner of linear progression, as it is not possible to place the same level of the certainty on the projects that will be happening in the near future (in 2–3 years) and those for distant future (10 years from now). Rather, she suggested that leaders should think about four distinct categories when making future projects: (a) tactics (projects that will be happening in 1–2 years and more certain); (b) strategy (projects that will be happening in 2–5 years with some level of predictability); (c) vision (projects that will be happening in 5–10 years and with less certainty); and (d) systems-level evolution (projects that will be happening in 10+ years and least certain). The last category contains lots of ambiguity, since it is just impossible to predict what will happen in the future. Leaders need to be able to embrace such uncertainty, but still be capable of re-evaluating and re-considering their strategies constantly. In the traditional way of thinking about organization's strategy, leaders often assign rigid, specific deadlines to organization's projects. While this approach can give the organization a clear sense of direction about where to go on the one hand, it could deprive them of flexibility on the other hand. The futurist's framework for strategic planning will give leaders more space of being flexible when unexpected events occur and easily engaging in re-strategizing some of their business plans when necessary.

9.3 Case Studies on Organizations: Re-strategizing and Preparation for Its Future Business

An example of a company that managed to adapt and turn around is Lego. For 66 years since its founding, Lego had never experienced a considerable amount of loss. However, by 2003, sales were down by 30% year-on-year and the company was $800m in debt. Consultants advised diversification, which Lego attempted by introducing jewelry for girls, clothes, theme parks, and video games. This strategy unfortunately caused them to almost go bust. Lego's CEO Jørgen Vig Knudstorp shared that they were "on a burning platform" and that they were "running out of cash … [and] likely won't survive" (Davis, 2017). Yet, slightly more than a decade later in 2015, Lego overtook Ferrari to become the world's most powerful brand. It had £660m in profits and became the number one toy company in Europe and Asia, and number three in North America. The company was revived by the leadership of CEO Vig Knudstorp who transformed the strategic approach of the company. He removed the company from things they had no expertise in, such as the Legoland amusement parks which are now owned by a different company. He also reduced inventory by reducing the number of individual Lego bricks they produced by half. Further to that, he recognized the importance of the company's fans, loyal customers, and the relevance of the technology and Internet. As a result, he encouraged fans, loyal and potential customers' interaction which used to be considered forbidden in the company. One way he did so was by allowing fans to share their creations as well as promote their events online. They also started making popular toys again by conducting intensive research on their target audience. Lego was saved as they stuck to and focused on developing what they did best – making toys, while outsourcing whatever projects they knew they did not have the capabilities and expert resources for. Despite the initial bleak outlook, Lego's CEO pulled through by transforming their strategy and propelling towards the future. Indeed, not all companies may be able to spontaneously manage to re-strategize and prepare for the future. For instance, Nokia was once a leading mobile phone manufacturer that experienced early success due to their visionary and courageous management choices that took advantage of the company's innovative technologies. However, in 2013, Nokia's mobile phone division was sold to Microsoft and again in 2016. Nokia's failure can be attributed to several factors such as poor management decisions, dysfunctional organizational structures, growing bureaucracy, and deep internal rivalries (Doz, 2017). Nokia had overlooked threats posed by other companies in the industry such as Apple due to overconfidence (Lauer, 2021). In a nutshell, their success had prevented them from exploring alternative growth areas, making it easier for their competitors to overtake them in terms of market share. Success breeds conservatism and hubris (Doz, 2017) and this in the long-term, resulted in a decline of the strategy processes enabling poor strategic decisions at Nokia that resulted in their downfall.

Another example of a future-ready company is Tesla. The recent report from the Institute for Management Development's (IMD) Future Readiness Center revealed that Tesla is one of the companies that are expected to thrive amidst frequent and unexpected changes and ranked top among the companies in the automotive industry (Lun, 2021). IMD ranked 86 highest-grossing companies from various industries such as retail, automotive, financial, and technology industries worldwide, including the United States, China, Germany, Japan, and Singapore. According to the report published by McKinsey consultants (De Smet, Gagnon, & Mygatt, 2021), one of the things Tesla has done to become future-ready involves adopting an ecosystem view. In 2014, Tesla decided to implement the strategy of open-source patents. By doing so, Tesla was able to create an ecosystem of their partners and become the center of the entire system, which accelerated further innovations and developments of new products. Tesla recognized the value of extending their products to others, which would eventually create greater values to themselves as well as those involved in the ecosystem. Such partnership also safeguards Tesla from being susceptible to a crisis. Organizations cannot effectively navigate through external shocks if they did not invest in building sustainable relationships with other partners in the industry. No matter how technology-driven Tesla is, the organization would not have achieved their exponential growth if they did not allow other companies to use their technology.

In the same IMD report, the company that ranked second in the automotive industry after Tesla was Toyota. Toyota has been a forerunner in the industry and thriving for a long time, despite having experienced a number of external threats in the company's history. What makes the company so distinctive from others is their unique philosophy called the Toyota way. This famous, yet inimitable set of values and beliefs deeply embedded within their employees has enabled organizations to achieve consistent growth. In particular, the Toyota way emphasizes the importance of continuous improvement (Brady, Gagnon, & Mygatt, 2021) which is also called *kaizen* and employees are constantly encouraged to proactively look out for any potential issues and areas of improvements at work. Such an organizational culture prevents both organizational leaders and members from being complacent of past achievements and successes. Toyota also values their employees and is committed to fostering exceptional talents. Although the Toyota way may not be easily copied or transferred to other organizations, it highlights some of the important characteristics that future-ready and future-proof organizations have, such as not being overly satisfied with the status quo and identifying weak spots. Even if organizations might not be able to adopt the Toyota way entirely, organizational leaders might adopt part of it as their mindsets so that they can become more prepared and adaptable to any future challenges.

The following recommended strategies assist organizations to re-strategize and prepare for future business. Figure 9.1 presents a visual representation of the re-strategizing and preparing for future framework.

9.4 Strategy 1: Upskill and Re-train Employees

The recent COVID-19 pandemic has re-iterated the importance for organizations to upskill and re-train their employees so that their workforce becomes more adaptable to market changes. This becomes crucial especially during times where even major industries cannot afford to hire new talent (Elfond, 2020). Organizations such as Amazon and Mastercard have invested in upskilling programs for their employees long before the pandemic began. Upskilling is not useful only during challenging times, but it also increases employee engagement and retention, enables reaching out to new talent, increases collaboration between departments, as well as accelerates the adoption of new trends within the company in the long run. For employee upskilling and reskilling, organizations collate data to plan, analyze, and implement strategic talent decisions. Knowledge sharing is also encouraged as transitioning existing employees into new positions is more cost-effective than hiring new ones. Google is

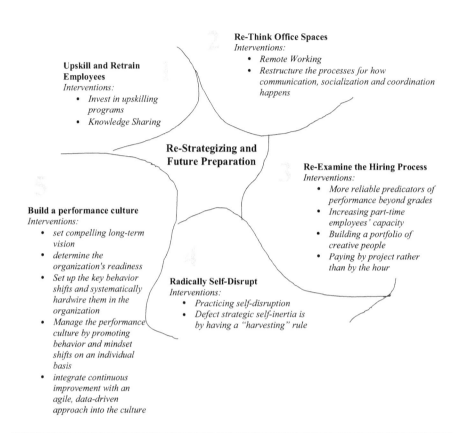

Re-Think Office Spaces
Interventions:
- *Remote Working*
- *Restructure the processes for how communication, socialization and coordination happens*

Upskill and Retrain Employees
Interventions:
- *Invest in upskilling programs*
- *Knowledge Sharing*

Re-Strategizing and Future Preparation

Re-Examine the Hiring Process
Interventions:
- *More reliable predicators of performance beyond grades*
- *Increasing part-time employees' capacity*
- *Building a portfolio of creative people*
- *Paying by project rather than by the hour*

Build a performance culture
Interventions:
- *set compelling long-term vision*
- *determine the organization's readiness*
- *Set up the key behavior shifts and systematically hardwire them in the organization*
- *Manage the performance culture by promoting behavior and mindset shifts on an individual basis*
- *integrate continuous improvement with an agile, data-driven approach into the culture*

Radically Self-Disrupt
Interventions:
- *Practicing self-disruption*
- *Defect strategic self-inertia is by having a "harvesting" rule*

Figure 9.1 Re-strategizing and Preparing for Future Framework

a prime example of a company leveraging on knowledge sharing through their G2G (Googler to Googler) program where employees volunteer to attend classes taught by their fellow co-workers.

Given that employees' skill development greatly contributes to organizational agility and flexibility for potential future crises, it plays a crucial role when organizations re-strategize their business goals, models, and operations. If employees possess skills that are only relevant to their current jobs and do not extend to other domains of organization's business, organizations cannot easily change their strategic focus. Organizations can foster employees' skill development in various ways. Vroman and Danko (2022) provided three suggestions: (a) empowering employees to own their career development, (b) showing where ideas go, and (c) providing a roadmap. As in expectancy theory of motivation, organizations must emphasize (a) that their employees are sufficiently capable of building new skills and (b) how organizations would benefit from employees' upskilling. Unless employees understand the need for skill development and have personal reasons for doing so, they are not expected to put efforts in upskilling or reskilling. At the same time, organizations should give enough time for employees to learn new skills and provide them with rewards when they complete skill development (Roslansky, 2021). Upskilling will not complete within a day or a month. It is thus crucial for organizations to consistently encourage their employees to engage in upskilling. Organizations can also provide an apprenticeship program whereby employees can receive skill-based education and offer skill development programs or workshops through partnering with external vendors (Waddill, 2021). In so doing, organizations can send a message to their employees that they care about employees' career while fostering a learning culture, both of which should help the organizations continue to thrive when unpredictable events occur.

However, helping employees to successfully upskill and/or reskill is not easy for organizations. Research with 65,000 employees and 75 HR leaders showed that most organizations approach employees' skill building in a reactive or predictive manner (Wilde, Smith, & Clark, 2021). Reactive manner concerns that organizations demand employees to build new skills when the need arises; however, reactive skill building does not help employees and organizations much, because by the time employees learned new skills, those skills had become already obsolete or outdated. Predictive skill building concerns that organizations predict future skill needs and invest in training and skill development of employees; however, the downside is that most skills employees learn based on the predictive approach are not much applied to their daily work, because accurately predicting future skill needs is very difficult. Wilde et al. (2021) proposed the dynamic approach as a more effective option for skill development of employees. This approach is defined as a dynamic exercise that embraces ambiguity, makes peace with imperfection, and frees up Human Resource, managers, and employees to move fast in responding to the things they know and can anticipate (Wilde et al., 2021). Specifically, they suggested that organizations should regularly ask for the inputs from their employees and other relevant stakeholders such as customers about any skill needs so that they can closely observe if there are any changing skill needs. Once organizations identify new skill needs, they need to take swift actions to provide opportunities for employees to build these skills. The focus should not be on providing a perfected training but the training that is good enough, so that skill development can happen more rapidly. Organizations should not simply invest in training and skill development of employees but need to carefully observe external environments to identify what skills are really needed for them.

9.5 Strategy 2: Re-think Office Spaces

The COVID-19 pandemic has re-iterated the way employees' function and carry out their responsibilities at work. Remote working has become the norm with most employees working from their own homes. While this new norm and working environment could potentially raise health concerns if not dealt with a balanced approach, most employees prefer working remotely and would want to continue to do so even after the pandemic ends. In a survey commissioned by the Straits Times in Singapore, eight out of ten workers said that they prefer to work from home or have flexible working arrangements (Lai, 2020). This highlights how remote working may become the new normal. In fact, it may be more beneficial for organizations to allow their employees to work from their homes if there are able to do so and fulfill their responsibilities rather than ask them to report to an office. Research indicates that productivity increases with employees operating from remote work settings. It is very effective if the organization restructures the processes for how communication happens, how socialization happens, and how coordination happens.

As telecommuting or remote work gained more traction among employees, organizations are required to think how they can maintain the quality of employees' communication and relationships, despite the reduced amount of time employees work face-to-face in the same office space. Given its highly contagious nature of the COVID-19 pandemic, it is difficult to foresee that organizations mandate employees to work in the office at the same level as the pre-COVID-19 anytime soon. There are varying strategies that managers can implement for better communication amongst employees who work remotely (Glaveski, 2021). For instance, managers can utilize task boards whereby managers and employees can update the status of project tasks about the progress of the tasks as well as those who are currently working on them. The task boards do not only enhance transparency and provide a quick overview of the project but they also help employees spend less time on emails and texts by collating the information about the given tasks on one platform. This is particularly effective as employees might have to spend lots of time on offline communication tools like emails and texts because of less time spent in the office. Organizations also need to consider such things as how they can maintain a company culture, what Human Resource policies need to be updated to adapt to the era of remote work in terms of recruiting, hiring, as well as compensation, and what trainings, and how they should be delivered to employees (Makarius, Larson, & Vroman, 2021).

Although telecommuting may have become a new normal already, and many employees prefer to work remotely as much as they could, completely switching to remote work may likely do more harm than good. For example, Bloom (2021) raises two concerns which organizations should take note of. First, it is extremely more difficult to manage a hybrid team that consists of office-based employees and the employees who frequently work remotely. The issue of a hybrid team is that a potential divide between office-based employees and remote employees will emerge, which would likely bring about various negative consequences such as less effective communication among team members, less transparency about team members' work, reduced trust in each other, and so on. If employees do not know what their team members are doing, it is highly impossible to fully trust in them, presenting a difficulty in collaborating with each other too. Furthermore, things such as office chit-chat or watercooler conversations do not likely happen between office-based employees and remote employees, hampering the development of amicable relationships among them. Second, given that those who *choose or want* to work remotely could be part of a certain population (for example, employees with kids or parents to take care of, employees from racial and/or ethnic minority groups), organizations might become characterized by less diversity in the office space. Moreover, many perceive that working remotely while their colleagues work in the office could potentially lower the chance of promotion (Bloom, Liang, Roberts, & Ying, 2015). In addition, letting employees work remotely for an excessive number of hours could eventually cause unexpected legal consequences too. Organizations need to be beware of the potential implication of the practice of telecommuting in dealing with workforce diversity.

9.6 Strategy 3: Re-examine the Hiring Process

In accordance with Vivienne Ming, Co-Founder and Managing Partner at Socos, human talent will significantly increase as a differentiator in the future workforce (EY Global, 2018). This implies that future-forward organizations should look beyond grades which are not exactly accurate and great predictors of future success in the workplace anyway. Instead, organizations should use more reliable predictors such as motivation, sense of purpose, and creativity. Though traits like these are harder to measure, but when these are incorporated as performance measures, it is certainly worthwhile. For instance, a company that wants to measure potential employees on their persistence could intentionally give them a test that is very challenging and highly demanding to have it cleared. Executives could examine the persistence, the length of the duration taken and how much consistent efforts are inputted to avoid failing and keep trying without giving up. Depending on the specific needs of an organization, similar tests could be designed and executed. Other consideration includes increasing the capacity of part-time pool by hiring less full-time employees, building a portfolio of creative people and paying by project rather than by the hour, and so on.

One of the strategies proposed by Roslansky (2021) emphasized that hiring should be based on a skill-based approach. Many companies and their executives might still focus on candidates' past records of education, experiences, as well as achievements because they are quick indicators of their capabilities which can be used by the organizations to predict their future work performance and successes. However, they do not necessarily reflect their potential. Instead, organizations can begin focusing on the skills that are desired to help them address their current and potential future issues and tailoring their job postings and hiring processes to the specific skill needs. If organizations pay attention to only candidates' experiences, they would likely overlook someone of great potential, and therefore, hiring processes should be designed in such a way that goes beyond immediate needs of business units and organizations (Harvard Business Review, 2021). Also, organizations need to develop the hiring practice where they can identify candidates who are capable of adapting to new situations quickly and properly handling issues and challenges (Kavitha & Suresh, 2021). In order to prepare for future business, organizations must have individuals who can work under ambiguous circumstances. Research has also shown the link between human resource flexibility and firm performance (Bhattacharya, Gibson, & Doty, 2005), suggesting that organizations should be able to re-design the hiring process whenever the need arises to keep pace with dynamic environments. Organizations thus should develop their capability of assessing their needs and identifying the potential talents that can fill the needs in a prompt manner.

There are unique and different ways for organizations to be adaptable and responsive to crises through re-strategizing. For example, Fuller, Wallenstein, Raman, and de Chalendar (2019) made an intriguing proposition: collaborate to deepen the talent pool. They suggest that organizations "work together to ensure that the talent pool is constantly refreshed and updated". As all companies strive to acquire talents, the pool of excellent talents will run out quickly, leading to suboptimal outcomes for everyone. Rather, Fuller et al. (2019) suggested that organizations should consistently explore to collaborate with others. Identifying and developing talents are often thought as an internal thing that organizations handle in their own respective ways, but this does not necessarily preclude that organizations cannot partner with others to find out the best talents. For instance, United States (US) (utilities companies which have collaborated with each other and established the Center for Energy Workforce Development in 2006. CEWD not only helped the utilities companies fill their vacancies for jobs but also developed training toolkits and materials which were shared with the companies for free. Furthermore, although the recommendations from research scholars and practitioners tend to be geared towards what organizations want, in order to acquire right talents, organizations also need to consider what future employees want as well. For example, Minahan (2021) shared that many employees might have different expectations than organizations about their employment. For example, they want to have greater flexible options and value the quality or impact of output rather than its volume. They might also want to work in a diverse team. If organizations cannot address such needs from employees, hiring processes that are designed around organizational needs might be of no use. Organizations thus need to pay close attention to (a) what they want and (b) whether what they provide actually matches with the preferences of their potential employees.

9.7 Strategy 4: Radically Self-disrupt

In an era of technology disruption, organizations must be willing to disrupt themselves before the pressure from their competitors arises (Dobbs, Koller, & Ramaswamy, 2015). This means that they must overcome the fear that a new product or channel will cannibalize an existing business. Practicing self-disruption can help a company conquer strategic self-inertia and enable them to better equip themselves for the future. Firms that are able to reallocate capital in response to changing conditions would have significantly higher growth rates and returns to shareholders than those who do not. One way that firms defeat strategic self-inertia is by having a "harvesting rule" that involves putting an amount of assets up for sale every year unless a well supporting argument can be made in favor of keeping them. It is crucial that organizations stay ahead of the curve by becoming their own competition.

The value of self-disruption has been recognized and acknowledged by practitioners. For example, McKinsey recently published a few articles on how companies engage in self-disruption. Amed, Balchandani, Beltrami, Berg, Hedrich, and Rölkens (2019) described that self-disruption is one of the key considerations among the industry leaders of fashion brands. In the fashion industry, younger consumers prefer novelty, and therefore, organizations that simply follow the fashion conventions would be likely competed away. Also, the advancement of technology and social media is another factor that drives self-disruption in the fashion industry. In particular, social media and e-commerce play vital roles, which fundamentally transformed how the brands advertise and sell their products. Amed et al. (2019) argued that continued innovation is undeniable for established brands so that they can better situate themselves in the industry characterized by unpredictability in customer trends as well as advancement of technology. Deloitte (n.d.) suggested that organizations engage in disruptive M&A so that they can effectively obtain resources and technology that could enable them to fundamentally change their business and supply chains. Furthermore, making a change to the core of organizations' business such as value propositions, people, processes, and technology could help organizations adapt to novel situations and find new solutions (Dahlström, Ericson, Khanna, & Meffert, 2017). Overall, organizations might have to actively destroy their current business models so that they can keep thriving even amid rapidly changing circumstances.

Woodward, Padmanabhan, Hasija, and Charan (2020) also emphasized the value of self-disruption for companies in an unpredictable world. The authors explained the process of self-disruption called the Phoenix Encounter Method (PEM) which is characterized by three steps: (a) groundwork, (b) battlefield, and (c) breakthrough. Woodward et al. suggested that executives can engage in the PEM for a couple of days in a workshop setting, so that they can effectively transform their thinking style to be more radical and future-oriented. In terms of groundwork, organizational leaders need to first identify their status quo. Specifically, the leaders need to ask about things such as their visions, strengths, weaknesses, stakeholders, as well as the ways in which they capture values. They also need to introspect about their own mindsets and readiness about responding to crises and attitudes towards disruption. It is also useful to proactively look out for novel trends and tools which could potentially disrupt the organizations' current business models (for example, AI, 3D printing). The second step is battlefield. This phase is also characterized by three strategies, namely, launching the scenario, thinking like your enemy, and developing a defense. In other words, they need to imagine what their competitors would do. It is critical to consider the most devastating attack to the organizations during this phase, because they will develop a plan a defense in the next stage. In other words, the leaders need to consider how they would come back from destruction to rebirth. Self-disruption may be critical for the organizations to overcome inertia, but this does not guarantee that the organizations bounce back from it, and therefore, thinking ahead about the plan for regaining is important. Finally, the third phase is breakthrough. The organizations need to make a blueprint for the future based on the previous two stages, and the executives need to try not to go back to the old way of thinking.

9.8 Strategy 5: Build a Performance Culture

During times of instability, organizations that focus on culture and organizational health can overcome crises faster. Building a performance culture can help leaders future-proof their company where organizations with a strong culture attain three times higher total return to shareholders compared to those without (DiLeonardo, Phelps, & Weddle, 2020). Five actions were advocated that help an organization establish a successful performance culture. The first is to aspire by setting compelling long-term vision. The second is to assess by determining the organization's readiness and identifying specific behavior and mindset shifts. Thirdly, the organization should set up the key behavior shifts required and systematically hardwire them in the organization. Next, the organization should manage the journey towards a performance culture by promoting behavior and mindset shifts on an individual basis. Lastly, the organization should integrate continuous improvement with an agile, data-driven approach into the culture. Overall, by transforming the organizational culture by embedding relevant values and mindsets, organizations can better prepare their employees for the future.

A high-performance culture does not emerge in one day, but it would require time and efforts to develop the culture within organizations. One useful model towards this end is McKinsey's 7S framework (Baishya, 2015). This framework covers seven interdependent elements – namely, shared values, strategy, structure, systems, skills, style, and staff. Shared value or superordinate goal is essential, as employees would not be likely motivated to excel at their work unless their organizations provide a shared purpose that everyone is expected to pursue. Strategy and structure are also relevant as they can provide a clear direction and expectation about what employees are supposed to do to contribute to the organizations. System concerns rules and procedures about how things are done in the organizations. Style concerns "pattern of action taken by top management over a period of time" (Baishya, 2015, p. 167). The last two considerations are staffing and skills. Staffing is related to how the organizations select and train their employees, and skills broadly refer to the competence that the organizations possess. These seven aspects of organizations should be clearly defined and aligned with each other, as a performance culture will not be germinated if the organizations fail to communicate with employees such things as their values and strategies. Gallup also presented three key components that are necessary for a high-performance culture (Abdallah & Ahluwalia, 2013). First, organizations need to implement an effective performance management process. Second, they should create empowerment and authority. Last, it is essential to increase leadership capability at all levels of the company. As such, top management's strategy and attitudes are a deciding factor of the emergence of a performance culture.

On top of these factors, Dewar and Keller (2012) introduced what they called organizational health, which concerns three factors that drive a high-performance culture. The three factors include an ability to align, execute, and renew. Organizations with a high-performance culture can effectively align their vision with strategy and employees' behaviors. But they are also competent at executing their strategies in a way that would not cause friction – for example, employees are clearly communicated about what the metrics for performance evaluation and appraisal, thereby enhancing their motivation and willingness to be committed to performance in the organizations. High-performance organizations are also capable of making changes and improvements constantly. Oakes (2021) provided another interesting view concerning organizational culture that contributes to enhanced performance. He argued that encouraging organizations to have their talents move around different teams and division and to create a culture of mobility. Organizations are often characterized by immobility, as the employees with a long tenure and more experiences tend to stick to one area of organizational businesses, potentially making the organizations parochial and rigid. However, research shows that high-performance organizations tend to value talent mobility more compared to low-performance organizations (Lykins, 2016). Such talent mobility should enhance encourage growth and development of employees by having important talents move around the organization and share their experiences with others. Those who move around can also gain more diverse perspectives from working in less familiar positions or teams, which should contribute to greater creativity, and hence, greater organizational innovation and performance. Most notably, talent mobility could make employees feel more comfortable with changes (Oakes, 2021). A culture of mobility, as well as a high-performance culture, could thus stimulate the changes in employees' mindsets and make organizations become more adaptable and future-ready.

References

Abdallah, E., & Ahluwalia, A. (2013, December 12). The keys to building a high-performance culture. *Gallup.* https://www.gallup.com/workplace/236546/keys-building-high-performance-culture.aspx

Amed, I., Balchandani, A., Beltrami, M., Berg, A., Hedrich, S., & Rölkens, F. (2019, February 15). Self-disruption in the fashion industry. *McKinsey & Company.* https://www.mckinsey.com/industries/retail/our-insights/self-disruption-in-the-fashion-industry

Baishya, B. (2015). McKinsey 7s framework in corporate planning and policy. *International Journal of Interdisciplinary Research in Science Society and Culture, 1*(1), 165–168.

Bhattacharya, M., Gibson, D. E., & Doty, D. H. (2005). The effects of flexibility in employee skills, employee behaviors, and human resource practices on firm performance. *Journal of Management, 31*(4), 622–640.

Bloom, N. (2021, May 25). Don't let employees pick their WFH days. *Harvard Business Review.* https://hbr.org/2021/05/dont-let-employees-pick-their-wfh-days

Bloom, N., Liang, J., Roberts, J., & Ying, Z. J. (2015). Does working from home work? Evidence from a Chinese experiment. *Quarterly Journal of Economics, 130*(1), 165–218.

Boston Consulting Group. (2019). *How to thrive in the 2020s.* https://www.bcg.com/featured-insights/how-to/thrive-in-the-2020s

Brady, D., Gagnon, C., & Mygatt, E. (2021, June 17). How to future-proof your organization. *McKinsey & Company.* https://www.mckinsey.com/business-functions/people-and-organizational-performance/our-insights/how-to-future-proof-your-organization

Davis, J. (2017, June 4). How Lego clicked: The super brand that reinvented itself. *The Guardian.* https://www.theguardian.com/lifeandstyle/2017/jun/04/how-lego-clicked-the-super-brand-that-reinvented-itself

Dahlström, P., Ericson L., Khanna S., & Meffert, J. (2017). Reinventing your business by transforming the core. *McKinsey and Company.* www.mckinsey.com/business...mckinsey/.../from-disrupted-to-disruptor-reinventingy.Article. February 2017.

Deloitte. (n.d.). *Disruptive M&A: Are you ready to define your future?* https://www2.deloitte.com/la/en/pages/financial-advisory/articles/disruptive-manda.html

De Smet, A., Gagnon, C., & Mygatt, E. (2021, January 11). Organizing for the future: Nine keys to becoming a future-ready company. *McKinsey & Company.* https://www.mckinsey.com/business-functions/people-and-organizational-performance/our-insights/organizing-for-the-future-nine-keys-to-becoming-a-future-ready-company

Dewar, C., & Keller, S. (2012, January 26). Three steps to a high-performance culture. *Harvard Business Review.* https://hbr.org/2012/01/three-steps-to-a-high-performa

DiLeonardo, A., Phelps, R. L., & Weddle, B. (2020, July 27). Establish a performance culture as your secret source. *McKinsey & Company.* https://www.mckinsey.com/business-functions/organization/our-insights/the-organization-blog/establish-a-performance-culture-as-your-secret-sauce?

Dobbs, R., Koller, T., & Ramaswamy, S. (2015, October). The future and how to survive it. *Harvard Business Review.*

Doz, Y. (2017, November 23). The strategic decisions that caused Nokia's failure. *INSEAD Knowledge.* https://knowledge.insead.edu/strategy/the-strategic-decisions-that-caused-nokias-failure-7766

Elfond, G. (2020, December 21). Why employee upskilling and reskilling is so important right now. *Forbes.* https://www.forbes.com/sites/forbestechcouncil/2020/12/21/why-employee-upskilling-and-reskilling-is-so-important-right-now/?sh=1b138b713302

EY Global. (2018, April 26). *How can you prepare now for the work of the future?.* https://www.ey.com/en_sg/workforce/how-can-you-prepare-now-for-the-work-of-the-future

Fuller, J., Wallenstein, J. K., Raman, M., & de Chalendar, A. (2019). Your workforce is more adaptable than you think. *Harvard Business Review.* https://hbr.org/2019/05/your-workforce-is-more-adaptable-than-you-think

Glaveski, S. (2021, December 1). Remote work should be (mostly) asynchronous. *Harvard Business Review.* https://hbr.org/2021/12/remote-work-should-be-mostly-asynchronous

Hahn, T., Kolk, A., & Winn, M. (2010). A new future for business? Rethinking management theory and business strategy. *Business & Society, 49*(3), 385–401.

Harvard Business Review. (2021). *Reengineering the recruitment process.* https://hbr.org/2021/03/reengineering-the-recruitment-process

Kavitha, R., & Suresh, M. (2021). Agile practices in human resource management. *Advances in Materials Research, 5,* 713–721.

Lai, L. (2020, October 12). 8 in 10 in Singapore want to work from home or have more flexibility. *The Straits Times.* https://www.straitstimes.com/singapore/8-in-10-in-singapore-want-to-work-from-home-or-have-more-flexibility

Lauer, T. (2021). *Change management: Fundamentals and success factors.* Springer. https://doi.org/10.1007/978-3-662-62187-5

Lun, T. N. (2021, December 15). Tesla, Lululemon, Mastercard among top future-ready companies on aggressiveness, digitalization: IMD. *The Business Times.* https://www.businesstimes.com.sg/companies-markets/tesla-lululemon-mastercard-among-top-future-ready-companies-on-aggressiveness

Lykins, L. (2016, April 13). Talent mobility matters. *i4CP.* https://www.i4cp.com/surveys/talent-mobility-matters

Makarius, E. E., Larson, B. Z., & Vroman, S. R. (2021, March 24). What is your organization's long-term remote work strategy? *Harvard Business Review.* https://hbr.org/2021/03/what-is-your-organizations-long-term-remote-work-strategy

McKinsey & Company. (2020). *The future of business: 2021 and beyond.* https://www.mckinsey.com/about-us/covid-response-center/leadership-mindsets/webinars/the-future-of-business-2021-and-beyond

Minahan, T. (2021, May 31). What your future employees want most. *Harvard Business Review.* https://hbr.org/2021/05/what-your-future-employees-want-most

Mygatt, E., Steele, R., & Voloshchuk, M. (2020, July 29). Organizing for the future: A focus on three outcomes. *McKinsey & Company.* https://www.mckinsey.com/business-functions/people-and-organizational-performance/our-insights/the-organization-blog/organizing-for-the-future-a-focus-on-three-outcomes

Oakes, K. (2021, August 20). Let your top performers move around the company. *Harvard Business Review.* https://hbr.org/2021/08/let-your-top-performers-move-around-the-company

Pauga, S. (2020, April 16). Five steps for preparing your business for a future crisis. *Forbes.* https://www.forbes.com/sites/forbesbusinesscouncil/2020/04/16/five-steps-for-preparing-your-business-for-a-future-crisis/?sh=129e5c71fbad

Reeves, M., & Deimler, M. (2011). Adaptability: The new competitive advantage. *Harvard Business Review.*

Roslansky, R. (2021, June 8). You need a skills-based approach to hiring and developing talent. *Harvard Business Review.* https://hbr.org/2021/06/you-need-a-skills-based-approach-to-hiring-and-developing-talent

Vroman, S. R., & Danko, T. (2022, January 18). How to build a successful upskilling program. *Harvard Business Review.* https://hbr.org/2022/01/how-to-build-a-successful-upskilling-program

Waddill, D. (2021, December 10). 4 strategies for upskilling and reskilling your workforce. *Harvard Business Review.* https://hbr.org/sponsored/2021/12/4-strategies-for-upskilling-and-reskilling-your-workforce

Webb, A. (2019, July 30). How to do strategic planning like a futurist. *Harvard Business Review.* https://hbr.org/2019/07/how-to-do-strategic-planning-like-a-futurist

Wilde, S., Smith, A., & Clark, S. (2021, November 26). Organizations need a dynamic approach to teaching people new skills. *Harvard Business Review.* https://hbr.org/2021/11/organizations-need-a-dynamic-approach-to-teaching-people-new-skills

Woodward, I. C., Padmanabhan V., Hasija, S., & Charan, R. (2020, September 8). Disrupt your own business first: Planning the future for your company begins with knowing how to destroy it. *MIT Sloan Management Review.* https://sloanreview.mit.edu.remo-texs.ntu.edu.sg/article/disrupt-your-own-business-first/

Index

Note: Page numbers in *italics* refer to figures.

Printed in the United States
by Baker & Taylor Publisher Services